Designed with Care:
Creating trauma-informed content

Designed with Care

CREATING TRAUMA-INFORMED CONTENT

Rachel Edwards, Editor

Print ISBN: 9798300551575

Imprint: Independently published

Published by Badger and Sett Publishing

Copyright © 2024
All rights reserved.

Published December of 2024

Edited by Rachel Edwards

Grateful acknowledgement to the following for permission to reprint previously published material: Lora Mathis "If There's A Way Out I'll Take It" *Instinct to Ruin* © 2016. Used with permission.

All rights reserved. No part of this publication may be reproduced or transmitted in any form or by any means, electronic of mechanical, including photocopying, recording, or any information storage or retrieval system, without prior permission in writing from the publishers.

DesignedWithCare.org

First Edition

Contents

Foreword i

Introduction iii

A note about content and references vi

Trauma-informed principles vii

Chapter 1 1
What is trauma?   Jax Wechsler

Chapter 2 20
Clarity is kinder: Michelle Keller
Designing content for bereaved and dying people

Chapter 3 36
Designing questions   Rachel Edwards, Jane McFadyen, and Steph Mann

Chapter 4 48
Trauma and technology   kon syrokostas

Chapter 5 73
The case for content warnings   Rachel Edwards

Chapter 6 87
Trauma-informed research for content design   Sarah Fathallah

Chapter 7 114
From principles to practice: Kate Every
Using trauma-informed principles to design services

Chapter 8 128
Working with and for young people   Steph Mann

Chapter 9 146
How trauma-informed principles can work in government   Jane McFadyen

Chapter 10 161
Content design in high-risk digital spaces   Owen Leigh

Chapter 11 .... **174**
Does this feel dignifying?   Morgan Cataldo
Considering, telling, and sharing more ethical stories

Chapter 12 .... **188**
So you want to decolonise trauma?   sahibzada mayed (صاحبزاده مائد)

Chapter 13 .... **203**
Vicarious trauma: Jenny Winfield
Protecting your spirit when doing trauma work

Chapter 14 .... **218**
Crisis communication: A crisis is more than a moment in time   Miriam Vaswani

Chapter 15 .... **241**
Compliance is just the start: Josh Kim
Accessibility for trauma-informed outcomes

Chapter 16 .... **255**
Trauma literacy in content design   Rachael Dietkus

About the authors 271

Thanks 276

Foreword

When I hear the word trauma, I immediately see a scene from *Buffy the Vampire Slayer*. Cordelia is screeching "what's your childhood trauma?" at the slayer gang after a particularly tricky night hunting demons.

It's ridiculous.

Cordelia said it with flippancy. As we often do. Do we make light of trauma? Sometimes. Trauma is a word that is bandied about with flippant disregard or whispered through sobs. Trauma itself is ignored. It's under-diagnosed. It's missed. It causes untold pain. It takes lives. It's brushed under the carpet in many ways by many people because it can be uncomfortable.

The main thing about trauma is that no one chooses it. It happens. It can happen to anyone at any time.

If it's a sibling or best pal who is affected, and you know what they need in that moment, sure, you can try to provide it. But what if you're producing content for strangers on the internet? When trauma is so complex, when so many people are affected in so many different ways, how can you produce content that is useful, usable, and safe?

Trauma has an infinite number of ways that it can show up, just as the human reaction to trauma is infinite. And with so many causes and so many reactions, how can we produce content that caters for all eventualities?

We can't. And we know that. But what we can do is make content using trauma-informed principles that explicitly care for our audience.

Caring about people isn't new. Being user-centred isn't new. But as humans change, trauma changes; and as tech changes, we need to change. This book shares expertise, ideas, and personal experience to help strengthen the single most powerful skill content people have available: we produce content that is accessible, usable, safe, and makes the world a little easier for our audience.

Sarah Winters
Founder, Content Design London

Introduction

Imagine for a minute you are being chased by a bear.

As you race through the woods, bear in pursuit, you see in front of you a sign that says "Being chased by a bear? Read this."

The sign has several columns of detailed text, explaining the history of bears, famous people who have been chased by bears, and the types of bears that are particularly fond of chasing. At the bottom of the poster is a QR code you can scan to fill in a report of your bear-chasing experience.

It's an absurd idea, isn't it?

If you are being chased by a bear, your body is full of adrenaline. Your heart is thumping, your stomach is in turmoil. As you race down the path, the only information you want — or can take in — is a sign reading "Get help here!"

When we are threatened by a present or past danger, our bodies and our minds change. Flooded with stress hormones, we can find it harder to read, make decisions, and understand information. Even when we are out of danger, thinking about the experience can cause unpleasant physical reactions and the feeling that we are back in danger again.

But whether we are actively running from the bear or remembering the experience, we might need information. The challenge for content designers, and anyone giving information to people, is how to do that when their users feel in danger.

I first came across trauma-informed practice in 2021 while working on a service for survivors of abuse. I was part of a wider design team made up of user researchers, service designers, interaction designers, and business analysts. They had completed a thorough and thoughtful discovery when I joined as a content designer for the alpha phase.

Throughout discovery the design team had used trauma-informed principles. They committed to keep using the principles as the service developed. But what did that mean for content?

Trauma-informed practice is often based on building a relationship: between a service provider and a person who has experienced trauma, for example. But content is different. Content is usually one-way: a website, a form, a letter. There's not often the chance to adapt to the user's needs, tailor the communication, or provide support if they are distressed.

So how did I apply these trauma-informed principles to content design?

I learned by doing, making mistakes, and adapting. I worked with an excellent team of user researchers, service designers, and survivor liaison officers. Together we launched the service, and I moved on.

But as I went on to my next project, I realised 2 things.

The first was how much I had learned about working in a trauma-informed way.

The second was that these trauma-informed principles were applicable to almost every setting, and every piece of work, I have done since.

Content designers create information that people can understand. We do that by thinking about people's needs. Trauma changes those needs, and we need to know what to do to design content that helps instead of harms.

Trauma can show up anywhere, often where we don't expect it. It's not enough to say that trauma-informed content design only applies to certain situations or certain people. If you are creating information for people, you need to be trauma-aware and trauma-informed.

This book shares the experiences of 15 authors across 3 continents. It covers topics from trauma-informed design research (chapter 6) to decolonising trauma-informed practice (chapter 12) to vicarious trauma (chapter 13). But it also includes experiences from content designers who have worked in areas like:
- crisis communication,
- government information,
- hospice care,
- information for young people,
- domestic abuse.

The authors extend beyond content designers, too, to include service designers, software designers, social workers, and accessibility experts.

In 2021 there was not a lot being said or written about trauma-informed content design. Since then, the conversation has been growing. This book is both a much-needed resource for content designers and evidence of how far we have come in just a few years.

Rachel Edwards
Editor

A note about content and references

This book, by its nature, mentions topics that may be difficult for some people.

We write about these topics in the context of our work. We do not share personal information about the people we have designed for, or go into detail about their experiences.

We know the nature of trauma means that people experience it differently and find different things difficult. For this reason, we have chosen not to list the topics that we think you may find challenging.

As you go through this book, you may experience a range of feelings and responses. We encourage you to choose how and when to engage, or not, with each chapter and its contents.

References

Each chapter contains a list of references and further reading. These are listed in the order they appear or are addressed in the chapter.

You can visit our website or scan the QR code to find linked versions of these references: designedwithcare.org/references

Trauma-informed principles

Trauma-informed principles often guide trauma-informed practice. They are not meant to be used as a checklist, but as a way of working that recognises and helps people with trauma.

Many organisations have developed their own sets of trauma-informed principles. The Substance Abuse and Mental Health Services Administration (SAMHSA) principles come from the U.S. Department of Health and Human Services. They are often cited as the original set of principles, and some organisations adopt them as they are or with slight variations.

The authors of this book also reference the Chayn principles of trauma-informed design. Chayn is a global nonprofit that creates resources to support survivors of gender-based violence.

Both sets of principles are referred to throughout the book, and are set out here for ease.

SAMHSA principles of a trauma-informed approach

6 key principles of a trauma-informed approach:

1. Safety
2. Trustworthiness and transparency
3. Peer support
4. Collaboration and mutuality
5. Empowerment, voice, and choice
6. Cultural, historical, and gender issues

Substance Abuse and Mental Health Services Administration, U.S. Department of Health and Human Services.

Chayn's trauma-informed design principles

- Safety
- Privacy
- Power sharing
- Agency
- Accountability
- Equity
- Plurality
- Hope

Developed by Chayn, a global nonprofit that supports survivors of gender based violence, and collaborators.

Chapter 1
What is trauma?

by Jax Wechsler

Trauma is very common, more common than you may think. While certain groups — such as people experiencing mental health challenges, people with disabilities, Indigenous people, and people from marginalised racial groups — are at higher risk, it's estimated that 70% of the global population has experienced a traumatic event.

Trauma can affect anyone, no matter their age, background, or culture, with profound impacts on social, physical, and emotional well-being. Trauma-informed practitioners understand the far-reaching effects of trauma and are committed to creating environments and engagements that are safe, supportive, respectful, and empowering for those affected.

At its heart, being trauma-informed means being aware of how trauma may affect people.

Trauma can manifest in unexpected ways and is not limited to specific groups or topics. Adverse life events that commonly lead to trauma include:
- accidents,
- large-scale disasters,
- physical or emotional abuse,

- war,
- witnessing or experiencing violence,
- natural disasters,
- neglect,
- the death of a loved one.

However, more subtle experiences can also cause trauma, and people can have trauma-related associations to things that may not seem particularly sensitive. This is why it is crucial for designers and researchers to work in trauma-informed ways — always. It is important to know how to respond should traumatic distress arise for someone. They also need to be aware of the risks of vicarious trauma, and understand that trauma can impact people's ability to process information, communicate, be with stress, and relate to themselves and to others.

In this chapter we will explore:
- what trauma is,
- different causes and types of trauma,
- how it is experienced in the body,
- its relationship to the brain, memory, and the nervous system.

We will also touch on triggering, signs of distress, and the core principles of trauma-informed practice. It's likely that trauma will show up in your work, but with the right understanding, you can be prepared to respond sensitively and effectively.

What is Trauma?

The term "trauma" originates from the Greek word "traumatikos," meaning "wound." Initially used in the mid-1600s to describe physical injuries, the concept of psychological trauma emerged in the late 19th century, when it was considered to be a cause of "neurosis" and "hysteria." Thanks to the more recent contributions of trauma experts such as Bessel van der Kolk, Peter Levine, Stephen Porges, and Patricia Ogden, along with advancements in neuroscience and neurobiology, we now understand that trauma is in fact an embodied experience. Today, trauma is recognised as having both physiological and psychological aspects.

Trauma versus traumatised

While most people encounter some form of traumatic event in their lives, not everyone becomes traumatised. Trauma results from an embodied response to an experience that makes us feel unsafe and that our brains and nervous systems can't process. It commonly involves a loss of power or control. Trauma is not tied to a specific event, but rather to how the event affects a person's physiology and nervous system. If an individual can self-regulate their nervous system after a traumatic event, the experience may not result in trauma.

Trauma is embodied and significantly affects one's nervous system, leading to physical, behavioural, and emotional changes. Emotionally, people might feel anxious, easily overwhelmed, or disconnected from their feelings. They may live in a constant state of hypervigilance, feeling as if something bad is always about to happen. They could struggle with mood swings, irritability, or a sense of numbness. Physically, trauma can show up as chronic tension, trouble sleeping, headaches, and digestive issues.

Cognitive impacts include difficulty concentrating and processing information, as well as memory issues. People can find it hard to trust others and feel safe, avoiding certain places, people, or activities. Trauma can shape a person's thoughts, worldviews, relational capacity, physical health, memory, imagination, and creativity.

Trauma is not about an event in the past, but rather how that event shapes present day experience for people, preventing them from feeling safe, worthy, loved, and trusting in others or themselves.

Trauma types and causes

It's impossible to predict who may be affected by the ongoing impacts of trauma.

In today's world, marked by large-scale challenges like global pandemics, climate change, and an escalating mental health crisis, people's ability to cope is being challenged. We tend to think of trauma as something that affects individuals. However, it also manifests in broader forms, such as intergenerational, collective, systemic, and racialised trauma. These affect groups, communities, family lineages, and even societies.

Many people may not realise they've experienced trauma, yet their nervous system has been impacted, and trauma is carried in their bodies. Even for those who know they've been affected, there's commonly a lack of awareness about how deeply trauma influences their behaviours, their ways of seeing the world, and how they move through life.

There are many different types of trauma. Some common types are listed below. They are not mutually exclusive, and people can experience several of these at the same time.

- **Acute trauma** is the intense distress that happens immediately after a sudden, short-term event, like witnessing an act of violence.
- **Chronic trauma** refers to the prolonged and repeated exposure to traumatic events over an extended period, such as experiences of family violence.
- **Relational or interpersonal trauma** happens within close relationships, often involving caregivers and those meant to provide safety and support.
- **Post-traumatic stress disorder** (PTSD) is a mental health condition triggered by experiencing or witnessing a traumatic event such as war or a large-scale climate event, like a fire.
- **Collective trauma** affects groups of people, from small communities to entire societies, as we saw with the psychological impact of COVID.
- **Intergenerational trauma** refers to the transmission of trauma from one generation to the next.
- **Historical trauma** refers to the collective emotional and psychological harm experienced by a group of people over multiple generations from significant collective traumas such as colonisation, forced assimilation, and cultural genocide.
- **Racialised trauma** emerges from the emotional and psychological harm caused by racism, discrimination, and oppression.
- **Systemic trauma** occurs when large structures like institutions, policies, or cultural norms wield power that can oppress or harm marginalised groups.
- **Vicarious trauma** occurs when people are indirectly exposed to trauma through their interactions with people who have experienced trauma. It is common amongst helping professionals but can also affect those who hear trauma stories, such as researchers.

"Big T" and "small t" trauma

Trauma experts often distinguish between "big T" and "small t" trauma.

When most people think of trauma, they often think of trauma manifesting after significant, life-altering events such as war, violence, natural disasters, or physical abuse. These types of events commonly lead to post-traumatic stress disorder (PTSD). This is what's commonly referred to as "big T" trauma.

In contrast, "small t" trauma arises from repeated exposure to more subtle stressors, like:
- bullying,
- emotional neglect,
- chronic illness,
- absence of physical affection or attention as a child,
- ongoing financial hardship.

While these events may not seem to threaten life or bodily integrity, they can, over time, reduce one's ability to cope, disrupting emotional and psychological functioning. These smaller traumas have a cumulative effect. A single incident may not cause significant harm, but when multiple small traumas add up, especially in a short period of time, they can have lasting emotional and physiological effects.

Trauma isn't just about the event, but one's experience of an event, and is deeply subjective. Gabor Maté explains, "Trauma is what happens inside of us as a result of what happened to us." The same event can result in trauma for one person but not for another, depending on how the experience impacts the person's nervous system and what resources they have available. For example, imagine 2 children experiencing the same difficult situation at school. One child, with secure attachment to their parents and low overall stress, is able to go home, process the experience, and metabolise the stress held in their nervous system. They can integrate the experience. The other child, without these resources, is left unable to discharge that energy, leading to a high likelihood of trauma. As Peter Levine explains in *Waking the Tiger: Healing Trauma*, "Traumatic symptoms are not caused by the triggering event itself. They stem from the frozen residue of energy that has not been resolved and discharged."

This trapped energy lingers in the body, disrupting both physical and emotional well-being.

Trauma, brain, and body

Trauma arises from the body's response to overwhelming experiences that leave our brains and bodies struggling to process the experience. The brain and body are inseparably interwoven via the nervous system. It is through the nervous system that we make sense of the world.

The vagus nerve, part of the parasympathetic nervous system, plays a central role in the functioning of the nervous system. This long and complex nerve carries information from all the major organs to the brain. About 90% of its traffic flows upwards, giving the brain a sense of what the body senses.

The brain uses this information to try to make sense not only of what's going on physiologically, but also what's going on emotionally. This translation happens in the autonomic nervous system (see Figure 1), which comprises the sympathetic nervous system (managing the "fight or flight" response) and the parasympathetic nervous system (managing the "rest and digest" functions).

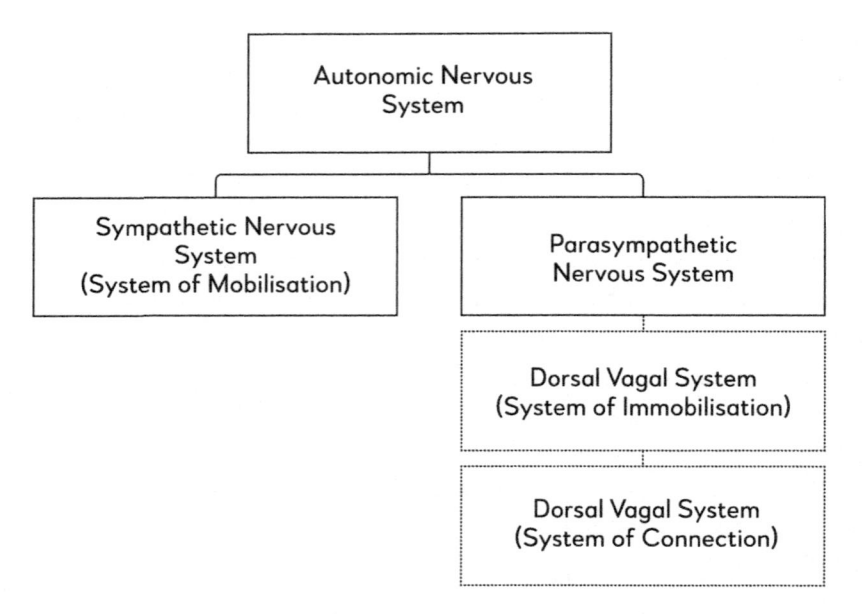

```
                    Autonomic Nervous
                         System
          ┌─────────────────┴─────────────────┐
   Sympathetic Nervous              Parasympathetic
        System                      Nervous System
  (System of Mobilisation)
                                           │
                                   Dorsal Vagal System
                                  (System of Immobilisation)
                                           │
                                   Dorsal Vagal System
                                   (System of Connection)
```

Figure 1. The different elements of the autonomic nervous system

The parasympathetic nervous system is made up of 2 parts:
- the dorsal vagal complex, responsible for immobilisation or the "shutdown" response,
- the ventral vagal complex, governing social engagement and connection.

You can think of the autonomic nervous system as a control system that unconsciously regulates bodily functions, such as the:
- heart rate,
- digestion,
- respiratory rate,
- immune system.

It helps to keep our body in "homeostasis," or the equilibrium of the body's systems.

Our nervous system monitors our environment, internally and externally, through millions of sensory receptors. It is always attuned to what's happening both inside and outside of our bodies, constantly scanning for any signs of threat. Polyvagal theory expert Deb Dana likens this to an inner surveillance system. Should we sense danger, our sympathetic nervous system switches on, preparing us for action. Our autonomic nervous system responds by sending messages to different parts of our body to ready us to take action. For example:
- our heart rate and blood pressure increases,
- more blood is sent to our muscles to mobilise them,
- our body floods with adrenaline and cortisol to sharpen our focus and give us the energy we need to fight the threat or run from it.

However, in certain situations of overwhelm, when neither fighting nor fleeing seems possible or effective, the body may instead go into a freeze or "fawn" response.

This system is vital for keeping us safe when real danger is present. The challenge comes when we perceive threats that aren't actually there. Trauma can significantly influence the brain's capacity to accurately assess threats. People who have experienced trauma tend to perceive danger where none exists in the present, resulting in exaggerated responses that do not serve them in day-to-day life.

The window of tolerance

Dr. Daniel Siegel's concept of the "window of tolerance" helps explain this further. When we're in our window of tolerance, our nervous system is in its optimal state. Our ventral vagal complex, part of our parasympathetic nervous system, is active. We feel calm, grounded, and able to think clearly. We can navigate life's challenges with ease, and our bodies function smoothly. We're breathing, sleeping, and digesting food well.

If we are unable to self-regulate, our nervous system can become dysregulated and move into hyper- or hypoarousal. In Figure 2, you can see how a regulated nervous system responds to a stressor. If we sense a potential threat, whether from something sudden like a loud noise or something else more subtle, our sympathetic nervous system switches on, activating our fight or flight response.

If we have a regulated nervous system, after we assess the situation and realise there is no present threat, our parasympathetic nervous system, responsible for rest and digestion, will activate to calm us, bringing us back into balance.

It can be helpful to think of the parasympathetic nervous system as our calming system, and the sympathetic nervous system as our activating system.

A REGULATED NERVOUS SYSTEM

Hyperarousal: Exaggerated response, anxiety, hypervigilience, can't relax, emotional flooding, etc.

Sympathetic system ON (Activating)

Parasympathetic system ON (Calming)

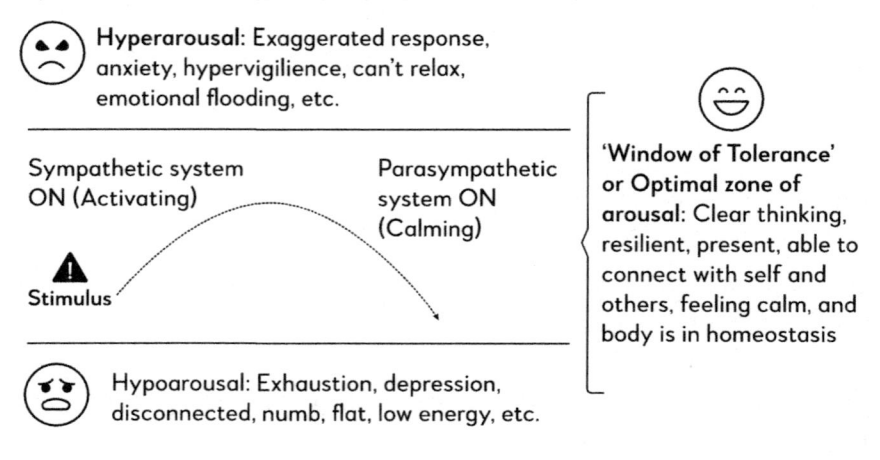

Stimulus

'Window of Tolerance' or Optimal zone of arousal: Clear thinking, resilient, present, able to connect with self and others, feeling calm, and body is in homeostasis

Hypoarousal: Exhaustion, depression, disconnected, numb, flat, low energy, etc.

Figure 2. A regulated nervous system is able to keep in the window of tolerance

We all have a window of tolerance, and we can all become dysregulated at times. If we are experiencing a lot of stress in our lives and not taking care of ourselves, our window of tolerance can narrow. Our nervous system may move into dysregulation more easily, leading to:
- irritability,
- digestive challenges,
- mood swings,
- low energy,
- difficulty concentrating,
- oversleeping or difficulty sleeping.

Trauma can shrink our window of tolerance, making us more easily dysregulated and prone to getting stuck in that state. This means that people who have experienced trauma can be in a dysregulated state a lot of the time, often without knowing it.

Nervous system dysregulation can show up in many ways. The good news is that we can all work to widen our window of tolerance and our capacity to stay in regulation. Practices that engage the parasympathetic nervous system can help calm the nervous system, build resilience, and widen our window of tolerance. This includes activities like:
- meditation,
- yoga,
- grounding techniques,
- time in nature,
- laughter,
- massage.

Deb Dana suggests that resilience grows when we can self-soothe and move more fluidly between states of regulation and dysregulation.

Dysregulation: Hyperarousal and hypoarousal

For someone who has experienced trauma, the window of tolerance can narrow. Figure 3 illustrates a dysregulated nervous system. After encountering a stressor, the sympathetic nervous system activates, but the parasympathetic nervous system does not switch on to calm and re-regulate the nervous system. As a result, the person may frequently feel as though they are under threat, leading to emotional dysregulation and a heightened response to stress. This can reduce their capacity to tolerate stress and make it difficult to stay in a regulated state.

A DYSREGULATED NERVOUS SYSTEM

Hyperarousal: Dysregulation: stuck ON

Stimulus

Sympathetic system ON (Activating)

Parasympathetic system can not keep the system calm

Hypoarousal: Dysregulation: stuck on OFF

For a dysregulated nervous system **'Window of Tolerance' or Optimal zone of arousal** becomes narrow. Person can become dysregulated easily and have difficulty returning to their optimal zone.

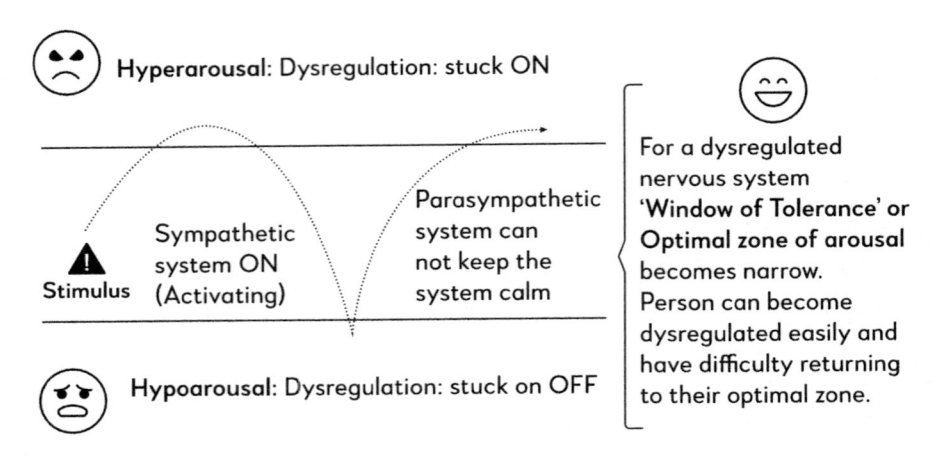

Figure 3. A dysregulated nervous system is unable to keep in the window of tolerance

People can become stuck in hyperarousal, experiencing anxiety, panic, or hypervigilance, as if they're constantly "on." In this state, it's like the nervous system is revved up, making it hard to relax, sleep, or regulate emotions.

If hyperarousal becomes overwhelming, the nervous system may flip into hypoarousal: the body's way of shutting down. In hypoarousal, people might feel:
- numb,
- disconnected,
- exhausted,
- dissociated, as though they've emotionally "checked out,"
- stuck in an "off" state.

Trauma often disrupts the nervous system's ability to return easily to the window of tolerance, causing people to cycle between hyperarousal and hypoarousal. Having a dysregulated nervous system makes it challenging to connect with others, engage meaningfully, or feel safe. It also creates more cortisol in the system, which can impact health. People are not always aware when their nervous system is in a dysregulated state and that it can be influencing their thinking, emotions, and behaviours.

Traumatic stress responses

When people are dysregulated, they commonly exhibit traumatic stress responses. Traumatic stress responses are the brain's and body's built-in way of trying to protect us. These automatic reactions show up both physically and emotionally when experiencing or remembering something distressing. Five types of traumatic stress responses are:
- **fight:** facing the threat head-on. This can look like anger, irritability, or a need for control. The sympathetic nervous system is dominant, preparing the body to confront a threat.
- **flight:** escaping the threat, physically or mentally. This can look like anxiety, restlessness, or avoidance. The sympathetic nervous system is dominant, preparing the body to escape from danger.
- **freeze:** feeling stuck, unable to act. This can look like numbness, dissociation, or paralysis. The dorsal vagal complex (part of the parasympathetic system) activates, immobilising the body, "playing dead."
- **fawn:** trying to appease others to avoid conflict. This can look like people-pleasing or difficulty setting boundaries. The ventral vagal complex (parasympathetic system), which is connected to the social engagement system, activates to help diffuse threats by pleasing others.
- **flop:** collapsing completely in response to the threat. This can look like shutting down, becoming unresponsive, or feeling helpless. The dorsal vagal complex (parasympathetic system) is heavily activated here, but this is a more extreme form of shutdown.

While these responses are protective when we're in real danger, people who have experienced trauma feel threatened a lot of the time, even when a threat is not actually there. When you're a trauma survivor, your defensive states can hijack your brain. Instead of helping you survive, trauma responses can become dysfunctional, harming your health, impairing your ability to effectively handle problems, and disrupting your relationships.

Trauma, memory, and the brain

After trauma, the brain starts devoting more energy to staying on high alert, constantly scanning for potential threats. This heightened focus can cause physical changes in the brain, affecting how people:
- process and recall information,
- think,
- relate,
- make decisions.

Trauma impacts 3 areas of the brain. These include the:
- amygdala,
- hippocampus,
- prefrontal cortex.

The amygdala is the brain's emotional and instinctual control centre, helping to perceive and regulate emotions. It's like an alarm system. When someone perceives a threat, the amygdala goes into overdrive, reacting just like the trauma is happening all over again. Their blood rushes away from the prefrontal cortex, responsible for creativity, problem solving, and higher-level thinking. It rushes to the amygdala to fuel the fight-flight response.

The prefrontal cortex becomes suppressed, leaving it with less capability to manage the fear, to focus, and to think clearly. The hippocampus, which is associated with memory and learning, is also impaired, leading to a reduced capacity to assess whether a situation is based on the present moment or from the past. This is important to understand for those of us working with creativity and idea generation. When anyone feels unsafe, their prefrontal cortex isn't fully available, making it harder for them to think clearly, problem-solve, learn, or tap into their creativity. Creating safety isn't just important for people who have experienced trauma — it's essential for everyone.

Trauma can also affect people's memories. In *The Body Keeps the Score*, Bessel van der Kolk explains how trauma alters how people store and recall memories. Traumatic experiences often aren't remembered in a clear, sequential way. There are often gaps, and memories tend to be fragmented and disjointed. When people try to share these memories, their emotions can feel overwhelming, making it even harder to process the memory and recall details.

Trauma is also stored in the body as sensory memories. This means that sounds, smells, or physical sensations can trigger intense emotional or physical reactions, even when the current situation isn't actually threatening. This is referred to as "triggering."

Triggering, distress, and co-regulation

Participating in design processes can be emotionally challenging for people, leading to uncomfortable emotions, stress, or even distress. This potential is increased for people who have experienced trauma.

Experiences of trauma commonly involve a lack of choice, control, and power, and can cause people to be sensitive to uncertainty, power dynamics, or triggers that may arise during design processes. A trigger refers to anything that reminds a person of a past traumatic experience, often bringing back the emotions, thoughts, or physical responses associated with that trauma. Triggers can cause a person to feel as if they are re-living the traumatic event, even if they aren't consciously aware of the connection between the trigger and the trauma. Sights, sounds, smells, and physical sensations related to a traumatic event can become deeply imprinted and reactivated when a person encounters something similar, often leading to intense emotional reactions. For example, hearing a loud sound may lead a person's body to react as if the danger is still present.

Triggers aren't always predictable, which makes it difficult to anticipate what might lead to someone feeling distressed. When engaging with individuals who have a history of trauma, it's crucial to stay mindful of the potential for distress. Distress can be suggested by subtle changes in how someone is presenting. For example, if someone who typically speaks with energy suddenly becomes flat in tone or appears flustered, it may signal distress. In those moments, a gentle, respectful check-in can make all the difference in supporting their wellbeing. Being able to recognise early signs of distress, whether it's hyperarousal (feeling overly activated and stressed) or hypoarousal (feeling shut down or detached), is key to preventing escalation.

Signs of distress are not limited to these symptoms, but these symptoms are common. Most importantly, be aware of changes in people's way of being. Should someone show these signs, it's best to check in with them to see how they are doing.

Physical signs
- turning pale or turning red,
- tears,
- faster or slower breathing,
- vacant look,
- clenching tightening muscles or fists,
- shivering or feeling cold,
- profuse sweating,
- gritted teeth,
- monotonous voice,
- fixed or glazed eyes.

Cognitive and emotional signs
- difficulty remembering,
- difficulty concentrating,
- confusion,
- long silence,
- disorientation,
- sudden mood change,
- overreacting to a situation,
- restlessness,
- changes in communication style (from extroverted thinking to long silences).

Signs in the social environment
- cool or heated discussion,
- dominating the conversation,
- difficulty making eye contact or connecting with others,
- withdrawing from conversation,
- rising or lowering energy levels,
- escalation of power differentials.

People often experience stress before it escalates into distress. If we can reduce stress early on, we can potentially prevent it from intensifying. A powerful question to consider is: how might we reduce stress at every step of the way to lower the chances of distress?

By consciously thinking about where stress might arise for people, and actively working to reduce it, we can potentially help prevent distress before it happens. When facilitating design processes, you never know when you might encounter distress, but having a plan in place helps you stay prepared. Knowing exactly what steps you'll take not only supports the person affected but also helps alleviate stress for you and your team, enabling you to respond with care and confidence when it matters most. This can also help you to manage your own nervous system, and your responses in the moment.

Co-regulation: How our nervous systems communicate

As we've discussed before, our nervous systems are always on alert, scanning for potential threats and keeping us safe. They constantly take in information, not only from our environment and our bodies but also from the nervous systems of those around us. This process is known as "interoception," a term introduced by Stephen Porges. At our core, we are relational beings, connected nervous system to nervous system. You know how when you ask someone how they are doing, and they say "great," yet you feel that's not true? Your nervous system is reading their nervous system, and telling you something different.

Our nervous systems influence each other, and we have the potential to "co-regulate." Think about a baby: they can't self-regulate and rely entirely on a caregiver to help soothe and balance their nervous system.

This is an example of co-regulation. Our nervous systems are constantly communicating with one another, which means that by calming your own nervous system, you can positively influence the nervous systems of those around you. This is something we are wired for — it's instinctual.

Co-regulation is the process where we help each other manage emotions, particularly in moments of distress, through empathy, support, and calming interactions. It's about offering a calm, reassuring presence that allows a person experiencing distress to calm and come back into regulation.

This connection works both ways. If someone else becomes dysregulated and we allow ourselves to become dysregulated too, it can amplify their distress. When your nervous system becomes dysregulated in response, the other person won't feel safe, and this can hinder their ability to regulate themselves.

That's why self-awareness and attention to your own physiological state are so critical. If someone begins to show signs of distress, first focus on calming your own nervous system through:
- deep breaths,
- grounding techniques like wiggling your toes,
- noticing sensations in your body.

Next, adjust how you're relating. For example:
- slow down your speech,
- soften your tone,
- adjust your body language,
- focus on your own breathing.

These shifts can help the other person co-regulate with your calm, grounded state. You need to ensure your own nervous system is in a steady place before you can effectively be the empathetic, supportive presence they need in that moment. This is where self-awareness and self-care can help you to navigate distress and work in more trauma-informed ways.

Trauma-informed principles and practice

Being trauma-informed is about understanding the dynamics and impact of trauma, rather than focusing on treating the trauma itself. It's a strengths-based approach that centres on responsiveness to trauma's effects, creating environments where physical, psychological, and emotional safety is prioritised for both providers and those we serve.

In service settings, trauma-informed practice has 3 main aims:
1. raising awareness about the widespread and often hidden impacts of trauma among staff and services,
2. preventing re-traumatisation in spaces that are supposed to offer support,

3. developing policies and practices that foster healing.

There are key principles that guide this work, for example:
- safety,
- trustworthiness and transparency,
- peer support,
- collaboration and mutuality,
- empowerment, voice and choice,
- cultural, historical and gender issues.

There are a few different models for trauma-informed principles, but the fundamental goal remains the same: to create environments where individuals feel safe, respected and supported.

Trauma-informed practice is also a practice. It's a way of being that asks us to constantly engage in our own inner work by developing our self-awareness and becoming attuned to our own needs, triggers, and emotions so we can be more present and sensitive to the needs of others.

Some questions you might like to consider in your journey:
- How might we reduce stress for people at every step of the way?
- How might we apply trauma-informed principles in our design processes and what we create?
- What potential harm might we be causing through our designs, content, and research?
- Have we involved people with lived experience in our design processes in a trauma-informed way?
- Am I aware of my own nervous system, and am I taking care of my own wellbeing?
- How did we learn? What worked, what didn't, and what might we try next time?

Building these trauma-informed muscles takes time, and yes, you will make mistakes along the way. But through reflective practice, you can strengthen your ability to respond to trauma with care and intention.

References and further reading

- Ronald C Kessler et al, "Trauma and PTSD in the WHO World Mental Health Surveys." *European Journal of Psychotraumatology* (October 2017)
- Nick Haslam and Melanie Joy McGrath, "The creeping concept of trauma." *Social Research: An International Quarterly* (November 2020)
- Bessel van der Kolk, *The body keeps the score: Brain, mind, and body in the healing of trauma* (2014)
- Peter A. Levine, *Waking the Tiger: Healing Trauma : The Innate Capacity to Transform Overwhelming Experiences* (1997)
- Stephen Porges, *The polyvagal theory: Neurophysiological foundations of emotions, attachment, communication, and self-regulation* (2011)
- Pat Ogden, Kekuni Minton, and Clare Pain, *Trauma and the body: A sensorimotor approach to psychotherapy* (2006)
- Intergenerational trauma: Rachel Yehuda, a neuroscientist, has written extensively about intergenerational trauma. Her studies of Holocaust survivors and their descendants, has focused on trauma, PTSD, and its transmission across generations. She has provided groundbreaking insights into how trauma can be passed down epigenetically.
- Historical trauma: see the work of Native American scholar and social worker Maria Yellow Horse Brave Heart.
- Vicarious trauma: recommended text about navigating vicarious trauma is Laura van Dernoot Lipsky and Connie Burk, *Trauma stewardship: an everyday guide to caring for self while caring for others* (2009)

- "Big T" and "small t" trauma: Gabor Maté talks about "Big T" and "Small t" trauma in several of his books, including *In the realm of hungry ghosts: Close encounters with addiction* (2008), *When the body says no: The cost of hidden stress* (2003), *The myth of normal: Trauma, illness, and healing in a toxic culture* (2022). Peter Levine points to this idea, without using this terminology in *Waking the Tiger: Healing Trauma* (1997), as does Bessel Van de Kolk in *The body keeps the score: Brain, mind, and body in the healing of trauma* (2014).
- Gabor Maté and Daniel Maté, *The myth of normal: trauma, illness and healing in a toxic culture* (2022)
- Deb Dana, *The polyvagal theory in therapy: Engaging the rhythm of regulation* (2018)
- Daniel J. Siegel, *The developing mind: How relationships and the brain interact to shape who we are* (1999)
- We all have a window of tolerance and it can be widened. This is where self-care practices and practices that strengthen our parasympathetic nervous system can be helpful. I feel this understanding of the nervous system is helpful for all humans. If you are interested in this further, look up resources by polyvagal theory expert Deb Dana. I particularly like her experiential book *Anchored: How to Befriend Your Nervous System Using Polyvagal Theory* (2021).
- Stephen Porges, *The Polyvagal Theory: Neurophysiological Foundations of Emotions, Attachment, Communication, and Self-Regulation* (2011)
- Substance Abuse and Mental Health Services Administration (SAMHSA) Concept of Trauma and Guidance for a Trauma-Informed Approach, U.S. Department of Health and Human Services (2014)

Chapter 2

Clarity is kinder: Designing content for bereaved and dying people

by Michelle Keller

After my mother died, I remember sitting around the table with my father and reading the volumes of cards he had received. The people who sent those cards loved my father. They wanted to offer some measure of hope and comfort. While everyone meant well, the messages printed in the cards were generic and not always helpful.

But there was one card that my father treasured. It was a handwritten note, not a polished, commercial sympathy card. The writer simply shared a beautiful memory of an interaction with my mother and the effect that it had on her life.

This experience was unique because, in a mountain of professionally crafted sympathy cards, this one friend had taken the time to actually talk about the person who died. Many people find it hard to talk about death. I work for a national hospice in the US. Talking and writing about death is my job. But despite dealing with death every day, each death is still difficult to process. Every loved one's death is traumatic for the people involved. Whether the relationship was happy or strained. Whether the person was old or young. Whether the death was sudden or drawn out. The death of someone close to us can also cause other traumas we have experienced to resurface.

In my own work, I have taken the principles outlined by the Substance Abuse and Mental Health Services Administration (SAMHSA) and Chayn and formed the core principles that guide my organisation's practice of trauma-informed design for bereavement.

Those principles can be summed up as:
- trust,
- agency,
- welcome,
- hope.

I'll discuss the principles in detail and give examples of what they look like in practice. Each section will offer some questions for your own reflection as you seek to incorporate similar principles into your trauma-informed practice. My hope is that you will come away with a better understanding of how to design trauma-informed content for the difficult subjects of death and grief.

A note on hospice care

Hospice care can vary from country to country, but the shared goal is to maximise the quality of life when a cure is no longer possible or treatment has become too difficult.

In the US, when a person's life expectancy is 6 months or less, they may choose hospice care, which is usually provided in the family home. The family members serve as the primary caregivers for their loved one who is dying. Hospice care provides a team of medical, social, emotional, and spiritual support professionals to assist the family in providing comfort care. Hospice will continue to provide support for 13 months following the person's death.

A note on language

In hospice, "family" is anyone the patient defines as family. Family is not limited to biological relationships. The word "family" helps us remember the reality of those who use the content we design. We cannot practise trauma-informed design without the input and partnership of our families.

These are real people. They're not "users" from whom we can extract data. They're real people who have experienced the death of someone in their lives. We need to listen to them and allow their stories to shape our content design. Throughout this chapter, I will refer to them as "families."

Moving towards a trauma-informed approach

In our content design for people who are grieving, we want families to feel heard and find hope so they can flourish. We want to provide the best help to people who are grieving. But the reality is that change is slow. It can be easy to become overwhelmed and impatient. There is so much to do, so much to explore, so much to think about, so much to change. And we often want it all changed now. Or even better, yesterday.

When moving towards a trauma-informed approach, it's even more important for change to be slow and incremental. Even if we have dozens of content and design workers with endless time and energy, changing all our bereavement websites in one rush would be devastatingly unsettling to our families. We need to think deeply. We need to talk freely and often with families. We need to listen to their stories.

Trust

The principle of trust encompasses ideas of:
- safety,
- transparency,
- clarity,
- consistency,
- comfort,
- accountability.

In my work, if the families using our service don't trust us, our content is useless. Many people come to us not knowing what to expect with death and hospice care. They are frequently overwhelmed, upset, emotional, and stressed. Building trust through our content means we can start to guide their journey through death and grief.

My team and I do this by conducting everything openly with the families we support. We do not hide information from them. We are clear and consistent in the way we communicate, both with our words and with our visual design.

Safety and transparency

Safety is a challenging concept as we think about designing content for grieving families. Everyone's approach to grief is unique. Grief ebbs and flows like waves, often rising up without warning. Families come to our website at any point in their grief journey. We want families to be able to access help whenever they need it. We also recognise that the subject of grief feels unsafe to many families. Families are coming to our website in a state of trauma, so safety must be paramount.

We have created a button on every page for families to access our crisis intervention resources. A link to those resources is also available in the menu at the top of every page. The page itself has numbers available for crisis hotlines, and the telephone number for the local hospice office. Family members who are accessing the site on mobile can call the hotline simply by touching the button. We provide multiple access points to crisis intervention to protect the safety of the families who visit our website.

We can also offer safety by being transparent with what we can and cannot do, and how we use information. I am transparent in my approach. I am upfront about the support our hospice can and cannot provide. I am honest about what I do with families' data. I work to make information easy to find, understand, and use.

When I collect information from families, their consent needs to be explicit. Families need to have the opportunity to approve or deny any cookies and information we collect from them. When I'm designing a cookie notice, I want the wording to be clear about what cookies we'd like to collect. Families, in turn, need to have the option to choose which cookies to accept.

Being explicit about what information we collect on a form, why we need it, and what we will do with it helps families to know their data is safe. They also have the opportunity to opt out if they choose. If they don't want to fill out a contact form because they don't want to give that information, we can provide other ways to contact us. For some families, what feels the safest is to talk to a live human. That must be an option.

Clarity, consistency, and comfort

When we're talking about content surrounding death and grief, it is especially important to use plain language. The Center for Plain Language defines plain language as "communication with clear wording, structure, and design for the intended audience to easily find what they need, understand what they find, and use that information." The US government says that "plain language is communication that is clear and easy to understand for your target audience, regardless of the medium used to deliver it." Can the families who are grieving and who access our website find information easily that can be understood and that will help them in their grief? That is the guiding question for us as we continually work to improve our bereavement content.

Family members who have been caring for their loved ones through death need honest, clear, straightforward information. They don't want to sift through jargon or flowery sentiment. Hospice, death, and bereavement raise an enormous number of questions, many requiring immediate answers. I want families to be able to find what they need quickly and to understand the resources they find.

When talking about death, we need to speak plainly and clearly. In the Monty Python sketch "Dead Parrot" there are roughly 16 different euphemisms for death, including:
- pining for the fjords,
- gone to join the heavenly hosts,
- passed on,
- is no more,
- has ceased to be,
- expired and gone to meet [h]is maker,
- bereft of life,
- shuffled off this mortal coil,
- run down the curtain,
- joined the choir invisible.

In the Monty Python context, it's hilarious. But faced with the death of an actual loved one (rather than a stuffed parrot), it's anything but funny. We don't like to say someone died, so we've come up with innumerable ways to say "died" without actually saying the word.

Here's the reality: changing the word doesn't make the person less dead.

For me, saying "my mom died" felt so much harsher than "my mom lost her battle to cancer" or "I lost my mom." Death is harsh, though. Death is final. Until we can come to terms with that finality, we will have difficulty learning to incorporate grief into our lives. To serve grieving families well, we need to help them do that. We don't want to smooth over the uncomfortable in the hope that they will feel better. Clarity is kinder.

Sometimes, this idea of clarity feels at odds with our desire to speak the language of our users. Most of our families use euphemisms to refer to death. It is difficult for them to say the words "my loved one died." So how do we navigate the balance between clear, direct language and the words our families use? On our website, we developed a soft onboarding sequence that helps families navigate our site. They self-select a particular grief journey to begin their search for resources.

For example, if a family member selects the option "I am grieving a recent loss," they are taken to a landing page with resources. The family member is "speaking" the words "I am grieving," and so the phrase "a recent loss" is used. The content is speaking in the family's voice, and so the euphemism "loss" is used.

However, from that selection, the heading on the landing page is "Did your loved one recently die?" At that point, we do not use euphemisms, but speak clearly about the death of the loved one. The content switches to speaking in the hospice voice. It's a delicate balance, and we are still working through the best approach.

Accountability

If the families who come to us are to trust us, then we must be accountable to them. We are not perfect; we will make mistakes. When we do, we need to acknowledge them and correct them.

When we first launched our website, we received immediate feedback that it was overwhelming. Grief makes it difficult to focus, to remember, and to process information. Our website was presenting a tidal wave of resources to families that was impossible for them to process. We listened to their feedback, we conducted interviews, and we changed the design of the site. The onboarding sequence was developed as a direct result of feedback we got from families.

I also received feedback that families found the navigation structure too complex. We thought by listing multiple options, we were making it clear where to go to find a specific resource. We were wrong. I conducted 2 card sorts with families. They took our 15 menu items down to 3 categories. We changed the navigation to reflect their language and structure.

By listening to the people we design our services for and correcting our mistakes, we show that we are accountable to them. By writing in a way that is clear while also respecting families' own language, we provide comfort. By making access to crisis intervention readily available, we help ensure the safety of families. All those factors build trust with the families we serve.

Questions to consider in your own work:
- How do you build trust with your users?
- If they experience a crisis while accessing your content, can they find help immediately?
- Do you have multiple ways for users to contact you if they have questions?
- Do you have a cookie notice that lets people choose what cookies they want to accept?
- Take a careful look at your forms. Do you really need to know all the information you are asking your users to provide?
- Do you ask for consent explicitly and often?
- What words are your users using? How can you balance the comfort of using their words with the clarity that is needed?
- How often are you talking to your users about your content? What do you do with their feedback?

Agency

Agency includes ideas of:
- choice,
- decision-making,
- collaboration,

- dignity,
- humility.

The concept of a "good death" is often talked about with hospice. What a "good death" looks like is up to the patient and their family. A terminal diagnosis can make you feel like nothing is in your control, you have no voice, and you are powerless. Hospice works diligently and compassionately to listen and to provide choices at every step of the journey.

People who are dying, and those who are grieving their deaths, often feel as if their agency has been taken away from them. It is vital that our content design does not take away their voice, their choice, their capacity for making decisions, or their dignity.

Hospice has agency, voice, and choice as core principles of the work we do. By electing hospice, the patient and their family are immediately involved in developing their specific care plan. Each week, that plan is revisited and updated. What are the patient's goals? Maybe there is one last trip they want to take. Perhaps they want to finish that quilt they started for their granddaughter. Maybe they want a little more time to say goodbye to all the ones who are important to them. The entire hospice team is then focused on helping the patient achieve their goals.

In contrast, when families are faced with a sudden, unexpected death, they may not have had the opportunity to make choices about the death itself. They now find themselves almost immediately overwhelmed with choices they never wanted to make. What about a funeral? Burial or cremation? Who do we need to call? What about the house? The dog? The partner? The kids?

But those questions do not actually represent agency in a trauma-informed sense. They represent decision overload.

Grief affects more than just your emotions. The idea of "grief fog" is very real. When you're grieving, it's difficult to think, to categorise or sort information. Even the simplest tasks seem to require more concentrated effort to complete.

How can our content design reflect more of the philosophy behind hospice and less of the decision overload most of us experience with the death of a loved one? Part of the way we can address that in our content design is through the principle of agency.

I mentioned in the previous section on accountability that we made changes to our website based on feedback from families. Those changes were not just a way to build trust with the families we serve, but also a way to restore agency to them. Now when families come to our website, they are able to self-select a path to guide their interaction with our site.

They can choose from the following options:
- I have not yet lost my loved one
- I am grieving a specific loss
- I am grieving a recent loss
- My grief feels like it's all too much
- I want to connect with others who are grieving
- I am helping someone who is grieving

When they choose an option, they are provided with a sample of resources on that topic, and additional options to return to the home page or search for something specific. They are also free to browse the site rather than selecting a defined path. How they interact with the resources we provide is up to them. They get to choose.

Collaboration

We include collaboration and partnership under the principle of agency. We don't just want to talk about giving families a voice. We want to work with them — alongside them — as we design content. Collaborating with people who are grieving must be handled in a way that protects their dignity.

Who is better equipped to tell a story about a grief journey after the death of a loved one: the user researcher who has talked to the person, or the person who actually experienced the death of a loved one? When I write it like that, it seems obvious. If we want to share the grief stories of families, we need to partner with them to tell those stories. We need to work with them to think about how to do that in a safe way that avoids re-traumatisation. We need to learn how to co-design.

Here's a true confession. When I first began learning about co-design, I had several immediate concerns:
- What if people don't want to talk about the death of their loved one?
- Content design isn't something everyone can do; that's why companies hire designers. How will our families know what to do?
- But the style guide . . . the writing for the web tips . . . draft, edits, publication deadlines . . . how do I follow those with people who are not my employees?
- It sounds like it takes a lot of time, money, and people resources; we don't have that.

I was thinking of co-designing as having families do the exact same work that I do. But that's not quite right. Co-design begins with user research done in a trauma-informed way. We talk with families about their experiences; we listen to what was helpful and what was not helpful. But our collaboration doesn't stop there.

Together, we look at our current website and see what works and what doesn't. Where families identify things that don't work, or things that are missing, we work together to come up with a solution. No, we don't need to teach them to use Figma to do a wireframe or give them access to our design system. But we could make a quick sketch of what a better content structure might look like. They can point out if the visuals are helpful or harmful or irrelevant. They could jot down a brief outline of some specific content or topics. Could we invite them to write a personal story in their voice rather than trying to make their voice fit into our company style guide?

We often say that everyone grieves in their own way, but families want to know that their own way is "normal." Several family members mentioned that hearing the stories of others whose loved ones had died was helpful in reconciling the uniqueness and normality of their own experience. We want to share those stories.

We have a place on our bereavement website where friends and family can leave a brief note for or about their loved one who has died. But simply having the space is not sufficient. We want to encourage families to share their stories in that space for others who might find it helpful.

However, we need to ensure that we are sharing stories in a way that is safe for both the author and the reader. We don't want to re-traumatise other family members by compelling them to read someone else's story. There needs to be the opportunity to opt out of seeing those stories if someone chooses.

We think we can do better with listening to the voice of families and empowering them to be the leaders in their own healing. Yes, we are the "professionals," but they are the ones living in the midst of death and grief. Valuing agency in our content design magnifies the dignity of the families we serve. They matter. Our content design must keep them and their stories at the centre.

And we can only do that if we listen to them. Incorporating collaboration, agency, voice, and choice as part of our trauma-informed design takes an incredible amount of humility. We have to be willing to acknowledge that we don't have all the answers. We cannot solve every problem, right every wrong, fix everything that is broken. But we can listen; we can learn; we can welcome and include families. They are the real experts.

Questions to consider in your own work:
- Where and how are you providing choices for your users?
- Are those choices real choices or just superficial?
- Can they opt out of content that might be re-traumatising?
- Do you practise co-design? What might it look like to do so?
- How can you protect the dignity of your users who are preparing for a loved one's death or trying to manage details of a death in the midst of great grief?
- How can you listen more to your users?

Welcome

Grief is global. No matter what our identity is, we will all experience grief. But at the same time, the way in which we address that grief will be uniquely shaped by who we are.

Every family member who visits our site has a unique set of experiences, knowledge, successes, and trials that shape who they are and how they respond to grief. We want them to feel welcome when they come to our website. We don't want them to be re-traumatised by what they encounter. We want them to know that they can find help that is for them.

In order to practise the idea of welcome, we need to be able to look seriously at how the issue of identity affects our response to trauma, and how we can be mindful of those effects when designing content for people who are grieving. Our identity is multifaceted and includes our personal history, our culture, our race, our gender, our ethnicity, and a host of other variables.

While it would be impossible for every piece of content to include all the possible variables that affect a family member's identity, we can — and must — look for ways to serve, in some way, all family members.

Chayn states: "Designing for inclusion must consider how position, identity, vulnerabilities, knowledge, and skills shape trauma and recovery." The National Hospice and Palliative Care Organization (NHPCO) references the idea of "community presence."

We can start by asking some basic questions. Do:
- families see themselves represented on our website?
- we show multiple ages, genders, ethnicities in our images?
- the authors of our content come from a wide variety of backgrounds and contexts?
- we have specific resources available to address some of the cultural differences in the way families view death and grief?
- we offer a variety of ways to engage with our resources?

Localisation and translation are concrete ways to create welcome. One important place to begin is to understand what the "heart language" is of the families who use our site. We don't currently have reliable information on the languages our families speak, but once we do, we will look at providing resources in those languages.

We want resources that better represent the wide variety of backgrounds of our families. Here is where welcome overlaps with collaboration. There are communities of people who have been historically underserved by hospice and who are actively distrustful of hospice. We want to cultivate a community of presence where they are welcomed and invited to share their stories.

Accessibility matters greatly in terms of promoting welcome. Clear language, solid information architecture, appropriate colour choices, and simple layouts all serve to make our site more accessible. Sites that are accessible benefit everyone. People who are grieving need design that is accessible.

It is challenging to find the best way to make our site equitable and inclusive. Having segmented resources for every identity does not necessarily promote inclusivity. The segmentation itself can reinforce the idea that some communities are "other." We do not want families to feel lost, excluded, and on the outside when they come looking for support. We want our content design to reflect the beauty of diversity without the harshness of segmentation.

We do not ask for demographic information in the forms on our website. We have access to that information through the health information we collect. We do not need to ask again in our bereavement content.

Some of the families we serve live in areas where internet access is spotty or non-existent. Many of these families do not feel comfortable using the internet. People who are grieving often want to come back to resources multiple times. It is helpful to have a way to provide a printable option of our resources.

Trauma-informed design for people who are grieving provides a space where all are welcomed. Through words, images, layouts, colours, and organisation, we can be present with families at all phases of their grief by designing content that reflects their unique identity.

Questions to consider in your own work:
- Is your content welcoming to your users? This can be especially difficult if you are managing the more logistical details of a death. How can you make the process of filing a life insurance claim feel welcoming?
- Is your content accessible for everyone?
- Do you have options for non-digital resources and info?

Hope

When we are working with families in hospice, hope seems in desperate need, and all too often it is absent. Death doesn't seem to coexist with hope for most people who are grieving. Grief itself often feels unending and hopeless. By working towards a more trauma-informed approach to content design, we can offer hope and healing to grieving families.

When we work towards trust, agency, and welcome, we create an environment where hope can grow. When hope grows, families can thrive. That is our ultimate goal. It's not site visits or revenue generated or reviews left. Those things are helpful and important. But the reason we do what we do is to offer support, hope, and healing to families.

In his book *Designing Hope*, Jeremy Cherry defines "hopeful design" as "a framework that creates hope by practising in an ecosystem, honouring that community with its solutions, and sharing in the responsibility of its outcomes." In that definition are echoes of trust, agency, and welcome. Trauma-informed design ought to be hopeful. Cherry's 3 principles for hopeful design are:

- **be curious:** learn from your surroundings from within an ecosystem,
- **be compassionate:** form solutions from experiential learning,
- **be humble:** share responsibility, no matter the outcome.

As we apply those principles to our content design for grieving people, we can help to foster hope. We have to start where we started in our previous 3 principles — with understanding our families. We need to learn from them and what their experiences are with death and grief. Not to exploit them, but to honour them.

We cannot fix grief. We can offer hope for a life that can still flourish with grief, not just in spite of it. Compassion is more than being aware of another's distress; it is being moved to take action to lessen their load. As we are conscious of the distress experienced by families who are grieving, we experience the desire to make it better.

Do all our images present people who are sad or angry or in despair? Can we provide images of people who are thriving and even happy without lacking compassion for those we aren't yet there? Is our colour scheme soothing without being sad? Can it be hopeful without being frivolous? Those are difficult questions to answer, and should be answered through user research.

Families who have experienced the death of a loved one in hospice often have a strong desire to give something back to hospice. They are looking for ways to donate their time and their money in support of hospice. But they are not looking to do that in the immediate aftermath of the death. We provide information about volunteering and donating, but not on our home page. In fact, not even at the top of any page. We have access to it via footer links, and at the bottom of a page about life after loss.

For the families who have not yet experienced the death of their loved one, hopeful design has a different focus. We want to point families toward finding hope in making the most of the time they have left. We want to highlight opportunities for sharing and saving memories of their loved one.

We are currently working on some research and designs for a page that will focus on the logistical aspects of death. That may not at first seem hopeful. Helping our families accept the reality of a loved one's coming death and taking time to ensure they know their loved one's wishes is a way to promote hope in grief and dying. We can help families prepare with their loved one so they can handle all the necessary tasks, knowing they are doing what their loved one wanted. We also offer hope to the dying as well, a confidence in knowing they have prepared their family as well as possible.

Questions to consider in your own work:
- How can you learn from your users, especially when they have experienced a death?
- How can you lessen the load of grief through your content?
- What does a hopeful outcome look like for your users?
- How can your content reflect the serious nature of death and grief while still offering hope for the future?

Balancing hope and death

Our content design should reflect the serious nature of death and grief. That doesn't mean it needs to be dark and sad. Balancing hope and death in our content design is not easy. But it can help families move towards a place of hopeful flourishing, when they are ready.

We won't always get it right, and that's why we need to be humble. We will be accountable to the families we serve. We will own our mistakes and correct them. We will work to better understand how families approach death and grief. In doing so, we will offer them hope.

References and further reading

- "Five Steps to Plain Language," The Center for Plain Language
- "An introduction to plain language," Digital.gov (United States Government)
- "12 questions on Trauma-informed Design at Chayn," Chayn (2024)
- "Inclusion and Access Toolkit," National Hospice and Palliative Care Organisation (2020)
- Jeremy D. Cherry, *Designing Hope*

Chapter 3
Designing questions

by Rachel Edwards, Jane McFadyen, and Steph Mann

We ask, and answer, countless questions each day. Many questions lead to seamless interactions, things we answer without stopping for thought. Others might be more intimate, and require a level of trust.

Asking questions is a careful process, especially when you aren't actually speaking to someone. Instead, you might be asking questions through a form or a website. Those questions might seem harmless: what is your name? What is your date of birth? Or they might be questions about some of the most difficult things someone has experienced.

Designing a service usually means we need to get information from people. And content designers are often at the heart of how we get that information, forming the questions and the guidance to help someone answer them.

But questions add cognitive load. They also require an element of trust: what will an organisation do with the answer? There needs to be safety. Is there support to answer this question, or if the question brings up previous trauma? And can a good question empower someone to do what they need to do?

As we say throughout this book, there is no checklist you can follow to produce a perfect, trauma-informed question or form. We 3 authors have worked on services that ask questions about death, abuse, and difficult topics for young people. Here are some of the things we have learned about writing questions for people who have experienced trauma.

Have a question protocol

Start by determining if you really need to ask the question at all. One of the best ways to do this is with a question protocol. The GOV.UK service manual explains:

> "Make a list of all the information you need from your users.
>
> Only add a question if you know:
>
> - that you need the information to deliver the service,
> - why you need the information,
> - what you'll do with it,
> - which users need to give you the information,
> - how you'll check the information is accurate,
> - how to keep the information up to date and secure.
>
> ... A question protocol forces you (and your organisation) to question why you're asking users for each item of information. It gives you a way of challenging and pushing back against unnecessary questions if you need to."

Write your question protocol down somewhere. Complete it as a team: involve business analysts, service designers, and policy or subject matter experts. You can refer back to it if you need to explain why the question is, or isn't, there. This can be particularly helpful with stakeholders who might want to ask extra questions. You can use the question protocol to:

- get early agreement about the questions you are asking,
- push back on requests to include additional questions.

Having the protocol means you have a consistent agreement about what you are asking and why. If the team changes, the protocol is a useful way of bringing new members up-to-speed and ensuring consistency.

Remember that questions add cognitive load. The best thing we can do for someone is to take away any unnecessary questions and additional cognitive load. Avoid gathering any "just in case" information. Ask yourself whether you really need to capture things like:

- title,
- middle name,
- marital status,
- education,
- addresses, including postcodes or zip codes.

Say why you are asking

If you have a question protocol, you will already know why you are asking each question. But the person completing your form doesn't.

You can build trust with them by saying:

- why you are asking,
- what you need it for,
- who you will share the information with,
- what you will do with their answers,
- what they can do if they need to change their answer or add more information.

This doesn't have to be a long explanation (it could even be hint text), and you might not need to do it for each question. But if, for example, you ask for information about previous addresses, you could include an explanation like this:

> "We need this information to check you are eligible for this service. We may share it with any housing authorities you name to confirm dates. If you do not want us to share this information, tick the box below and do not complete these questions. We will contact you to discuss your options."

This solution may not be practical in every case or for every question. But it can help establish some trust with someone who is worried about why you are asking and what happens with their answer.

Think about when to ask questions

It's also worth thinking about *when* you ask a question. Make sure there is a logic behind your question order that supports the person answering the question.

For example, a person filling in a form for compensation might need to give some background information to determine their eligibility. Ask these questions first, before you move on to ask more detailed questions. If they are not eligible, why gather more information?

It's better for users if we direct them in the right way. By asking the right questions in the right order, we remove the burden from the users. If they aren't eligible, we don't need to gather the rest of the data.

Directing people out of a service that would be a waste of their time and effort can actually be helpful. Establish the most important eligibility first, so you can filter people out if they are in the wrong place. If someone is directed out, make sure you explain why, and if there are any alternative options for them to take.

While it's always annoying to complete countless questions only to find you are not eligible, this has an extra importance for questions around trauma. Disclosing details about trauma can be harmful, as can forcing someone to relive an experience and recount it to a stranger (or computer screen). Doing this and then discovering they are not eligible can create new trauma and harm for someone.

Use branching to get users to relevant points

Whether you are using a paper or a digital form, you can still filter users to the right areas of your form. This means that they only answer questions relevant to them.

For example, if your service is only for people over 18 years old, this is a good starter question. You can then immediately redirect younger users somewhere with more relevant content. (If you are redirecting someone, be sure to explain where you are sending them and why.)

Or, if you are asking about location-specific information, you can filter out users who are not in the right area to somewhere more relevant to them. This saves people from filling in unnecessary information. It also keeps your organisation from collecting and storing data it doesn't need.

Repetition — perceived or real

If you have a question protocol, you should know why each question is included, and you should avoid any repetition. But sometimes repetition happens. This could be because:

- you have to ask similar questions in different parts of a form (for example, name and date of birth),
- the questions are not actually the same but appear to be because they aren't well-worded or explained.

At best, this is annoying for someone completing the form. But it can have another result.

> "I was once developing a multi-part form that had similar questions in different parts. There was a good business reason for this, and we thought at worst it would be a little annoying.
>
> "But if someone doesn't trust you, or your organisation or service, they may perceive it differently, as became clear when we tested the form. The service users who had experienced trauma saw this repetition as questioning. They became suspicious of the service because they thought they were being asked the same thing twice to see if their answer changed. Some even likened it to being cross-examined."

If you need to ask a question twice, explain why. And if your questions are very similar, consider combining them or removing one.

People might answer every question

> "The form I was working on included optional questions, and in some places the choice to skip a section or only complete 1 of 2 sections. But people did not want to leave an answer empty. This was a surprise to me. They said they didn't want to do it wrong and have their form rejected. So instead, they used their time and emotional energy to answer questions they didn't need to."

Telling people they don't have to do something, or that they can choose between options, is tricky design. It's not impossible, but people may get confused or misunderstand. Don't just hope that people read the instructions at the top of the page. Work with your research team, if you have one, and test wherever possible to see how people actually behave with your form.

In this example, the problem was partly because the form was hard copy, not online. A digital solution might allow someone to bypass questions that aren't relevant to them by using proper branching.

You can add optional questions if there is a clear user need for them. Don't mark fields that are required, but do mark your optional fields. We are used to forms using an asterisks (*) to show required fields, but this can be overlooked or ignored. Clearly marking optional fields instead takes away this anxiety and gives the user a choice.

For example:

Do you want to learn more about us?

Phone number (optional) _____

Email _____

Ask different questions

Many topics can be sensitive for different reasons; for example, information around a person's:

- marital status,
- religion,
- contact information,
- children or number of children,
- health concern.

The person completing the form might be completing it alone. Or they might have help from a social worker, teacher, or family member and not want to give personal information in front of them.

If you can, give users options to capture general rather than specific information. For example:

- give an age range instead of specific years,
- have a salary range instead of an exact amount,
- ask if someone has children rather than how many they have.

Provide guidance and support for answering questions

It can be hard to ask a good question. You can ask the same question of a dozen different people, and they might answer it in 12 different ways. Try it and see.

But your goal for your form is that someone completes it successfully. To do this, they're likely to need some guidance.

In its simplest form, this might be how to format a date or phone number. Or it could be more complicated information about what to include in a statement.

There are several ways you can provide guidance. Which you choose will depend on your resources, your channels, and what works best for your users. You could try:

- adding guidance next to the questions, or the option to select for more information (if it's a digital form),
- having separate guidance to refer to when completing the form (this can be a good option for a paper form),
- giving contact details so someone can ask questions directly (if you choose this option, make sure to give opening hours or an estimate of how long a response will take).

Provide choice

Where you can, provide choice. Some users will want support while others will prefer to complete the form independently. If you can, design for both options. Do not assume that everyone can or will ask a friend or family member for help if they need it. This is disempowering, and presupposes everyone has friends or family to ask. It also assumes the:

- person answering the question is comfortable sharing their answers,
- friend or family member can understand what is needed, which may not always be the case.

In some cases you can also give a choice about how to answer or provide information. If you give options, let the user know if there are consequences associated with those options.

For example:

Do you have details of your insurance provider?
- ☐ If yes, please provide them.
- ☐ If no, you do not need to provide them now. However, this might delay your application by 1 to 2 weeks.

Yes and no are not the only options

Sometimes people need more than 2 options. "Yes" or "no" aren't always helpful. What if they don't know the answer? Offering a third or fourth option can reassure them, give them choices, and help them to complete the form.

For example:

Do you know your national insurance number?
- ☐ Yes
- ☐ No
- ☐ I'm not sure (if selected you could direct them to GOV.UK to help them find their number)

You can make the outputs for "no" and "I'm not sure" the same: the difference is it gives the user visual options that match their mental model.

Tone is important

You might be asking questions that are difficult to answer. You might even be asking questions that seem unusual as a way to get the information that you need.

The tone of how you ask these is very important. Your tone needs to:
- build trust,
- sound supportive,
- not sound like it is blaming.

Open-ended questions have a softer tone and allow people more control over their thoughts and answers. Remember to:
- explain why you are asking any questions that might be difficult to answer,

- give people the opportunity to ask questions if they need clarity — this is much easier in person, but you can do it online, too, through email, phone, or live chat,
- reframe how you ask questions. Instead of "why," try "are you able to" or "can you." Instead of "How," ask "would you" or "could you."

Using clear language that removes any ambiguity is also important.

> "While researching with bereaved people, we learnt that people really valued and appreciated clear use of language.
>
> For example, when describing a bereavement, people often naturally want to avoid using words in a service like 'died.' By trying to use 'softer' words, they might instead use 'late' or 'passed away.'
>
> But this is tricky, because not everyone understands euphemisms like 'late,' and they are hard to accurately translate for many languages."

A preference for euphemisms can depend on language and culture. But unless you have research that tells you otherwise, avoid euphemisms in your digital service; be clear instead.

Be contactable, and helpful

Let people know how to contact your organisation if they have questions. Make it clear that they are welcome to get in touch, and someone will help them with their questions.

This may seem obvious, but for people with a distrust of service providers or government services, it can be important. In our experience, people who had experienced trauma often considered forms and questions to be a test. They felt like they were being judged or graded and did not want to "get it wrong" and miss out on accessing a service or benefit.

To help counter this worry:
- be approachable and contactable,
- make contact information clear and visible,
- manage expectations by providing opening hours and estimated response times.

No easy questions

How someone experiences trauma is unique to them. So are the questions they might find difficult.

> "In the service I worked on, the application forms were long. To make the process simpler, we decided to start with the easy questions: name and date of birth. We thought everyone could answer them effortlessly and without thought. This would get them off to a good start before we moved on to the difficult questions about their abuse.
>
> But then we tested it. And it turns out, for a lot of people who were applying to the scheme, these were not easy questions.
>
> Some of them had had their names changed — by adoption, or because they were called a different name in the care setting.
>
> Some of them didn't know their date of birth, because records had been lost, destroyed, or not kept.
>
> These easy questions were actually not easy at all.
>
> What could we do? There was no way of getting around the fact that we needed a name and a date of birth. We had to ask the questions.
>
> But we could put words around them that recognised there might be some difficulty answering. We put a note that explained 'In some cases, your name or date of birth may have changed or be unclear. Please give the name and date of birth you regularly use for official documents.'
>
> We couldn't get rid of the trauma. But we could do our best not to add to it."

For many people, this assumption would have been right. They could have easily answered questions about their name and date of birth. But not here.

Don't make assumptions about what will and won't be difficult.

Questions around title, for example, can often be difficult for people to answer if they:
- are divorced,
- never married,
- have a different title than the one they were assigned at birth,
- don't associate with binary title options.

Security questions that ask about favourite teachers, first pets, or previous addresses can be difficult for someone who had an unstable childhood.

Questions that ask for a first and last name can be challenging to answer accurately for people who:
- don't have a surname,
- have different names on different documents.

Think carefully about each question, and apply trauma-informed principles to every question you ask.

Question with care

Asking questions often exaggerates or exposes power imbalances. Questions can provoke memories, reactions, and feelings that may be unexpected.

When you are designing questions or a form, remember that you want the person at the other end of the screen (or paper) to succeed. You want them to complete their task, and you want to avoid causing them harm.

Starting your question design using trauma informed principles is, however, just the beginning. An early design question set is an assumption of what is needed, but you will not know if it works and how well it is understood until people (not your team) try it.

So test it with the users of your service. It's their lived experience, their pain points, and their barriers that will really show you how to iterate your design to meet their needs.

References and further reading

- "Structuring forms," GOV.UK
- Ashley Peacock, "Designing accessible security questions: a trauma-informed approach" (2023)
- "Names," GOV.UK
- "Why your form only needs one name field," UX Movement (2017)
- "Why Indian immigrants' 1st names sometimes end up as XXX on Canadian passports," CBC News (2022)
- "Heiltsuk woman unable to restore Indigenous surname on ID because system can't handle its spelling," CBC News (2021)
- Fibria Novytasari, "I do not have a last name" (published on LinkedIn) (September 2024)
- Helen Lawson, "The importance of empathetic language, voice and tone," *The Content Strategy Podcast*, episode 36 (2021)

Chapter 4
Trauma and technology

by kon syrokostas

Practising trauma-informed design

It was 2022 and I was in a Zoom call. The host, now a friend and a teacher, was a trauma survivor. When it was time to end the call, she shared with us that the red "end" button was activating (sometimes called "triggering") for her. It made her feel like finishing the call meant she was doing something bad.

At that time, I was working as a mobile and front-end developer. In my free time I was learning about trauma. So my friend's observation instantly caught my attention. I found myself asking: is there an intersection between trauma and technology? And is there such a thing as trauma-informed (UI/UX) design?

Not long after the call, I searched the Internet for "trauma-informed design." There weren't many things back then, but there were some. And those first videos and articles marked the beginning of my journey towards becoming a trauma-informed designer (and developer).

It's been a while since that time. I've joined calls. I read articles, papers, and books. I spoke with amazing people. I wrote a 20-week blog on the topic, and I took on more software projects related to mental health and trauma. There are a lot of things I learned and a lot of things I had to unlearn. I made mistakes, and I very often still do.

This is the nature of this work. Being a trauma-informed designer isn't something we become. It isn't something we can "finish" after taking a course, completing a certification, or reading a book.

It's a practice.

A practice of leaning towards the people who've been harmed and listening to what they need.

A practice of working with our own hurt and of grappling with our power and ability to cause harm.

And, ultimately, a practice of healing and connection.

I invite you to read this chapter with that in mind. The chapter includes principles and patterns that I and others have found useful when designing with and for trauma survivors. But they are not universal truths, nor are they the only ones. Not everything will resonate, and that's okay.

They are also not a checklist. Dr. Carol Scott, when talking about trauma-informed principles, often tells people that they can think of them as ingredients to a recipe. I intentionally don't go over the trauma-informed principles in this chapter, but I use the same metaphor. Not every ingredient is used in the same way in every dish. Figuring out how to use each is also a practice. Hopefully, this chapter will help you get started with that.

A note on the words I use

Throughout this chapter I use the word "technology."

Normally that word refers to any kind of technology, from a computer to a dishwasher, and from a printing press to a steam engine. That's not how I'll use it here. Whenever I use the word "technology," I am referring to information technology — that is, anything that has to do with computers.

I am not touching on all information technology, but I'm exploring the parts of it that most people directly interact with. This excludes things like servers, network switches, and so on. Unless a distinction is made, whenever you see the word "technology," you can think of your laptop or your phone and of the software that runs on it.

When I use the word "tech," I'm generally referring to the companies that work in information technology.

The word "Internet" written with a capital "I" refers to the World Wide Web. When written with a lowercase "i" (internet), it refers to any network of interconnected devices. In this chapter I intentionally use the word with a capital "I."

A note on my positionality

When reading any material, I believe it's important to stay aware of the positionality of the author. I am a white, cishet, currently able-bodied man who lives in Greece (Europe). I hold a master's degree in computer engineering and work as a developer. I also identify as a trauma survivor.

Most of these identities come with power. I've tried to stay mindful of that as I was writing this chapter. I don't know if I've always succeeded.

A note on why this matters for content designers

Content designers aren't often developers, so it may seem like there is limited value in reading a chapter about technology. But many elements of software design rely on working with content designers.

Wording for error messages and buttons, for example, are all things that should be designed together. Adding components and choosing colours and images are often better done in partnership.

My aim in this chapter is to show you where you might influence the creation of a software product, and the questions and issues you might want to raise with your developers to create more trauma-informed experiences.

Software: interacting with technology

When considering trauma, we need to acknowledge that in every experience there is room for harm, activation, and re-traumatisation. That's a hard reality to work with. At the same time, in every experience there is room for connection, restoration, and healing. I find hope in knowing that.

Software is what first piqued my interest around trauma-informed design. That's partly because I design and build software. But it's also because software is how we usually engage with technology. Software allows for experiences to happen, which means that software can both cause harm and support healing. Intentionality in how software is designed can make all the difference, and it's at the heart of a trauma-informed practice.

Here are some of the ways in which we can be intentional when designing software.

Reducing cognitive load

Cognitive load refers to the load placed on working memory by a range of cognitive processes. In short, it's how much "thinking" we need to do. When designing trauma-informed software, it's important to be extra attentive to it.

Creating software that isn't cognitively taxing isn't new. It has always been part of the role of design. But when working with trauma survivors, being brief and clear becomes even more important. Trauma can impair our cognitive abilities, which means that we might have a hard time concentrating, focusing, or making decisions. Emotional activations are also all too common with trauma. When we are activated, the thinking part of our brain shuts down. This can make engaging with information harder.

Some design patterns that can increase cognitive load (and should be avoided) are:
- large blocks of text or long sentences,
- long videos or audio files,
- large collections of items (for example, in a navigation bar),
- asking people to make multiple decisions at the same time,
- long onboarding flows,
- asking people to remember something that's not right in front of them.

Consider breaking down the information in smaller chunks or reducing the available options to only what's truly important. Research can be very helpful in this process.

Giving back agency

My friend, who is a sexual assault survivor advocate, told me how she would meet survivors at the hospital right after an assault. She would bring with her different kinds of food and ask them what they would like to have. In that way, she would give them a choice. Trauma strips us of our agency. Having a choice again, no matter how small, can feel empowering.

Our design can also equip survivors with choices, supporting them in recovering a sense of agency. Here are some examples of choice we can include:
- dark or light theme,
- ways of signing up or logging in (email, social sign-in, one time password, biometric authentication),
- levels of security (enabling or disabling encryption or multi-factor authentication),
- ways to view content,
- ways to ask for help (customer support chats, chats with an AI agent, phone calls),
- the amount of notifications,
- the amount of personal information shared publicly,
- the amount and types of data that are collected.

However, it's important to remember that too many choices can be overwhelming and tiring. Because of that, I like to distinguish between meaningful choices and burdensome choices.

A meaningful choice strengthens a survivor's agency by letting them decide about something they care about. The choice might be simple and optional, offering a survivor a sense of control without significantly increasing their associated cognitive load.

A burdensome choice is one that a survivor doesn't want to deal with. It's potentially too unimportant for them, it's asked of them too often, or it requires a lot of thinking. Sometimes it might refer to a situation in which they simply don't know what's best (for example, a very technical configuration option). Instead of helping them feel in control, it increases the cognitive load associated with using the design, making it harder to use. It can also cause stress.

The separation between meaningful and burdensome choices isn't always clear-cut or objective. What's important for me might be burdensome for you, or the other way around. In order to work with the subjectivity of this matter, you can:

- conduct research,
- gather data on how often people engage with each choice and consider adapting the ones that are rarely used or require unnecessary decision making - always see this data in the context of accessibility and safety,
- offer a choice of how much customisation (or, in general, how many choices) people would like to have.

Choices and safety

When there is risk associated with your design, offering choices can be a way to mitigate that. For example, Chayn has a feature that allows survivors to receive resources by email. Chayn also gives them the choice to select a custom email subject. This can help subscribers stay safe in case someone sees their email inbox.

Features like that can give survivors agency over their own safety. For someone who's experienced trauma, this can feel particularly empowering.

Choices and transparency

Choices can also go beyond direct ways of engaging with a design. Indirect choices can look like:
- picking which files to upload on the cloud,
- choosing which events to add on a calendar,
- deciding what information to disclose when chatting with an AI companion.

As designers, it's our responsibility to help people make informed decisions in cases like these. Being transparent and explicit about how data is used and stored can give people the information they need.

Intentional friction

When we talk about agency, we also need to talk about friction.

For years, designing digital experiences has meant making things so simple and seamless that people would naturally flow through them. Opening a video streaming platform provides us with the videos we'd want to watch without us having to search for them. Watching a video directly leads us to the next one. And the next one . . . and the next one.

With barely a click, we're able to interact with the platform and consume hours of "relevant" content. It's seamless, easy, frictionless.

In many cases, we have achieved that. We can now consume all the content we want with minimal action. We can find dates by simply swiping left and right. We can order food with fewer than 10 taps. And we can learn "everything" by talking with an AI companion on our phone.

If we consider where it all started (punched card and writing commands in a terminal), the evolution of software is impressive. And it's not only that software has become easier to use. What used to be a specific experience in time ("I will open my computer to do x") is now a fluid and pervasive part of our lives.

This isn't always bad. Technology now lets us do more, faster, and better. It's more convenient to use and, overall, it's often a better experience. But this convenience isn't always good either. Because when we make something frictionless, we can end up taking away people's choices in the process. Frictionless technology can imply choiceless technology.

If we can spend hours watching video content without taking any action, how much choice are we actively making over what we watch or for how long?

When the information we consume is filtered through social media algorithms, search engines, and AI models, how much choice do we have over our information sources?

And when popular apps are pre-installed on our phones, how much choice do we have over which ones we are using (and where our data goes)?

I'm usually quite optimistic when thinking about tech, so I'm not trying to paint an image of a dystopian tech world. I am, however, trying to point us to the idea that frictionless technology might not always be what we need. Especially when practising trauma-informed design.

And that's where intentional friction (or speed bumps) come in. Friction, because we break the continuous stream of automatic actions to create space for choice. Intentional, because we don't add it everywhere; we carefully place it where it can equip people with agency, or where its absence could cause harm.

What could this look like? Here are some ideas:
- directing people to another place for content that may be activating, so they have to actively choose to see it,
- social media feeds that stop after a certain amount of posts; we can see more, but we'll have to restart the app first,
- video conferencing software that forces us to pause for a few minutes after several hours of meetings (this can work for games, too),
- streaming platforms that stop autoplaying videos after a while,
- apps and websites that don't automatically "remember" us (this can also be good for safety),
- notifications that are disabled by default and can be enabled in the settings (also good for safety).

In general, intentional friction can help protect us from harm. When an algorithm or a technology becomes so automatic that it strips us of our agency and autonomy, harm can (and almost definitely will) happen. Intentional friction instils moments of pause and space that give us back choice.

But intentional friction is more of a pillow than a wall. It's extremely helpful, but it requires buy-in from the people developing and, most importantly, funding those technologies. As we'll see later, the real protection against harm requires a change in the culture of tech.

Ingredient shelf: software

In this section I include some specific practices for working with software. This isn't an exhaustive list nor a checklist. I once again use Dr. Carol Scott's ingredients metaphor here to convey that.

So, welcome to the first ingredient shelf! This one's for software.

UX fundamentals

Trauma-informed software is built on top of "good" software. The fundamentals of UX design are the basis of a trauma-informed practice.

Move towards
- usability heuristics,
- considering the intersections between accessibility and trauma in your product strategy and decision making.

Move away from
- deceptive patterns.

Communication

Warm, inviting, welcoming, and inclusive content and visuals help survivors stay regulated while engaging with a design. It's important to avoid content and visuals that can activate or re-traumatise a survivor.

Content

Move towards
- warm, inviting copy with language and tone that is validating, affirming, empathetic, understanding, and non-judgmental,
- inclusive and gender-responsive language. As Chayn recommends, "use gender-neutral language without being gender-ignorant."

Move away from
- shaming or blaming the person using your design,
- content walls and content that adds a lot of cognitive load. Make sure that this is true in both desktop and mobile designs; content that looks great on a large screen might be too long on a smaller one.

Typefaces

Move towards
- accessible typefaces with adequate letter spacing and minimised imposter shapes.

Move away from
- hard-to-read decorative or hand-written script font families.

Move with curiosity
- consider picking typefaces created by designers with marginalised identities.

Colours

Move towards
- warm and soothing colours,

- in light themes, softening the white background using your primary colour. In my experience, this results in a more soothing experience than softening with grey. Alternatively, use a very soft non-white background,
- accessible colour contrasts. Use tools that help you check accessibility of colour combinations, like "Who Can Use."

Move with curiosity
- be mindful of over-emphasising western associations with colours (for example, that red is a bad colour only used for errors and urgent notifications).

Images

Move towards
- using warm and inviting imagery that makes trauma survivors feel calm and welcomed,
- inclusive images or illustrations of people,
- images of nature and animals.

Move away from
- using images that directly depict harm or suffering which can activate and re-traumatise survivors,
- images of items that are often involved in traumatic events or that many people have negative associations with (for example, guns).

Motion and animation

Move towards
- allowing animations to be disabled, ideally at the operating system level.

Move with curiosity
- use animations, moving images, videos, and motion sparingly. Trauma can make concentrating harder. Animations and motion can be distracting, and that can be emotionally activating,
- animations can cause vomiting and intense discomfort for people with vestibular disorders.

The "exit this page" button

The "exit this page" button is a component designed to provide a fast and safe path out of a website. It's often used in websites that could place people in physical or emotional danger if they are seen browsing them. When the "exit this page" button is clicked, it sends people to another predetermined, "safer" website, like a search engine or the local weather.

The button should work like this:

1. I'm in `searchEngine.com`,
2. I go to `website.com`, which has the "exit this page" button,
3. I press the button,
4. I am navigated to the local weather website (let's call it `localWeather.org`),
5. I press the browser's back button and am navigated back to `searchEngine.com` (`website.com` is skipped).

Move towards
- make sure that when the "exit this page" button is pressed, it disables the ability to return back to the original website,
- opening a second tab or using an overlay to quickly hide the open website, using a keyboard shortcut (for example, `Esc`, triple `Shift`) to activate the button,
- using the "exit this page" pattern in some situations. The "exit this page" pattern includes 2 additional pages, 1 that explains how the "exit this page" button works and 1 that provides more information for safety online. This pattern can be useful when the "exit this page" button only appears in specific parts of the website (for example, a form to report domestic abuse in a government website) or when you have found in your research that people are misunderstanding how the "exit this page" button works.

Move away from
- making the button hard to access. Don't hide it behind dialogs or inside navigation drawers.

Move with curiosity
- be mindful of where you send survivors. News or weather websites often include negative headlines that can be activating. Consider using websites with soothing content, such as images of small animals, instead,
- the most common implementation of the "exit this page" button can fail when someone visits multiple pages of the website that contains it. Using the above example, consider the following flow: `searchEngine.com` > `website.com` > `website.com/resources` > `localWeather.org`. Because we're implementing an "exit this page" button, we want to make sure that navigating back from `localWeather.org` takes us to `searchEngine.com`. However, this isn't the case. Instead, we will be navigated to website.com, only skipping the last page viewed (`website.com/resources`). To fix this behaviour, consider closing the current tab and opening a new one when the button is pressed.

Adaptive and responsive design

Not everyone has safe access to every type of device. Some survivors may only have private access to a phone. Others might not have a phone or may worry that spyware has been installed on it. The only safe option for them could be something like a PC in a public space (like an internet café or library).

Designing for all types of screens and devices allows us to meet people where they are.

Move towards
- designing for phones, tablets, and desktops, and testing the final product on multiple devices,
- considering if designing for less common screen types (like smart watches or smart TVs) could also benefit survivors,
- designing for touch screens first (mobile devices lack many input accelerators such as right click, mouse hover, and keyboard shortcuts),
- designing to the strength of each platform and screen.
- testing accessibility with real people using the screen readers on multiple devices and operating systems.

Move away from
- conducting fast, convenient, or "guerilla" research (research conducted quickly in public spaces). These techniques tend to over-emphasise certain types of devices and often exclude people with disabilities,
- locking orientation when designing for phones and tablets. Some people may be unable to turn the orientation of their phone from either a portrait or landscape perspective easily.

"Stressful" components

There are some UI components which tend to cause more stress or discomfort. Pop-ups and timers are prime examples of these. Designing them with care can result in a smoother experience for survivors. Microsoft, in their resource "Mental Health and Cognition: Design pattern guidance," provides some useful ways to achieve that.

Pop-ups

Pop-ups often interrupt an individual's intended action. The resulting distraction and cognitive overload can activate stress and anxiety.

Move towards
- timing pop-ups to appear at appropriate times so that they are aligned with what a person is trying to do,
- providing the option to disable pop-ups,
- including the relevant actions inside the pop-up window; for example, a pop-up warning someone about their battery running low should include a button that activates the battery saver mode.

Timers

Design timers carefully. Engaging with them can contribute to anxiety.

Move towards
- counting up rather than counting down to zero,
- soothing colours that can help minimise feelings of anxiety,
- using calming and figurative imagery for a timer, like a tree that grows over time, rather than a stopwatch,
- providing choices to manage a timer, such as adding more time or pausing it.

Data: being known by technology

Data has been recently dominating the conversation around technology. Of course, data existed long before that. But when we use this word now, we mostly associate it with digital information. Very often the conversation is around people's data and how that information is shared. Or better: how, with whom, and for which purpose. Questions of ethics, value, trust, and safety arise when we talk about it. And some of these questions are critical to trauma-informed design.

Privacy

One of my favourite things in Chayn's trauma-informed design principles is the inclusion of privacy. Privacy is a fundamental right. Also, it's intertwined with safety and trust, which makes it even more important for survivors.

Unfortunately, more often than not technology is used to strip people of their privacy. Our obsession with data and targeted advertisements can lead us to see "users" as a collection of data points to extract instead of people to serve. And when working with trauma survivors, this isn't only unethical, it's also unsafe.

For people who are living in situations of crisis, for people who have been (or still are) targeted by abusers, or for people who have had their personal information exposed, a data leak or a misplaced targeted ad could make the difference between life and death.

Of course data will keep existing, and we will keep collecting and using it. But what's important here is the way we approach data. Are we being extractive or are we being consentful?

The FRIES of consent

In the past few years, consent has taken a more central role in the world of tech. Regulations like the European Union's general data protection regulation (GDPR) have helped establish basic rules on how consent and data should be managed. But there's more work to be done.

When we practise trauma-informed design, consent can both support and damage the trust-building process. When done right, people can feel seen and respected. For many, it can be a restorative experience. When done wrong, people can feel frustrated, used, or taken advantage of. This can re-enact the dynamics that left them traumatised in the first place.

But what does right or wrong mean when looking at consent? American sexual health organisation Planned Parenthood has defined 5 characteristics of consent. According to them, consent should be:
- freely given,
- reversible,
- informed,
- enthusiastic,
- specific.

Yes, FRIES!

The Consentful Tech Project has adapted these characteristics for tech. Let's go over them:

Freely given

This means that a design shouldn't mislead us into doing something we wouldn't normally do. An example would be pre-filling a checkbox or using deceptive language ("I do not want to receive marketing communication emails"). These cases are misleading partly because they assume consent before it is given, and partly because they deviate from what people expect.

Reversible

Even if we initially agree to something, we should be able to change our mind about it. A great example here is the unsubscribe button in most email lists. Another great one is "user preferences" that allow for changes in how our data are managed. However, the latter can sometimes be problematic if that option is hard to find.

Reversible consent is also very important when conducting research.

Informed

Clarity is important when it comes to consent. Unfortunately, we rarely see this in tech, where consent is usually built around people agreeing to long legal documents like terms of service or privacy policies.

This practice makes informed consent harder, creates walls of content, and fuels inequity through inaccessible language ("legalese").

Enthusiastic

This is my favourite one. It refers to our wanting to give consent instead of being forced to do so. If our workplace uses Slack or all of our friends are on Facebook, it's unlikely that we'll be able to avoid agreeing to their terms of service. But it's unfair to assume that we want our data to be used for targeted ads or to train AI models just because we need to use a service.

Specific

Agreeing to our data being used in one way doesn't mean that we agree to its being used in another way. This is a common problem with most terms of service; they don't allow for specificity in what we are agreeing with. And when they change, it's often hard to track what happened. In contrast, many cookie notices ensure this specificity by providing options around which cookies are accepted and which ones aren't.

Ingredient shelf: Data

Welcome to the second ingredient shelf. This one includes specific practices for working with data. Same as before, this isn't an exhaustive list, nor a checklist. Take what resonates, and leave the rest.

Access

Not everyone has an email address or a phone number. Some people might be accessing our services from a shared device. The need for authentication creates a barrier for them and risks excluding information from the people who need it the most.

Move towards

- providing access to your content (or part of your content) without the need for authentication,
- allowing people to view the devices that accessed their account, so that they can know if they have been hacked,
- enabling biometric authentication, which can be more secure and reduces the cognitive load associated with remembering a password. Keep in mind, however, that not everyone is comfortable with sharing biometric data, so make that feature optional.

Move away from
- remembering people's credentials by default if you are working with at-risk populations. Do offer it as an option, however, since it makes the log-in process significantly easier and it reduces the cognitive load associated with remembering passwords.
- using only facial recognition for biometric authentication. Sharing facial information can be more vulnerable. There have also been reported cases of facial recognition failing for people of colour. Consider including it as an optional feature to make your design more accessible.

Move with curiosity
- modern password requirements can be cognitively overwhelming, so consider also including alternative authentication methods like one-time passwords (OTP) or social sign-in,
- have clarity on the intention behind using authentication: is it truly a needed feature that makes our design work? Or is it a tool that we use to extract people's email addresses and capture data?

Anonymity and encryption

Both anonymity and encryption can protect survivors. At the same time, they can hide or enable abuse. It's important to be intentional and transparent in our decisions around them.

Anonymity

Move towards
- encouraging or enforcing anonymity, if protecting the identity of survivors is a priority for your design,
- disabling or discouraging anonymity, if it can be used to hide the identity of abusers.

Move away from
- storing data in people's devices, as this can put them at risk.

Move with curiosity
- when collecting or publishing data, be aware that anonymisation can be ineffective. For example, using 1990s US census

summary data, Dr. Latanya Sweeney has estimated that 87% of the US population can potentially be identified using only their 5-digit ZIP code, their gender, and their date of birth.

Encryption

Move towards
- using encryption when working with sensitive data,
- informing people about the use of encryption, and especially about its absence.

Move with curiosity
- mindfully consider when to use encryption, since it can be used for storing illegal data or abusive content.

Hardware: being in space with technology

When I was first engaging with trauma-informed design, I heard about a small device that can be used to provide location data, similar to how a phone does. At first, it didn't occur to me that this was problematic. Then, someone pointed out how this device could very easily enable stalking.

When discussing trauma-informed design, we rarely extend the conversation to hardware. Since this is primarily a book on content, I won't go into details either. But I believe that it's important to at least point out the need for trauma-informed hardware.

Here are some examples of where trauma and hardware intersect:
- devices that can access people's location can enable stalking, expose survivors' data, and put them at risk (this also includes personal cameras that attach the location as metadata to a photo or video),
- devices that include microphones or cameras can be used to spy on people, and the idea of them being used in that way can make many survivors very uncomfortable. Hardware and software that disable those features (like camera covers) can provide survivors with some comfort,
- public cameras and other public sensors collect vast amounts of data without consent.

Artificial intelligence: Exploring the futures of technology

At the time of writing this book (2024), everyone is talking about artificial intelligence (AI). The future of this technology is unclear, and there is so much noise surrounding it. Writing about it risks adding to the noise or creating content that will soon become obsolete or inaccurate. But not including it would be a notable miss.

That being said, it's important to acknowledge that the underlying principles of designing software and working with data also apply here. AI also has specific nuances that we need to take under consideration when practising trauma-informed design.

Machine learning

Artificial intelligence isn't a new concept, and neither is the hype around it. Different approaches to developing AI systems have existed since the 1960s, and even though most of them found little to moderate success, there have been periods of high interest in the past.

Currently, the most popular way of developing AI systems is called machine learning. A subcategory of it, deep learning, is also frequently used. Arguably these 2 ways perform better and are more successful than anything done before. They have only become possible recently because they require a large amount of data and a lot of computational power. In many ways, contemporary AI is only possible thanks to modern hardware.

Machine and deep learning are not the only ways of developing AI systems today. But they dominate most of the AI conversations. So I will only be focusing on them in this section.

Inherent issues of machine learning

If one were to oversimplify machine learning, they could use the term "fancy statistics." In machine learning, a computer program receives a large amount of data and creates a statistical model to represent that data. This process is called training. After the training, when new data is given to the AI system (input), it uses that representation to generate an output. Deep learning is similar, but uses a lot more data and fancier statistical models.

This way of working with AI creates 2 fundamental problems which are relevant for trauma-informed design. First, the output of an AI system isn't always accurate. Second, what is deemed as "correct" by the model (and thus what is produced as an output) is defined by the dataset used to train it.

The first problem is important because it undermines safety and trust. Since machine learning models are using statistics under the hood, their output is always an approximation of the data used to train it. The statistics used now are very sophisticated, but an approximation is never the same as reality. This means that every time we choose to use an AI system, we run the risk of providing inaccurate information to the people using our design.

Knowing how important trust is for survivors, this process has the potential to cause harm. But, even more importantly, if we are reaching out to an AI system in moments of crisis, the accuracy of information could significantly impact our safety.

The second problem is trickier. An AI system's output is heavily influenced by the data used to train it. If those data are biased, the system will replicate this bias. And because deep learning requires vast amounts of data, uncurated datasets from the Internet are often used. Unfortunately, there is a lot of bias on the Internet.

AI is evolving very fast, and it's hard to say where we'll be in 1, 5, or 10 years. Chances are that inaccuracy will still be a part of it, but we'll probably get better at managing it (as designers and as people). The bias problem is harder to solve. Of course we need better datasets, but this is very hard to achieve since the datasets need to be so large. And this isn't the only issue.

In their 2021 paper "On the Dangers of Stochastic Parrots: Can Language Models Be Too Big?," Emily M. Bender and colleagues conclude that language models "trained on large, uncurated, static datasets from the Web encode hegemonic views that are harmful to marginalised populations."

The bias in our datasets is not random. It has the potential to benefit the dominant social groups, and it points to how systemic issues affect AI.

Systemic issues affecting AI

```
Capitalism + White supremacy + Patriarchy = harmful AI :(
```

Everything from how AI is built to how it "acts" and the consequences it has is coloured by the systems it is created in: systems of capitalism, white supremacy, and patriarchy.

AI is built by extracting the data of the people who use it (often without consent) and by extracting the labour of annotation workers in the Global South. It's used to produce biassed and even intentionally abusive content, as in the case of deepfake porn. And it results in the loss of jobs, especially in the content design, graphic design, and customer support fields. All these are both impacts of trauma and sources of it.

And, to some extent, this is true for every technology. In her book *The Real World of Technology*, Ursula Franklin argues that every technology "ages" in a 3-phase pattern. This includes:
- advocacy (excitement and promises),
- adoption (acceptance, growth, and standardisation),
- institutionalisation (economic consolidation and stagnation).

Unfortunately, as Ethan Marcotte writes in *The World-Wide Work*, "The promise of liberation that's made in the first phase is never, ever fulfilled."

AI has existed for decades, but it has only become commercially mainstream in the last few of them. And yet it is already causing disproportionate harm to the ones who have historically and systemically been excluded and marginalised. No amount of content warnings ("AI can make mistakes") or output curation will fix that.

With AI dominating the conversation in tech, and with multiple emerging technologies on the horizon, it's worth asking ourselves: what is our role as trauma-informed designers? Can we advocate for fairer, more ethical, and more trauma-informed technology development? Can we interrupt the way technologies age? Can we work towards a more liberated world?

Ingredient shelf: AI

Trauma-informed practices won't fix the systemic issues of AI. But sometimes we have to work inside those systems and do the best we can to mitigate harm. Here are some practices that could help with that.

Especially here, because of how novel AI is, it's important to remember that this isn't an exhaustive list. I'm expecting things to become clearer and more standardised as the current way of building AI matures, and as the hype and noise go away. Everything is fluid now; we cannot know what will stand the test of time.

Move towards
- making it easy for people to double-check important information,
- including citations in AI's responses whenever possible,
- continuously testing the results of AI systems,
- including systematically excluded people in the development of AI and the design of AI solutions,
- advocating for AI regulations.

Move away from
- designing AI solutions that directly replace people's work,
- designing AI solutions that can directly cause harm (for example, deepfake video generators),
- using people's data to train AI systems unless they have consented to it (FRIES),
- using AI systems for use cases where the AI's inherent problems or biases can be amplified (for example, automatic profiling),
- using AI systems for surveillance.

Move with curiosity
- consider if AI is needed in the design and avoid using AI for the sake of it.

Creating a more trauma-informed world

Lately, I have been in plenty of calls on trauma-informed design, accessibility, and diversity, equity, and inclusion (DEI). More often than not, someone will ask about how we can push the adoption of those practices in the face of resistance. The question is valid, and also reveals a larger systemic issue.

For years, the culture in tech has been anti-trauma-informed. Maxims such as "design for the 80%" and "move fast and break things" have been used all too often. And countless apps and services have ended up causing more harm than good to both individuals and communities. In the face of such cultural and systemic barriers, we might ask ourselves if practising trauma-informed design is worth it.

I believe that it is. Because I see trauma-informed design as a practice that spans beyond the creation of interfaces and experiences. It's a practice of pushing against the culture and systems of oppression that dominate tech. Every time we avoid re-traumatising someone, every time we keep a survivor safe by protecting their privacy, and every time we help someone feel in control through meaningful choices, we are moving towards a more just and equitable world.

A practice of trauma-informed design alone might not be enough to get us there. But it is a much-needed start.

References and further reading

- Carol F. Scott, Gabriela Marcu, Riana Elyse Anderson, Mark W Newman, Sarita Schoenebeck, "Trauma-informed social media: Towards solutions for reducing and healing online harm," *Proceedings of the 2023 CHI Conference on Human Factors in Computing Systems* (2023)
- Paul Ginns and Jimmie Leppink, "Special Issue on Cognitive Load Theory: Editorial," *Educational Psychological Review* (2019)
- Elizabeth Woo, Lauren H. Sansing, Amy F. T. Arnsten, and Dibyadeep Datta, "Chronic Stress Weakens Connectivity in the Prefrontal Cortex: Architectural and Molecular Changes," *Chronic Stress* (2021)
- Rachel Edwards, "Using trauma informed principles in content design," (2023)
- Resmaa Menakem, *My Grandmother's Hands: Racialized Trauma and the Mending of Our Bodies and Hearts*, (2017)
- "Mental Health and Cognition: Design Pattern Guidance," Microsoft (2024)
- "Moving images," *Readability Guidelines* (2020)
- "Chayn's trauma-informed design principles," Chayn (2023)

- Lesley-Ann Noel and Melissa Eggleston, "Trauma-Informed Design: Leveraging Usability Heuristics on a Social Services Website," *Journal of User Experience* (May 2024)
- Gareth Ford Williams, "A Guide to Understanding What Makes a Typeface Accessible." *The Readability Group,* (2020)
- Aggie Toppins and Alison Place, "On the contradictions of feminist branding," *Feminist designer: On the personal and the political* (2023)
- Aasawari Kulkarni and Alison Place, "On fighting the typatriarchy," *Feminist designer: On the personal and the political* (2023)
- Facundo Corradini, "Accessibility for Vestibular Disorders: How My Temporary Disability Changed My Perspective," *Accessibility, User Experience,* (2019)
- Juliette Xing, "UI, Design, and colors in China" (published on LinkedIn) (2024)
- "Exit this page," GOV.UK
- "Summary of user research #2908," GOV.UK (2023)
- "Follow up on results of Exit this Page behaviour spikes," GOV.UK (2022)
- "Exit a page quickly," GOV.UK
- kon syrokostas, "A deeper dive in the "Exit this page" button," *the Trauma-Informed Design blog* (2024)
- "Best practices for adaptive design," Flutter (2024)
- "Understanding consent is as easy as FRIES," Planned Parenthood (2016)
- The Consentful Tech Project, *Building Consentful Tech* (2017)
- "Impact Model," Open Terms Archive
- Latanya Sweeney, "Simple Demographics Often Identify People Uniquely," (2000)
- "Uber's facial recognition is locking Indian drivers out of their accounts," *MIT Technology Review* (2022)

- "Study finds gender and skin-type bias in commercial artificial-intelligence systems," *MIT News* (2018)
- Fangxing Li and Du Yang, "From AlphaGo to Power System AI: What Engineers Can Learn from Solving the Most Complex Board Game," *IEEE Power and Energy Magazine* (March-April 2018)
- Emily M. Bender, Timnit Gebru, Angelina McMillan-Major, and Shmargaret Shmitchell, "On the dangers of stochastic parrots: Can language models be too big?" *Proceedings of the 2021 ACM Conference on Fairness, Accountability, and Transparency* (2021)
- Karen Hao and Andrea Paula Hernández, "How the AI industry profits from catastrophe," *MIT Technology Review* (2022)
- Karen Hao and Deepa Seetharaman, "Cleaning Up ChatGPT Takes Heavy Toll on Human Workers," *The Wall Street Journal* (2023)
- Hera Hussain, "Digital self-clones, self-deepfakes and trademarks — is reclaiming power possible?" *Chayn* (2024)
- Jo Constantz, "AI Is Driving More Layoffs Than Companies Want to Admit," *Bloomberg* (2024)
- Gerrit De Vynck, "Duolingo cuts workers as it relies more on AI," *The Washington Post* (2024)
- Jack Kelly, "Klarna's AI Assistant Is Doing The Job Of 700 Workers, Company Says" *Forbes* (2024)
- Paul Hatton, "AI is replacing artists, and here's the proof," *Creative Bloq* (2023)
- Ursula Franklin, *The Real World of Technology* (1990)
- Ethan Marcotte, "The World-Wide Work" (2019)
- "Accessible and Equitable Artificial Intelligence Systems - Technical Guide" Accessibility Standards Canada (2024)
- Eva PenzeyMoog, *Design for Safety* (2021)
- Cory Doctorow, "My McLuhan lecture on enshittification" (2024)

Chapter 5
The case for content warnings
by Rachel Edwards

If you have visited a theatre, watched a TV show, or read a news article, you will have seen a content warning. Content warnings (sometimes shortened to CW) are also known as:
- trigger warnings (or TW),
- activation warnings,
- guidance labels,
- content notes.

I call them content warnings because that's what they are. They let people know what content is coming up. But content warnings are maligned, misunderstood, and debated. They are used, mis-used, ridiculed, and appreciated.

Why have we got so much to say about the content warning? And when — and how — should we use them?

Content warnings in all their forms

One of the challenges of talking about content warnings is that we are talking about a whole range of things. In a very literal sense, a content warning could include a:

- line on a sandwich wrapper stating the item contains nuts,
- poster outside a play saying the production uses a smoke machine or pyrotechnics,
- note at a concert that there will be strobe lights,
- warning at the start of a TV show that the show has scenes of alcohol and tobacco use,
- line at the start of a news article stating the article has details of torture which you may find upsetting,
- few words at the start of a post on a forum,
- paragraph on a university course syllabus, outlining potentially difficult reading material in the course.

All of these warnings serve a purpose. Essentially, the same purpose: to protect someone. Think about the first 3 on that list: knowing a sandwich contains nuts protects someone with a nut allergy. Someone with breathing difficulties might be endangered by a smoke machine. Strobe lights may trigger a seizure in photo-sensitive people.

We seem to be okay with warnings like these. We understand they don't apply to everyone, but they apply to some people and can have serious physical effects. You won't find many people who would argue, for example, that we shouldn't label food allergens.

But the other content warnings seem to be more controversial. They relate to feelings, memories, and traumas. And while these things can also come with strong, physical symptoms, the reaction to using a content warning here is much more mixed.

Triggers

Before we talk about content warnings, we need to talk about triggers.

It's not a word I like, and there's some thought that the word itself can be harmful. But it's a word we use, and so let's look at what it means for a minute.

Trauma-informed designer and educator Jax Wechsler writes:

> "Triggering can occur when people are reminded of a past traumatic event or a stressor that leads to distress.
> Triggers can be sensory (sounds, smells, images), situational

(locations, activities, interactions), emotional (feelings, moods), or cognitive (thoughts, topics). They can be both internal and external."

Triggers can come from a range of exposures: sounds, smells, moods, and so on. They are not limited to words.

A content warning is intended to warn someone about the content that is coming up. In our general understanding, the reason for doing this is to prevent re-traumatisation. However, this is a complicated argument, for a number of reasons.

A personal story

A few days before my daughter was diagnosed with cancer, we took a train from Waverley Station in Edinburgh to York in the north of England. We were going away for a night: unknowingly, our last bit of normal for a very long time. On our return, we were faced with her lymphoma diagnosis and immediately moved into hospital to begin treatment.

We spent the better part of the next 4 months in the Royal Hospital for Children and Young People. As I drove there and back each day, my route took me past Waverley Station. And every time I passed it, my stomach would flip. My chest would tighten. I felt almost unbearable grief and panic.

There's no logic behind why the train station was my trigger. Or maybe there is, and I have yet to figure it out. But my mind and my body chose that train station as a symbol for the trauma that came when a consultant told me my daughter had cancer.

In the months after, as she went through her treatment, I had countless experiences that could understandably be called traumatic. But it was that train station that my mind and body fixated on.

One of the many difficult things about trauma is that what activates — or "triggers"— someone's trauma is often not what you would expect. Experts talk about a noise, a certain light, a smell bringing people back to their trauma. Some things might be expected to provoke a reaction. Other things, like my drive past the train station, are almost illogical.

Can you write a content warning that covers all the different triggers? No. You can't.

So maybe we need to think of their purpose a bit differently.

The origins of the content warning

The general consensus is that content warnings emerged in the 1990s in the infancy of the internet. They appeared on sexual assault forums warning about things that other forum users might find upsetting. Often abbreviated to "T/W" (for "trigger warning") and followed by a few words indicating what the trigger might be, their use soon expanded beyond these early forums.

The idea behind them was to warn people, and give them the choice to leave the content, or to proceed with awareness of what they were going into. This meant someone wasn't surprised by an unexpected topic and could instead prepare themselves if they chose to proceed.

The science

The use of content warnings grew exponentially, and so perhaps did our understanding of their purpose. They moved beyond just internet forums to television, the news, theatres, and course reading lists. And with that growth came research.

A number of studies have looked into the effect of content warnings on users. These have shown that using them to prevent stress and trauma does not have the desired effect. Instead:

- rather than lessening or preventing stress, a content warning can increase it, making someone more anxious about what might be coming than they would be if they encountered the topic without a warning,
- people might deliberately choose to read content knowing it might be upsetting, leading them further into the topic,
- content warnings can "contribute to a culture of avoidance at odds with evidence-based treatment practices" (as a 2023 article in Clinical Psychological Science describes).

These are perhaps unexpected findings. And they certainly go against our good intentions when we provide warnings.

Other criticism centres around the idea that we can't provide a warning for every trigger. This, too, is correct: someone writing about the history of train travel in Britain would never think to provide a content warning before mentioning Waverley Station. Triggers are often personal, and even if they are shared, someone's response to them might be different.

So why don't we just stop?

With a body of evidence and a vocal group of critics, should we persist with content warnings?

I think we should. But, we need to be clear about:
- how we're using them,
- why we're using them,
- what we expect them to do.

I am approaching this problem as a content designer — a person whose job involves finding the right words and trying to make information easy for people. So how do content designers take the aim of the content warning — to protect people from harm — and apply it to what we create?

Content warnings are intended to provide choice and safety. Someone can choose whether to continue with the content, and take measures to ensure their safety before they do. This can build trust and empowerment. These are all central features of trauma-informed content design.

And content warnings have their advocates, too. Writer and content strategist Sam Dylan Finch wrote:

> "We label the deep end of a swimming pool . . . so that folks who can't swim can make a smart decision about whether or not they should be on that end of the pool . . . We would never tell someone who can't swim that they're "too sensitive" for asking how deep the water is . . .
>
> Content warnings operate on the same principle. They're there to prevent danger or distress so that, like labelling the deep end of a pool, people can make smart choices about where they're going to swim."

Discussing their use in universities, Kate Mann (associate professor of philosophy at Cornell University) wrote, "Exposing students to triggering material without warning seems more akin to occasionally throwing a spider at an arachnophobe."

When I'm talking about trauma, I always give an introduction to the topics I'm going to cover. It usually goes something like this:

> "Before I start my talk, I want to make you aware of some of the topics I'll be mentioning. I'll be using examples from my work and will be touching on work with survivors of abuse and applicants to a redress scheme for children who were abused in care. I won't be going into the experiences of these people, but I will talk about some of the issues that came up. Towards the end of the talk I'll be mentioning user research around planning a funeral. I wanted to let you know these topics will come up. If you need to leave now or at any point, or do anything you need to support yourself, please feel free to."

And every time I have done this, someone has thanked me for doing so. They've said they weren't in a space to deal with that topic, or it meant they were prepared when it came up, or that it helped them relax knowing what was — and wasn't — going to be talked about.

Choice and safety

One of the trauma-informed principles we apply to content is about choice. We should give people the choice about if and when they want to access our content. This can include warning them if something difficult is coming up.

We also apply safety. We can give our users options to stay safe, from an "exit this page" button to support options. We do this so our users can take care of themselves in the absence of our being there with them physically.

I worked on a service where applicants were asked details about abuse they had experienced. The application form was paper, and it was long. Some applicants spoke about the process they went through to look at the application. It could involve self care or self-medication. Some wanted a supportive friend, others wanted complete privacy. But they all spoke of "bracing themselves" for the difficult questions.

We were asking them to go through pages of information, and each time they turned over a page, there was an intake of breath. They were waiting for the hard questions. When would they appear? What would they say? How would they feel when they saw them?

So we added a line to the bottom of each page of the form. It told them what was coming on the next page. We used clear, factual language about what topic was covered. We also reminded them of the support options. This meant they could decide if they were ready before turning the page over.

This was a content warning. It was helpful, and it gave people choice and safety.

If we took away those warnings, someone might feel increased anxiety and stress throughout the whole application. They might be on edge, worrying and waiting.

However, what made this warning work was its:
- location,
- wording,
- choice of next steps.

Here's what wouldn't have worked so well: a line at the top of the application form that said "This form asks questions about your abuse." Why? Because there is no indication of:
- when that content comes, meaning potentially elevated stress throughout the application,
- support options available, meaning if someone is triggered they have nowhere to go for help,
- the choices someone has: when can they take a break, or leave and return to the content?

Some good and bad examples

Blanket warnings

I recently watched the opening ceremony for the Paris Olympics. At the start of the 4-hour broadcast, the commentators announced that strobe lighting would be used in the ceremony.

If you were someone who was photo-sensitive, where would that warning leave you? You would probably have to turn off the television and miss the entire ceremony. A better option might be something like:

> "There will be short bursts of strobe lighting in the ceremony. We expect these to happen approximately 60 and 95 minutes into the production and last for about 5 seconds. We will remind you 2 minutes before this happens."

With this information, someone has a choice. They can watch in safety, knowing they will be reminded when to turn off — and when they can turn back on! Or they can choose to turn off now.

Another example of a real-life warning that does very little: at the start of a TV programme, I heard the warning "This show contains some scenes that some of you may find upsetting."

This statement does nothing other than create anticipation of Something Bad. There's no idea of what the bad thing is, when it will happen, or what we can do about it. So it makes sense that this kind of warning would increase stress and heighten anxiety.

Personalised warnings

Here's an example of a London theatre doing a content warning well. This particular production used several loud, bright, and dramatic effects. These were thought to be an essential part of the show. Rather than exclude people from the entire production, however, ushers would tap the shoulders of ticket-holders who had indicated a need, warning them an effect was coming.

This is obviously a very personal, labour-intensive solution. But if the other option is total exclusion, it seems a good compromise. And it shows that we can be creative with how we give warnings and care for people.

Choice, again

There is a difference between content that people can choose to engage with (for example, a film, an article, or a forum) and what they have to do: (for example, register a death or report a crime). In these cases, a content warning may not help. Telling someone that a form to register a death contains questions about death is not likely to help them.

We can't get rid of all discomfort. People still have to go through unpleasant things, and we can't always fix them. If you are designing in these sorts of areas, you can also draw on other trauma-informed principles and consider adding elements that provide trust and safety in your content.

Things to think about

I think there is a case to be made for content warnings: but for thoughtful, helpful, and supportive ones. When you're deciding whether to use one, here are some things to consider.

Placement

A content warning doesn't have to go at the top of your page. Think about where to put your warning.

At the beginning (or top of the page)

This might be appropriate if the content you are warning about runs throughout, or appears right at the start. Consider whether you need any reminders, or signposts to further support, throughout your content.

Throughout your content

You can use a design element or marking to indicate when the content you are warning about comes up. The Consentful Tech Project has an example of this in its zine, *Building Consentful Tech*. At the beginning of the publication they write:

> "We've tried as much as possible not to reproduce harm and violence in this zine, however we do make several references to sexual violence. We have used the symbol ◊ at the top of the relevant pages to indicate where this content appears."

The pages that contain this content then have a small orange diamond in the top corner, next to the page number. This makes it clear and easy for someone to skip those pages if they choose to.

Immediately before the content

This position works if the person can miss that particular piece of content without penalty. If you're choosing this, think about:

- how you let someone know when it's safe to come back in; for example, by leaving a page between your warning and the content, or marking the content with a sidebar,
- if you also need to tell them at the beginning that this content is coming and you will tell them when.

At the end

This is more about guiding someone towards support rather than warning them away from the content.

For example, I recently read an article about a convicted child killer. At the end of the article was the line:

> "This is a distressing case, so if you — or someone you know — need help after reading about this, you can find details of support organisations on our website."

There was no warning at the top of the page, possibly because it was assumed the killer's name was well-known enough that people who chose to read would know what was coming.

Positioning a statement at the end can acknowledge strong feelings and try to promote safety, rather than directing someone away from the content entirely.

How often you use a warning

One UK children's charity researched how content warnings on their website affected their users. Their website was almost entirely information on topics that were potentially harmful, and so every page had a warning.

However, testing showed that people using the site hated the warnings appearing all the time. Many of them were return users who had visited the site, or page, before and didn't want to keep seeing the warnings.

The solution was to create an option for users to clear all content warnings. This was added to each page in the following format:

> **Content warning: this page contains content on abusive relationships.**
>
> ☐ Dismiss this warning
>
> ☐ Dismiss all content warnings

What goes into the warning

Avoid going into too much detail about the potentially difficult content, as that can cause distress in itself. Be general, but specific enough to be helpful.

For example, if your content is information about a surgical procedure, you could say the content contains details of an operation without outlining the steps of the surgery in detail.

It can also be helpful to give an indication of:
- where the content comes (for example, at the beginning or end of a page, or on a specific page),
- how much detail is covered (for example, if it just mentions a topic or goes into details about it).

Adding a step

Content designers try to make information easily accessible to people. But there may be times where putting in a small barrier, or "speed bump," is helpful. This adds an extra element, making the user deliberately choose to take an extra step to access the content.

Here's an example.

When my daughter was diagnosed, one of the first things her consultant said was not to Google anything. He gave me some websites for trusted information, and advised me not to look beyond those.

One of those sites was Lymphoma Action UK. It had useful and helpful information about childhood cancer, but one thing it did not include was survival statistics. And while I wanted to know this information, almost more than anything else, I also didn't want to know.

Instead of publishing the statistics on their page, they presented the information this way in a section called "Outlook":

> "Your child's lymphoma specialist is the best person to talk to about your child's outlook, because they know all of your child's individual circumstances.
>
> Cancer Research UK has information on children's cancer statistics if you would like to learn more. If you choose to

look at survival statistics [link], remember that they can be confusing. They don't tell you what your child's individual outlook is — they only tell you how a group of people with the same diagnosis did over a period of time. Treatments are improving all the time and survival statistics are usually measured over 5 or 10 years after treatment. This means that statistics only tell you how people did in the past. Those people may not have received the same treatment that your child will receive. A lot of statistics are very general and include people of all ages. Cure rates in children are much higher than in older people so the information you find might not be relevant for your child."

This warning worked for several reasons:
- calling the section "Outlook" rather than "Survival rates" felt more positive and more reassuring,
- choosing to leave the site and go somewhere else was a deliberate action — it made me pause and think about if I really wanted to see the statistics,
- the information was contextualised and suggested where to get the best information for your own circumstances.

In the end, I did not click to go to the Cancer Research UK site. But had that information been on the same page, I almost certainly would have scrolled down to read it.

What next?

A good warning gives someone a choice. So think about what choices you are giving them. Are you:
- pointing them towards sources of support, or other resources,
- letting them engage with the information in a different way (for example, can they have a conversation with someone rather than reading through the information?),
- allowing them to disengage from the harmful content but return later,
- giving them the choice of when and how they access the content.

Is a warning what you need?

Finally, it may be that a warning isn't what you need. Does it create what your users want and need? Or will something else provide that choice and safety?

Remember that a content warning has the potential to cause harm as well as safety. It is not a one-step solution to keeping your users safe from re-traumatisation.

Redefining content warnings

What if we thought of content warnings as information that gives people a choice, rather than as a disclaimer that almost rids us designers of responsibility?

It may be that a content warning doesn't prevent re-traumatisation. But maybe that was never its original intent.

The message board users in the 1990s who first used "trigger warnings" were doing so to let people choose if they wanted to engage, and to provide them choice and safety. They weren't trying to heal the previous trauma or prevent re-traumatisation. They were reaching out with words as they would to a friend — to say, "Are you okay if we talk about this or would you rather not?"

Use a content warning in the same way you might talk to a friend about something difficult. "This is coming up. How do you want to deal with it?"

For me, a content warning is primarily about choice. It lets me choose when and how I engage with content that might be difficult. It lets me decide that I don't have the mental or emotional space for something just now, and I want to come back to it later.

And doing this keeps me safe.

References and further reading

- Jax Wechsler, "Navigating distress during design research" (published on LinkedIn) (September 2024)
- "Trigger warnings: what do they do?" BBC News (2014)
- Brian Duignan, "Trigger Warnings on Campus," *Encyclopedia Britannica* (2023)
- "How the trigger warning took over the internet," Buzzfeed News (2014)
- Victoria M. E. Bridgland, Payton J. Jones, and Benjamin W Bellet, "A Meta-Analysis of the Efficacy of Trigger Warnings, Content Warnings, and Content Notes" Clinical Psychological Science (2024)
- Payton J. Jones and Benjamin W. Bellet, "Helping or Harming? The Effect of Trigger Warnings on Individuals With Trauma Histories," *Clinical Psychological Science* (2020)
- Benjamin W Bellet, Payton J Jones and Richard J McNally, "Trigger warning: Empirical evidence ahead," *Journal of Behavior Therapy and Experimental Psychiatry* (December 2018)
- Emily Reynolds, "Do trigger warnings work as intended?" *The British Psychological Society* (November 2023)
- Jeannie Suk Gersen, "What if Trigger Warnings Don't Work?" *The New Yorker* (September 28, 2021)
- PJ Vogt, "What do trigger warnings actually do?" Search Engine podcast (2024)
- Sam Dylan Finch, "When You Oppose Trigger Warnings, You're Really Saying These 8 Things," *Everyday Feminism* (2015)
- Kate Mann, "Why I Use Trigger Warnings," *New York Times Opinion* (20 September 2015)
- The Consentful Tech Project, *Building Consentful Tech*
- "Lymphoma in Children," Lymphoma Action UK
- M. Slade, "Here's what trigger warnings are - and what they are not," *Everyday Feminism* (2016)

Chapter 6
Trauma-informed research for content design

by Sarah Fathallah

Design research plays a crucial role in shaping the designs that we interact with, including the content that we read, learn from, and consume. Through design research, designers engage people as co-creators, testers, and evaluators to explore new opportunities for intervention or improve upon existing designs.

Content designers often play an important role in shaping the questions that research needs to answer to make informed design decisions. They might facilitate or observe research sessions with participants, as well as analyse research findings to decide how best to include what they've learned into the designs.

However, engaging people in research can sometimes become a source of re-traumatisation or activation for the people participating in the research. So being a trauma-informed content designer means not only focusing on the outcomes that designers produce, but also on the process that designers use to arrive at those outcomes. This means considering trauma-informed design research as the collective responsibility of anyone involved in making it happen, from design researchers to content designers and others.

As the Campaign for Trauma-Informed Policy and Practice aptly cautions, "'Trauma-informed' is not a checklist or destination — it's an ongoing commitment to a process that is nearly always evolving." With this warning in mind, I urge you to read this chapter not in search of a list of research practices to adopt uncritically or prescriptively. Instead, I invite you to consider any potential practices as a proposal to evaluate and challenge with critical thought and your own beliefs ("reflexivity"). A reflexive stance is crucial to situating, assessing, and adapting your research practices to ensure they are aligned with the context you work in, the ethical commitments you uphold, and the competence you need to carry them out with adequacy and responsibility.

This connection between practice and critical reflection can be referred to as "praxis." A term popularised in liberatory movements, praxis was defined by Brazilian educator and philosopher Paulo Freire as the combination of "reflection and action directed at the structures to be transformed." Guided by this understanding, I invite you to develop, nurture, and realise 6 praxes when adopting a trauma-informed stance in your design research work:

1. praxis of preparedness
2. praxis of appropriateness
3. praxis of instructiveness
4. praxis of attentiveness
5. praxis of responsiveness
6. praxis of dutifulness

Together, these praxes take into account that trauma survivors need to:
- feel safe,
- feel in control,
- express their emotions,
- know what comes next.

Each praxis is presented with a set of proposed practices and possible reflection prompts that design researchers can use to practise self-reflexivity. You can use these prompts either individually or in teams.

Trauma-informed design research praxes

1. Preparedness

A praxis of preparedness invites designers to reflect on and establish the foundational conditions for a design research team to be trauma-informed. These range from team formation and staffing, to skill building and training, as well as organisational protocols and resources.

Reflection prompts around preparedness

- What is our understanding of trauma? Where do we draw our trauma expertise from?
- Are we familiar with the communities we plan to engage with in this design research? What do we know about those communities and their history of being involved in research?
- How could this design research make conditions worse for research participants and their families or communities? How are we prepared to mitigate that harm?
- What human resources do we have at our disposal? What skills, backgrounds, and training does each team member bring?
- What competencies or perspectives are missing? How can we fill those gaps? Who can give us advice or guidance if something is unclear?
- What timelines are we operating under? Are we likely to feel under stressful time constraints if issues arise?
- What protocols do we have in place for identifying and responding to participant distress? How confident are we about using those protocols?
- Do we have resources and referrals we can share with participants? Have we vetted those resources and referrals? Do we know what participants might expect if they use them (for example, wait lists, limitations around citizenship status, agency collaboration with law enforcement, language access)?
- What do we have in place to support our well-being as researchers? Who could we turn to for support?

Staffing and forming skilled research teams

Form teams with appropriate experiences and backgrounds

Design teams can benefit from having members with a combination of:
- lived experience,
- research expertise,
- trauma understanding (through team members with clinical or social work backgrounds, mental health professionals, or peer support or crisis support workers).

Value lived experience

Beyond simply engaging with those with lived experience through advisory boards or committees, this can look like employing a "peer researcher" model. This is where researchers who share lived experience with participants take the lead, especially with:
- participant relationships,
- facilitating design research sessions,
- tracking participants' affects, if desired and deemed appropriate by those researchers.

Researchers who have not engaged with the communities at hand may need to receive additional training before working with them.

Engage trauma specialists in consultative or supervisory capacities

If the design research team itself does not have sufficient expertise, it can engage experienced trauma specialists in an extended capacity. This could be in a consultative or coaching capacity, or through a supervision model. Design professor Tad Hirsch suggests that while it is "good practice to include mental health professionals in research sessions . . . at the very least, researchers should be prepared to make appropriate referrals to other needed services."

Staff teams so that researchers never facilitate sessions alone

Depending on the type of design research methods, it is best to make sure that design researchers work (at the minimum) in pairs.

Plan for researcher activation and vicarious trauma

When you are planning your research, think about situations where a team member may need to leave the research session.

This includes emergent needs, such as:
- having a backup plan in case a researcher is unable to continue with the research encounter,
- having explicit group discussions about what researchers need when they are feeling activated and what regulation and self-care strategies they can deploy,
- practising what to say or do during a session to signal that they need a break or to switch roles with someone else.

This should also consider longer-term needs, such as burnout or vicarious trauma that may result from prolonged exposure to traumatic material.

Building needed competencies and training

Receive training on listening and accessible facilitation skills

Team training can cover reflective and active listening, accessibility considerations, and other topics that will allow the research team to create a space where participants can show up fully and safely.

Build skills to recognise distress and support participants

Training may include learning about trauma and how it affects the nervous system. Ultimately, the goal is to help design researchers identify and respond effectively to symptoms of distress.

Prepare researchers for the potential to experience secondary or vicarious trauma

Secondary trauma can occur when someone is exposed to a traumatic event through a firsthand account or narrative, such as hearing someone's story once in an interview or research session.

Vicarious trauma is when someone is repeatedly exposed to traumatic material, such as researchers working with communities who have experienced trauma for extended periods of time.

Depending on the research topic and context, researchers should be prepared to be exposed to a wide range of traumatic material and potentially experience secondary or vicarious trauma as a result.

This can be achieved through thorough scenario planning as well as conducting role plays and mock research sessions to prepare team members for situations that may play out.

Build skills to recognise and navigate secondary and vicarious trauma

Making sure members of the design team learn about and recognise symptoms of secondary and vicarious trauma is crucial, as well as building skills in trauma stewardship. This is what trauma workers Laura van Dernoot Lipsky and Connie Burk describe as the "ability to evaluate one's response to trauma exposure." Because each of us respond differently when we experience "dysregulation" (becoming activated), it is helpful to recognise our individual symptoms so that we can respond with self-compassion or ask for support.

Understand the longer term impact of secondary and vicarious trauma

In addition to immediate dysregulation or strong emotions, secondary or vicarious trauma that isn't tended to can lead to longer-term trauma. This can not only affect design researchers themselves but also the work that they engage in, often appearing as:
- increased absenteeism,
- increased illness or fatigue,
- reduced motivation,
- lowered self-esteem and sense of work competence,
- loss of sense of control over work and life in general,
- difficulties with boundaries,
- reduced productivity.

Create personal wellbeing plans

Prior to starting any study, researchers can plan for and discuss how they navigate activation and dysregulation with their teammates. This means getting to know one another, learning about everyone's distress signs, and determining ways to support one another. Examples of prompts you can reflect on and plan for include:

- I know I'm activated when I notice . . .
- Things that help me cope when I feel this way . . .
- Things I could do if I was in a research session and this happens . . .
- How I will let a colleague know if it is becoming too difficult to continue . . .
- How I will take care of myself during the research study . . . (for example, sleep, time alone, exercise, taking baths)
- Things I can do after a particularly hard day . . . (for example, call friends, be alone, debrief with colleagues)

Putting in place resources, protocols, and support systems

Build more space in project timelines

Teams working in projects on sensitive topics or with vulnerable communities need additional time to, among other things:
- build rapport and trust with community members,
- recruit participants,
- properly train and prepare teams,
- collect and synthesise data,
- source and vet resources.

Plan at the very beginning to provide ample time for planned activities (like giving researchers more time to synthesise research findings so as to mitigate potential activation) and unplanned research activities (for example, a specialist to support with an issue that arises).

Set protocols for identifying and responding to signs of distress from participants

Team members can have an agreed upon protocol for what to do when participants are distressed or uncomfortable. These protocols should include:
- team roles (who is doing what based on their experience and skills),
- scripts and actions (what to say or do in response to what situation),
- resources (prepared materials like referrals and contact information for additional support).

Team members should be thoroughly familiar with these protocols ahead of time to avoid confusion or miscommunications during critical moments, which can negatively impact participants.

Establish self-care strategies for researchers

Teams can develop strategies they can use to care for themselves. These include both strategies that design researchers can deploy on their own (such as social support, life balance, or techniques to regulate their nervous system) or access through organisational resources (such as therapy or counselling).

With the appropriate resources for self-care, teams can be more compassionate and effective in tending to participants and engaging in "co-regulation." Co-regulation is what trauma educator Jax Wechsler describes as a researcher helping to calm the participant's nervous system by calming their own nervous system.

Prepare resources and referrals to support participants

Ahead of time, it's best to prepare resources and referrals that are relevant to the context and topics at hand to share with participants should they want support.

It's best if these resources are localised, translated, and vetted as much as possible. You might consider including confidential and private resources, in case participants are interested in talking with someone without the concern of being reported to the authorities.

Create accessible explanations of the design research study for participants

Prepare verbal and written explanations of the research team's design research study, which include:
- expectations for engaging in the research,
- informed consent protocols,
- data collection and privacy,
- compensation,
- other considerations.

These explanations should be in developmentally and linguistically appropriate language, as well as tested (for example, in mock interviews) beforehand, to ensure understanding and accessibility to participants.

Plan data privacy and storage safeguards

Teams should put in place the infrastructure necessary to ensure that data collection is safe and private, regardless of whether it is done online or in-person. This includes considering:
- data storage,
- anonymising identifiable or personal data,
- how long collected data will be saved.

2. Appropriateness

A praxis of appropriateness urges designers to consider their design research goals and questions. It asks them to make sure that the research study design, environment, and timing consider and protect participants' physical and emotional safety.

Reflection prompts around appropriateness
- Do our research methods ask for more than what is necessary for us to meet our research goals?
- How confident are we that our research and our language minimise harm to participants? Whom can we ask to provide input or review?
- Could our approach to asking questions and facilitating research sessions lead to unintentional disclosure from participants? How do we prevent that from happening?
- Is the research environment (physical or virtual) designed to promote the safety of participants?
- Does our research calendar allow for spaciousness in scheduling research sessions and ensuring critical timely follow-ups to participants?

Using prudent research study design

Minimise unnecessary or unwanted disclosure

Consider the potential for participants to disclose traumatic past experiences, and take that into account in designing the research approach and methodology. As Tad Hirsch says, this is particularly important for "researchers who employ psychotherapeutic techniques that encourage disclosure and reflection." This could mean, for example:

- not asking probing questions in an interview if they are not necessary for the goals of the study,
- not prying,
- not forcing stories.

This also means that screening for trauma should not be required unless directly linked to the goals of the study.

Avoid asking participants to recall memories in linear ways

Trauma fundamentally alters how the brain processes what's going on. Memory is encoded as intense sensory fragments, which then form the basis of future flashbacks. This means that participants may have trouble remembering their past experiences in a sequential, fully contextualised way.

This is important when considering design research tools like journey mapping, which linearise participant experiences and memories. Instead, participants can be invited to share however much or little they remember in whichever way they remember it.

Consider the methods, number of people, and format of research interactions

Depending on the goals and context of the study, you should carefully consider your methodology to prioritise participant wellbeing. Think about:

- **Research methods:** Participatory research activities (such as a fill-in-the-blanks prompts or a card sorting exercise) where participants don't have to make eye contact can feel more comfortable than a face-to-face interview.
- **Number of participants:** Group research sessions can provide opportunities for peer support amongst participants but may also introduce social dynamics that can be activating or uncomfortable. You may also invite participants to bring a support person with them to the session (in-person or virtual), but take that into account when you set up the research environment.
- **Number of research team members:** Aim to find a balance. Include the people with the skills needed to facilitate and document research sessions, but do not overwhelm participants or make them feel like they are being scrutinised by observers.

- **Synchronicity:** Research methods that participants can complete in their own time (like unmoderated studies or diary studies) can feel less stressful in the moment or be completed anonymously by participants. However, these don't provide opportunities for support and co-regulation from a facilitator.

Review research study design with survivors and advocates

When crafting specific design research methods and instruments, ask external people, ideally those with understanding of trauma and the subject matter, to:

- review the questions, language, or activities,
- make sure that the study design is appropriate for trauma survivors,
- flag anything that feels unsafe or potentially activating.

Creating safety in the research environment

Physical environments

For design research that takes place in person, host research sessions in physical spaces that are:

- private,
- quiet,
- inviting,
- comfortable.

Give participants the ability to see and access the exit. Substance Use and Mental Health Services Administration (SAMHSA) guidance suggest you should also try to "ensure that the individual has some control in the situation (access to drinking water, choice in seating arrangement, and the ability to take breaks with access to clean, preferably gender-neutral, bathrooms)."

If possible, provide self-care items that can help participants ground and soothe themselves as needed, such as:

- mindfulness and somatic activities,
- fidget toys,
- objects with different textures,
- colouring supplies,
- scents,
- nourishment, snacks, and drinks.

Virtual environments

For remote design research sessions, provide multiple ways for people to participate so they can choose what feels most comfortable, private, and safe. If video conferencing is used, participants should be allowed to choose whether they want to have video on or off, both for them and for the design research team.

It is also good practice to use video conferencing software that is encrypted and in line with privacy and security safeguards.

Try to meet the participants' access needs

Provide all participants with an upfront list of access preferences and accommodations to choose from and request before the session. SAMHSA says this "allows the person to make requests comfortably and not feel guilty about needing accommodation on the day of the interview."

These include commonly offered accommodations, such as:
- captioning,
- translation and interpretation,
- tech assistance,
- compatibility with assistive technology.

It can also include other trauma-informed and accessibility accommodations, such as:
- having a support person present during the interview,
- providing items that are helpful for stimming or fidgeting,
- arranging transportation,
- reimbursing childcare expenses,
- assuring that a staff person of a certain gender conducts the interview,
- anything else they may need to show up fully to the design research session.

Scheduling research sessions with spaciousness

Allow extra time for breaks

When planning the timing and agendas of research sessions, build in plenty of opportunities to pause and take breaks, both planned and unplanned.

When scheduling research sessions, it's wise to plan time for breaks between sessions. Allow sufficient time between sessions, plan non-activating activities between research sessions, and avoid scheduling sessions during personal time.

Build in time for debriefs

Similarly, it's important to prioritise regular debriefs for research teams to be able to process and surface any needs they may have. Expectations around attendance for these debriefs (for example, if attendance is optional or required, what the debrief will look like, and who will facilitate) should be made clear to team members.

Ensure research session timing allows for prompt participant follow-up

Consider the need to promptly follow up with participants after research interactions, and avoid scheduling sessions when follow-up may not be possible (like the end of the week or before a holiday).

3. Instructiveness

A praxis of instructiveness invites designers to set expectations and be transparent with research participants when communicating with them ahead of research sessions. This is to minimise participants' anxiety of the unknown and give them the information they need to make informed decisions about how they engage in the research.

Reflection prompts around instructiveness

- What do our participants know about the research they are about to participate in? What information could we share with them to set expectations and support them in showing up fully?
- How transparent are our recruiting and sampling processes to participants?
- How aware are participants of our data collection, safeguarding, and privacy protocols? Do they actually know what happens with what they share with us?
- How accessible is our informed consent process to participants? Are participants actually able to say no or revoke consent at any time?

Brief participants about what to expect

In early communications, participants can benefit from knowing what they should expect when coming into the design research session, including:
- what it will look like,
- who will be there,
- how long it will last.

This helps minimise the "unknown" and the anxiety it might induce. You can send participants questions or prompts in advance and specify if they need to prepare anything before coming to the session. This is also an opportunity to discuss with participants what their:
- options for engaging in the research are like,
- rights are,
- access needs might be.

Support participants in preparing for the design research session

You may want to send participants a participant wellbeing packet with resources and referral paths they might find useful during or after the research session. These may include:
- soothing exercises,
- self-care resources,
- referrals to organisations providing support around mental health, violence and harm, and basic needs.

You can consider providing the option to have a one-to-one call with participants to check in about anything they may be concerned about before the session. When relying on technology (like virtual whiteboards) that may be unfamiliar to participants, you may want to offer individual support to show them the platform and how it works. Doing this with the participant ahead of time can reduce any stressful last-minute adaptations to their technology needs or preferences.

Ensure continuity in communications with participants outside research sessions

Being involved in recruiting participants and scheduling research sessions can help designers build a relationship with participants as soon as possible. This relationship-building can be more difficult when teams rely on external recruiting firms instead of recruiting participants themselves. To avoid overwhelming the participants, communications should ideally be with the same team member.

Be transparent and seek informed consent

Participant recruiting calls should be open and transparent. Let potential participants know how many people will likely participate and how they will be selected. After participant recruiting is done, additional information around the recruiting and sampling processes might be beneficial to explain why some were selected and others were not. Psychologist Rebecca Campbell and colleagues suggest that as much as possible, "avoid deceptive or vague recruitment language that may invoke feelings of betrayal."

Ensure informed consent processes are accessible

Contextualise the informed consent process in a way and language that is familiar to participants so they can more fully understand and consent. Share any relevant consent forms or scripts with participants in advance.

Disclose how the design research data will be used and shared

To ensure complete transparency, be explicit with participants about how their data will be used, as well as how their privacy and confidentiality will be protected. This must include any requirements for researchers to be mandated reporters. Mandated reporters are people (particularly in the helping professions) designated by law to report to the relevant authorities any known or suspected cases of abuse or neglect of children, elders, adults with disabilities, or other dependent adults.

And similarly to informed consent language, privacy policies should be clear, specific, and accessible to participants.

Let participants have an active role in the research

Engage with the structure and pacing of the session

For research sessions that have an agenda, walk through the sequence of activities with participants and ask for their feedback before beginning. This helps frame the design research session as a collaborative partnership.

Provide opportunities for refusal and re-negotiation of consent

Participants can be given opportunities for refusal throughout research sessions, including by:
- stating upfront which topics are to be discussed,
- prefacing each transition to check if they want to talk about each topic or not.

In this way, consent is not a static or one-time decision, but rather an ongoing negotiation.

4. Attentiveness

A praxis of attentiveness requires designers to have the capacity and tools to facilitate sessions with care, actively listen, and be attentive to the needs of participants during research interactions. This allows them to watch for, notice, and recognise potential signs of distress or activation.

Reflection prompts around attentiveness
- Do we have the skills to facilitate research sessions with care?
- How do we centre the participants' autonomy and choice during research interactions?
- How comfortable are we setting and maintaining appropriate boundaries with participants?
- Do we feel prepared to gently interrupt participants in anticipation of a potentially harmful or activating disclosure?
- Are we familiar with the signs of participant distress and discomfort that we should be looking for during research sessions? Do we know with confidence what we are paying attention to and how to recognise it?

Facilitating research sessions with care

Ask participants what makes them feel safe

Depending on the research study topic, you can remind participants at the beginning of a session that some of the prompts or questions may be difficult or upsetting. Ask participants if there is anything the team can do or be aware of to help them feel safe.

Dr. Jasmine B. MacDonald and colleagues suggest teams can also empower participants upfront to "set their own boundaries about what they want to disclose or any topics or questions they would prefer to skip" as well as discuss signals participants would prefer to use if they want to stop or take a break (for example, raising their hand).

Outline what will happen during the research session

At the beginning of each research session, reiterate information about:
- expectations,
- participant rights,
- data sharing and confidentiality.

Emphasise their choice, autonomy, and control over what they decide to share.

Practise attunement and active listening

Author and psychotherapist Dr. Resmaa Menakem writes, "Being an active listener involves not interrupting; not making judgments . . . not giving advice or offering explanations; and not jumping in with a story of your own." These are important maxims for design researchers to consider. Teams can practise attunement and active listening by:
- being fully present,
- being respectful,
- ensuring that participants feel heard through body language and verbal affirmations,
- welcoming silence,
- restating what is said and contributed.

Acknowledge the needs participants express

If a participant is sharing that they are having a hard time meeting their basic needs (for example, if they're experiencing food or housing insecurity), acknowledge that they have shared something that feels important, even if unrelated to the topic being studied. Offer to put them in touch with someone who can connect them with resources, if possible. It's important to recognise the wholeness and humanity of participants, not just their contributions to the research.

Create and maintain appropriate boundaries

It's crucial for design researchers to build rapport with participants so that they feel comfortable without overpromising or misrepresenting the nature of the relationship. Researchers should reflect (and potentially disclose to participants) on the boundaries they want to hold. Remain attentive to signals that may indicate a boundary breach, and have a plan for how to respond.

Prefacing sensitive topics and making use of gentle interruptions

Announce the transition to a potentially activating activity or set of questions

Before transitioning to a new activity or set of questions that may be activating, ask the participant if they are okay to switch to that topic. For example, you could say, "Next, we would like to ask you questions about [insert topic]. Would that be alright with you?"

Make use of gentle interruptions when anticipating a disclosure

If a participant appears close to disclosing a past traumatic experience or something that can feel activating, you can try to gently interrupt and warn them before disclosure occurs. Ground the participant in the present moment, and allow them space to decide if they would like to share more information with you. Skillfully and gently nudging participants away from reliving traumatic experiences aims to prioritise their psychological safety, as recounting past trauma can increase participant distress. Indeed, psychotherapist Ayhan Alman suggests that interruptions can "slow the pace and help participants re-anchor in the present."

Watching for changes in participants' affect

Tracking changes in participants' affect

"Affect" is what we can observe about someone's emotional state through physical or observable traits, like:
- demeanour,
- facial expressions,
- gestures,

- speech,
- intonation.

Watch for signs of potential changes in affect in participants, both verbal or nonverbal. Is the participant breathing more heavily? Are they restless or fidgeting? Are they getting irritable? Are they becoming agitated? Are they spacing out? Are they dissociating? Are they suddenly sweating and feeling very hot or shivering and feeling very cold? Are you noticing a voice change? Are they experiencing a sudden loss of concentration or remembering? (Some of these may be harder to observe if the participant is off video during virtual research sessions.)

Understand how dissociation can manifest

Another form of detachment or disconnection, called dissociation, can be mild or severe. Mild forms of dissociation occur everyday for all of us, such as when we are driving a car and become inattentive or distracted while continuing to function as if on autopilot. More severe forms of dissociation are often related to a history of trauma. These are potential signs of dissociation:
- fixed or glazed eyes,
- confusion,
- fast speech,
- sudden change of mood to low or no emotion,
- long periods of silence,
- monotonous voice.

Proactively check-in with participants if they have shared a lot

Even if the participant is not displaying any signs of affect change or dysregulation, you can proactively check-in if you feel like the participant has just shared a lot. For example, you might say, "We have covered a lot of territory over the past hour. How are you doing right now?"

5. Responsiveness

A praxis of responsiveness calls on designers to be able to respond to participant distress or activation when it arises in a way that is trauma responsive: acknowledging and validating the participants' feelings, offering options for support, and deferring to their lead on how they want to move forward.

Reflection prompts around responsiveness
- How and when do we interrupt a research session to tend to participants' needs?
- Do we know what to say to participants when they are feeling activated? Have we rehearsed or role played scenarios to prepare?
- What protocols do we have in place for responding to participant distress? Do these protocols allow for participants to be involved in the decision-making around support and next steps?
- Are we aware of the options participants have at their disposal should they need or want support?
- Do we have the skills to support participants with safety planning, if needed?

Acknowledging and validating participant distress

Stopping to tend to the participant's distress

If a participant is feeling distressed or activated, do not continue business as usual! It's important to interrupt the research session, acknowledge and name what is happening (for example, "I noticed that your tone of voice shifted a little bit; is everything okay?"). Interruption should be as gentle as possible, taking into consideration potential group dynamics if the sessions include more than one participant. If possible and appropriate, the participant can be pulled aside by one of the design research team members to discuss with them individually.

If the participant dismisses the researchers' concerns or doesn't want to talk about it, do not dig further or force them to share more. If the participant shares how they're feeling, researchers must affirm that they are listening (saying something like, "Thanks for sharing that with me").

Validating and normalising the participant's feelings

It's crucial that design researchers do not interrogate, blame, voice doubts, or minimise the participant's feelings by saying things like "it will be okay," "it will pass," "everything happens for a reason," or even "I understand how you feel."

Instead, it's more advisable to validate what the participant is feeling. It could be as simple as saying: "I'm sorry that happened" or "I'm sorry you are feeling [use their own words]; that sounds [terrible / frustrating / difficult]." You can normalise the participant's feelings and experience by reminding them that it's not unusual for people to have strong feelings when recalling painful experiences or discussing topics like the one they just shared.

Approach grounding activities with caution

Research teams may be tempted to learn more about soothing and grounding techniques they can use in a research session to soothe and manage participant's affect dysregulation in the moment. However well intentioned, trauma experts do not agree on the benefits of grounding and other techniques for co-regulation. Psychology experts Laurence Heller and Aline LaPierre suggest something as seemingly innocuous as "deep breathing with someone who has experienced significant trauma can trigger regression and re-traumatisation."

Additionally, using these techniques typically needs people who are experienced and highly attuned, and who have built a rapport and relationship with participants beforehand, to minimise the risk of re-traumatisation or the potential to create discomfort.

Following participants' lead

Discuss options for how to move forward

Design researchers can ask the participant how they want to proceed, asking something like, "What would you like us to do next?" This makes it less cognitively difficult for the participant to decide by specifying a few potential options. These could include taking a break, stopping, or resuming the session.

If the participant wants a break, affirm that they can take all the time they need. You might say, "Take as much time as you need and let me know if there is anything we can do to support you. We will be here when you are ready."

If the participant wants to stop the session, make sure they know that it's okay to do so, and aim to minimise any feelings of guilt that they may have about it. You could say, "This is completely understandable and okay. As we talked about before, no one is upset about ending this session. We just want to support you in the best way we can. If you need information about people to talk to, we can send you some phone numbers or resources that may help."

If the participant wants to continue the research session, make a determination as to whether it's okay to continue. However, it is not necessary or recommended to probe for more information about trauma history at this point. As much as possible, researchers should provide the participant with opportunities to be in control of the lines of inquiry. "We could talk about X or Y. Which one would you prefer tackling first?"

That being said, if signs that the participant is feeling activated keep showing up, researchers can end the session without making them feel that they are to blame.

Provide the participant with opportunities to be in control

Make sure that the participant knows that they are in control, and most importantly, actually let them take the lead.

Offering resources and support

Ask for and use person-specific calming techniques

Ask the participant directly what typically helps when they are feeling this way. For example, some people may like to take a break and go for a walk to calm down, while others may say they need to call a friend. Using calming techniques specific to them works best.

Provide resources and referrals

These should be location-specific, and prepared and compiled ahead of time. If needed and appropriate, design research teams can support the participant with a safety plan.

6. Dutifulness

A praxis of dutifulness encompasses the work that designers must do to show follow through and accountability after design research interactions, particularly to those who may have experienced activation.

Reflection prompts around dutifulness
- How and when do we inform participants of next steps that we have agreed on taking?
- Do participants know what happens after a research interaction? Are there opportunities where they can be engaged later on in the design project?
- Do we have the capacity to promptly follow-up with and compensate participants?
- Do we have the ability and resources to hold spaces for debriefing and process as a research team?
- Whom could we turn to for help if we need to process or vent?

Ensure prompt critical follow-ups with participants

End research sessions on a caring note

As the session ends, you can thank the participant and normalise the feelings that may have come up during the session (for example, saying, "I want to acknowledge that talking about these experiences can be uncomfortable, overwhelming, or [use their own words].")

This is also an opportunity to check in with the participant ("How are you feeling right now?"), and encourage them to take some time for some self-care if they can. Affirm something that they did well — like telling detailed stories or providing helpful suggestions.

Offer to provide follow-up support

After the session, you can:
- offer follow-up support to the participant if they would like ("What else do you need today?"),
- discuss follow-up timeline (you can follow up in the future as things don't always come up immediately after the research encounter),
- assess whether the participant would like any program support, referral to other services, or additional resources or information.

Inform participants of next steps

At the end of the session, share with the participant what to expect in terms of any follow-up communications or referrals discussed, payment for their compensation, and any contact they should expect in the future.

Demonstrate follow-through and accountability

"Do what you say and say what you'll do" is the rule! If a researcher told a participant that they should expect a follow-up, they should make sure to follow up. Teams can demonstrate diligent and dutiful follow-through by being accountable for their actions, including fully acknowledging when mistakes are made and working to fix the problem.

Ensure prompt follow-ups and compensation

Depending on what was discussed with the participant, design research teams should check-in after the session and provide additional resources or referral paths. Teams should also make sure that payment to participants is processed as quickly as possible, typically within the next business day. Participants should be able to select their payment method during recruitment.

Hold team debriefs and spaces to process and evolve

Create a culture of peer support and consultation

Design research team members can be of support to one another. This could mean consulting with a trusted colleague before a big decision or action, or assigning specific roles for team members to implement trauma-informed practices. For example, a team member could be the go-to person for all things mandatory reporting, while another may want to be responsible for collating and vetting referrals and resource lists, or creating information or wellbeing packets to send to participants.

Hold regular team debriefs to process

Right after each research session, researchers should take time to debrief and decompress together. In addition to post-research session debriefs, the team can meet to discuss personal experiences with the research, process, vent, and, if necessary, surface the need to receive supportive therapy or other resources. Scheduled and impromptu wellness checks can be the container for such debriefs.

Adapt and revise research processes as evolving practice

As they experience and debrief new research encounters, design researchers should be encouraged to continue learning, seek additional training and resources, build new skills, update their processes and protocols, and practise critical reflexivity.

Provide participants with opportunities to engage with the project post-research

Allow participants to review findings before they become public

After synthesising the data and writing the design research findings, you can invite the study participants to correct, add nuance to, and react to findings as part of a participant review process (also called member check or respondent validation).

Consult participants about attribution and identifying information

For any design research that is shared publicly, Rebecca Campbell and colleagues note it is best to "consult with participants about de-identifying data, recognising that participants are in the best position to know what might be identifying to people in their lives." For specific contributions such as quotations or cultural probe artefacts (drawings, poems, photographs, or other), participants can determine how they want to be credited publicly (for example using their full name, first name, nickname or pen name, or initials).

Provide updates to participants post-research

As the study progresses, design research teams can update the participants on what is happening with the project, and potentially also invite participants to attend or engage in opportunities related to the design project (like a product launch or publication).

Conclusion

These trauma-informed praxes are a synthesis of my own experiences as a design researcher as well as recommendations from other researchers from whom I've learned along my journey studying trauma and the ethics of design. These praxes, and their accompanying practices and reflection prompts, are not meant to be prescriptive. Rather, I offer them as suggestions, and invitations for further discussion and critique that can challenge our collective thinking.

When considering these praxes with your teams, it is important to consider them as part of your broader commitments to responsible and ethical design. These include your approaches to transparency and disclosure, informed consent, data privacy, and more. It is also crucial to situate these praxes in the context of your work, particularly the sensitivity of the topics you research and the vulnerability of the communities you work with. Finally, assess these praxes against the knowledge, skills, and capacity that you have, or what designer and author KA McKercher invites us to think of as our "scope of practice." This means being honest with ourselves about:
- what we know how to do,
- what we don't do (and others know we don't do),
- how we keep growing and practising accountability,
- where we partner to extend our scope of practice.

References and further reading

- "Listen: CTIPP team discusses trauma-informed integration." *Campaign for Trauma-Informed Policy and Practice* (2024)
- Paulo Freire, Pedagogy of the oppressed (1970)
- Tad Hirsch, "Practicing without a license: Design research as psychotherapy," *Proceedings of the 2020 CHI Conference on Human Factors in Computing Systems* (2020)
- Laura van Dernoot Lipsky and Connie Burk, *Trauma stewardship: An everyday guide to caring for self while caring for others* (2009)
- Jax Wechsler, "Navigating distress during design research," (published on LinkedIn) (September 2024)
- "A guide to GPRA data collection using trauma-informed interviewing skills," Substance Use and Mental Health Services Administration (SAMHSA) (2015)
- Rebecca Campbell, Rachael Goodman-Williams and McKenzie Javorka, "A trauma-informed approach to sexual violence research ethics and open science," *Journal of Interpersonal Violence*, 34 (2019)

- Jasmine B. MacDonald, Kylie Butler, Melissa Willoughby, Pragya Gartoulla, Will Dobud, "How to do trauma-informed research and evaluation" *Australian Institute of Family Studies* (2024)
- Resmaa Menakem, *My grandmother's hands* (2017)
- Ayhan Alman, "Trauma-sensitive research for user researcher," *UXPA Magazine* (2023)
- Laurence Heller and Aline LaPierre, *Healing developmental trauma: How early trauma affects self-regulation, self-image, and the capacity for relationship* (2012)
- KA McKercher, "Why designers need a scope of practice," (published on LinkedIn) (November 2023)
- Edwards J. Alessi and Sarilee Kahn, "Toward a trauma-informed qualitative research approach: Guidelines for ensuring the safety and promoting the resilience of research participants," *Qualitative Research in Psychology* (2022)
- Matthew Bernius and Rachael Dietkus, "Cultivating resiliencies for all: The necessity of trauma responsive research practices," *Ethnographic Praxis in Industry Conference Proceedings* (2022)
- Sarah Fathallah, Anna Myers and Verónica C. Rabelo, "Adding friction to mandatory reporting: The case for survivor-centered research," *Ethnographic Praxis in Industry Conference Proceedings* (2023)
- Sophie Isobel, "Trauma-informed qualitative research: Some methodological and practical considerations," *International Journal of Mental Health Nursing* (2021)
- Christine Murray, "Protecting victims in research," *Center for Victim Research* (2018)
- Soraya Seedat, Willem P. Pienaar, David Williams, Daniel J. Stein, "Ethics of research on survivors of trauma" *Current Psychiatry Reports* (2004)
- Emilie Smeaton, "Trauma and trauma-informed researchers," *Social Research Association*

Chapter 7

From principles to practice: using trauma-informed principles to design services

by Kate Every

Cast your mind back to the summer of 2020. There was no toilet paper in the shops, and people were deep in the Zoom quiz craze. I was working as a service designer for NHS Test and Trace throughout the height of the pandemic. It was fast-paced and chaotic, with policy seemingly changing hour by hour. We were working in teams with people we had never met, all from our home offices or bedrooms. We were working long days, and there was intense pressure to get operational services live so that the public could access tests that would let them know if they were infected with COVID. Team members were often burning out and needing to take time off.

While this was playing out at work, all of us were also experiencing the pandemic in real time in our personal lives, just like everyone else. We were locked down at home; people got sick, or had relatives get ill and pass away. And when they logged onto work in the morning, they were faced with the reminder of what was going on everywhere.

This paints a pretty bleak picture, but it wasn't all bad. It was hard work and often very stressful, but there was also an amazing sense of camaraderie and pulling together. It was incredibly rewarding to be part of teams doing such important work.

Throughout this time, our teams delivered services that:
- helped the general public book appointments at testing centres — and send them a result within 48 hours,
- let isolating people receive tests at their home,
- got at-home tests to people when they became available, and helped them to report their results so the government could keep an eye on prevalence.

We delivered services that meant people could test before going into hospital for an operation to make sure they weren't bringing in an infection, even if they were asymptomatic. We delivered services to let care home workers test their residents several times a week and reduce the spread within care homes.

These services meant that people would know when to isolate if they were infected, reducing the risk of spreading the virus — particularly in those people who were asymptomatic and would have carried on their usual routine if they'd not known they were infected. It meant people could access care they needed, or financial assistance. It gave people peace of mind to know they could safely visit loved ones with the assurance that they weren't carrying an infection.

During this time we conducted over 200 rounds of research to ensure our services were user-centred. We delivered updates to our services every single week. There were things we did well, and there was a lot we could have done better.

I'll give you an example of one research encounter that stuck with me for the wrong reasons. We usually worked in "squads," or small teams focused on a particular service. But on this day I was observing and note-taking for a researcher who I didn't usually work with. What I didn't know at the time was that they were quite junior, and they weren't that familiar with the service I was the designer for.

They opened the video call as they always did, and I sat in the background with my camera off for note-taking as I always did. They started by asking some questions to get some context, one of which was around the participant's experience of the pandemic. The participant's voice shook a bit as they told us that they had lost their partner. That they had not been able to leave home in months because they were clinically extremely vulnerable. That they were struggling with the isolation. There was a pause for a moment as we took it in. Then the researcher moved directly onto the next question in the plan: "... And what is your experience of booking COVID tests?"

We continued through the session, doing a usability test with a prototype. We logged off and rushed off to our next meetings without a time to debrief. The notes and findings got added to our overall collection of insights to inform the next iteration of the service.

I left the call, but it stayed with me for days. I felt really uncomfortable. I kept thinking about the person on that call, the way they had shared their deeply painful experience, and how we had just moved on, business as usual.

Now I want to make something clear: I'm not trying to blame or criticise that researcher. We were working under immense constraints, and we hadn't thought about our research from a trauma-informed perspective. At the time, I didn't even know what that was. The researcher was not equipped to handle what came out on that call, and I was not equipped to support them better.

I tell you this story so that we can discuss the constraints in which we all work, and think carefully about how we can better equip ourselves and drive change in our organisations so situations like this don't happen. I also tell you this in case you have had similar experiences and felt that uncomfortable feeling I experienced. I want you to realise you're not alone.

Beginning the journey

Coming out of that experience, I wanted to ensure that I wasn't causing unintended harm when I was researching and designing around complex topics. I started by educating myself on trauma-informed principles and finding ways to apply them to my own practice. This exploration also meant having conversations with other designers about what they experienced in their encounters with their service users and people taking part in their research. The more I talked to people, the more I found that everyone had a story to tell about research that was potentially distressing for themselves as facilitators, or re-traumatising for the participant involved.

Their words echoed my own experiences. I had been unprepared for what might come up and how to handle the session to minimise harm for all involved. But these conversations with other designers also revealed strategies and approaches my colleagues had developed to bring care into their practice and equip themselves better for the future.

These experiences and conversations have led me to think of being trauma-informed in user-centred design as 3 distinct (but interrelated) areas.

1. Trauma-informed operations: How we practise

How do we ensure that we are approaching our interactions with care for both the user and the practitioner?

This is about the things we do as practitioners to ensure our interactions with people are trauma-informed, whether they're:

- users of a product or service,
- participants within research.

2. Trauma-informed design: What we create

How do we ensure that the touchpoint (website, form, app, help content) we create is as trauma-informed as possible, especially when we aren't there to mediate the interaction?

This is about the outputs we create as a result of our research and design. This includes the:

- choice of content we use,
- interactions we design,
- use of visual imagery and language,
- format and accessibility of the interface.

3. Trauma-informed infrastructure: How we enable trauma-informed operations and design to happen

How can we create environments in which trauma-informed operations and design can emerge?

This looks at the service infrastructure that sits beneath our operations and design, including how the team is funded, structured, and trained. This also includes the wider policy landscape and the organisational culture.

I am going to focus on trauma-informed operations, and I'll provide some practical ways to think about bringing trauma-informed principles into our work. Some of these suggestions can start to be incorporated into your ways of working immediately; others may take more time, and that's okay. As Rachael Dietkus and Matt Bernius remind us:

> "working to integrate trauma-responsive practices in design and research remains a bold endeavour. It requires all of us to willingly step into spaces that are often uncomfortable. After all, change is uncomfortable and often creates resistance (both in ourselves and in others). This work will take effort and should not be rushed. The journey is lifelong."

Trauma-informed operations: From principles to practice

Peer support and collaboration are 2 of the guiding principles of trauma work. It's important to me to work in a community with others and learn from their experiences and expertise. Using those principles, I have worked with peers and user-centred design (UCD) practitioners, facilitating co-design workshops where we shared ideas on bringing trauma-informed principles into our own practice. These workshops took place at conferences in 2023 (UX Scotland and Magnify Inclusive Design Conference) and within my own user-centred design team.

Within the workshops, the groups came up with a whole range of ideas for how we could bring trauma-informed thinking into our work. People discussed this in relation to their own roles and organisations. During the sessions, I was joined by people across professions like service design, content design, user research, and interaction design, as well as specialists in accessibility and diversity and inclusion. Practitioners ranged in their level of experience, and they also worked in a wide range of sectors from government to healthcare to funeral care and charities.

They used a range of lenses to inform their thinking:
- macro approaches (systems, policies, and processes) and micro approaches (for example, individual research encounters),
- things they already do in their work (like asking for consent before a research session) and things they've never done but could try in future,
- how things might be different in a physical setting to a virtual or online setting,
- what insights they might bring in from outside work to inform their thinking; for example, approaches they might use when volunteering, or as part of a hobby.

We used the Substance Abuse and Mental Health Services Administration's (SAMHSA) 6 trauma-informed principles as a guiding framework for generating ideas. Trauma-informed principles are interrelated and build upon each other. They should be considered holistically, meaning that you can't pick and choose; they're all crucial. This means that one practical idea can span multiple principles. For example, having a **collaborative** conversation with participants where you encourage them to make **choices** about how the research session is run can improve **trust** between participant and researcher, fostering a greater sense of **safety**. One idea, (at least) 4 principles.

Following the workshops, I analysed the ideas and identified several themes which I will dig into in more detail in the next section:
- ensure communication is clear and transparent,
- draw on experts and wider practitioner networks,
- move beyond trauma-informed operations.

Use the themes and ideas below as a guide to spark ideas within your own practice. There is no checkbox guide which will fit every situation. It's imperative that you think about how to apply trauma-informed principles within your specific research and design context. This always starts with understanding the needs of the people you are involving in the process: your users, your research participants, your team, your stakeholders.

In fact, for some of the ideas below, you may find the exact opposite approach is needed, depending on the context. For example, with some groups, people may only feel safe to engage if they can be anonymous on an online session, keeping their cameras off and using a pseudonym.

In other cases, creating a sense of trust and peer support within a group session may mean it's better for everyone to have cameras on and to share names with others. Rather than thinking of these as rules, use them to ask questions and find what is right in each situation.

Theme 1: Ensure communication is clear and transparent

In the co-design workshops, one theme came up again and again: communication. How we communicate with the people we design for is fundamental in opening space for safety, building trust, and enabling collaboration and choice.

Having clear and open communication applies to everyone you are working with:
- users of your services,
- people you research with,
- your team members,
- other stakeholders.

Take care with language, and collaborate with others to set appropriate boundaries for the conversation or engagement.

Establish boundaries and consent through open, honest communication
- Agree clear definitions of roles and responsibilities at the start of every stage of work, whether an interview, research session, or co-design activity.
- Be really clear with participants why you are doing the research, how data will be used, and how it will be collected and stored.
- Outline at the start of the session which topics will be covered. Establish consent to discuss particular events or subjects and allow people to say no to topics they don't want to discuss.
- Be clear about the types of support you have available for participants and the limits of the researcher to provide support.
- Give people the space to leave, to say no, and to withdraw their inputs at any time.

- Make content as clear as possible and make it available in multiple formats. Participants can't truly consent if they don't understand what they're agreeing to, so use plain English, and read content out or provide it in other languages or mediums if necessary, such as video or audio.
- For consent forms, think about if someone can sign them digitally so they don't have to print and return a document.

Create shared understanding around language, following the person you are researching or designing with
- Agree on shared definitions of important words or phrases with the participant. Share what you mean by a term and ask if that resonates with them. If it doesn't, ask what terms might be more suitable.
- Do your research to learn how to pronounce unfamiliar names or terms, or to find someone's correct pronouns.
- Be aware of the connotations of words. Words and phrases like "observer," "interview," and "collecting data" could all be difficult for people as they have other associations beyond your design engagement with them. Come up with alternatives that are better suited to the people you're working with.
- If a participant is uncomfortable with the words being used, rethink or reword questions based on their needs.
- Give people choice about the words you use. Follow their lead and reflect the language they choose to use.

Share your insights with the people who gave their time to come to research

Sometimes people give their time, effort, and energy by sharing their thoughts with us in research. Often they are vulnerable in the process. Within the busyness of our roles, we don't always take the time to reach back out and share with them the impact of their insights. This is an extractive practice, and we should strive to avoid this.
- Give participants an update before any final outputs. See if they're comfortable with how their data is being represented and give them the option to amend their contribution.

- Share your final synthesised findings back with the people you researched with, and tell them what is going to happen as a result of the findings.

Be transparent about the future of the product or service you are designing
- Communicate about the product or service, making a publicly accessible roadmap or update log if possible.
- Be honest about feedback you won't be taking onboard, and why.
- Publish the methodology you are using. Share your resources with the people you are researching with, the team, and other stakeholders, and ask others to share what they are doing.

Use good listening skills
- Put participants at ease — don't go straight into questioning or treat it like a clinical research setting. Acknowledge each other's shared humanity.
- Verbally summarise what you think you heard. This ensures you've understood someone correctly and have not misrepresented what they've said through your own lens or bias.
- Provide written summaries after the session to give the participant space to reflect. They could also then sign the summary if they are happy for their statements to be included. Sometimes people aren't aware of what they say in the moment, and on reflection would like to reword their statements to better reflect what they intended.

Make practical adjustments in research and design sessions

There are many ways to make practical adjustments to make research and co-design sessions more comfortable for the people you invite to take part. Taking care to provide adjustments helps to create a safer environment, and doing this through collaboration and dialogue with the participant provides them with choice, which can help to build trust.

Sarah Fathallah goes into depth about trauma-informed design research approaches in Chapter 6, so I will briefly touch on a few ideas.
- Prepare for the session in advance. The adjustments you make will depend on the context and setting. Communicate directly with the participant to understand their needs. Introduce yourself and the

team and find out key details they might want to share, like name and pronouns. Be aware of cultural considerations (for example, don't schedule research on certain culturally significant days or rest days, or take your shoes off in certain spaces).
- Enable choice for your participants wherever possible. Throughout your preparation, you should ascertain how you can best provide flexible options so the person you have invited to research has choices. Give them a choice about whether the session is in person or online. If the session is in person, can you give them a choice of venue? Are you able to travel to them, or will they need to come to you? And provide choice about how to receive compensation, if appropriate. Be clear about how and when compensation will be paid (ideally up-front, so they don't feel financially obligated to stay if they are triggered).
- Create a comfortable environment. If meeting in person, think about whether the space is accessible for the specific person and their needs. Consider how you can make the space more inviting and spacious, perhaps using calming colours, fidget toys, or materials to keep hands busy, or by laying out the space in a more friendly way.
- For virtual meetings, provide guidance on how to access the meeting and have experienced tech support on hand if the participant needs it. Use accessible and collaborative tools, with enough time for a walk-through and a back-up plan if online tools do not work for the participant.
- Consider the pacing and timing of the session as you prepare, and also remain flexible to make changes based on needs that arise when you're in the session. Plan more time for sessions than you think you need. This allows for breaks and the ability to go at the participant's pace. Build in time between sessions, and put a cap on the number you are able to complete in a day. Practitioners need time to debrief, decompress, and have a break after sessions, particularly where trauma has been discussed, or someone has become distressed.

Theme 2: Draw on experts and wider practitioner networks

A crucial but sadly underutilised practice is to draw on experts and wider networks to supplement your understanding and the support you can provide. As user-centred design practitioners, we can grow our understanding and awareness of trauma and trauma-informed approaches, but we are not (necessarily) experts in trauma. The UK Government "Working definition of trauma-informed practice" states:

> The purpose of trauma-informed practice is not to treat trauma-related difficulties, which is the role of trauma-specialist services and practitioners. Instead, it seeks to address the barriers that people affected by trauma can experience when accessing health and care services.

Being trauma-informed does not mean treating trauma. It means knowing your own boundaries and capabilities so you are prepared to hand over to a professional if and when needed. Draw on support from subject matter experts, charities, professionals from other disciplines, informal networks, and community groups.

Engage with experts when preparing for research

- Go through trusted community or charity groups, working with them to reach the participants and involve them in the process to act as an intermediary. When engaging with community and charity groups, it is really important to compensate them for their time. They are often working with very scarce resources, so they won't be able to support your research for free no matter how much value they see in it.
- When you don't know enough about a topic or a particular cultural group, reach out to organisations to learn more. Don't rely on them to do the labour for you. Start with any publicly accessible resources they have produced and use this as a jumping-off point to dig deeper.
- Start to establish partnerships with subject matter experts or charities. Ideally, get them as part of the team! Get their feedback on the wording of questions and framing of language or your use of visual imagery within artefacts. They will be able to anticipate potential issues that you might have missed.
- In some cases it will be appropriate to bring a specialist or support worker into the research or design session alongside the participant. Make it clear what their role is and how they can offer support.

Signpost to professionals and professional resources if participants need additional support

The most important point here: know your boundaries. If you are not a trained trauma professional, know when to step back and sensitively end the interview and signpost to the professionals. Have a plan in place for this eventuality, so you know the language you will use to draw the session to a close and any materials you want to share as part of your signposting.

Create a support pack with resources and signposting to local organisations that are available for the participant if they need it. An exemplar is an open-source wellbeing pack and post-session participant care created by Bright Harbour in collaboration with AndGood. This pack includes, in their words:

- "reassurance that help is available and that everyone deserves support,
- links to a huge range of different support organisations so that participants can pick what resonates — whether that's support with crisis planning or help with managing personal finances,
- DIY support like breathing exercises that could be used there and then to help alleviate stress or overwhelm,
- reminders about how to get in touch with us if they're feeling unsettled."

They also offer the option of a one-off, free wellbeing support chat with their Clinical Psychotherapist partner for the project.

Engage in communities of practice

Engaging in the wider trauma-informed community through communities of practice groups, or having space for discussions with colleagues and peers, can help build awareness of approaches taken by other practitioners, and also be a source of peer support for your own work.

Debrief with colleagues and other professionals after sessions — your own health and wellbeing are really important, too, and should not be forgotten.

Theme 3: Moving beyond trauma-informed operations

At the beginning of this chapter I spoke about 3 areas of trauma-informed UCD. This chapter has mainly focused on how we introduce trauma-informed principles into our own practice, what I've termed "trauma-informed operations."

Applying the principles in our own work is imperative as we strive towards becoming trauma-informed. It leads to better environments for ourselves and our teams to operate within, and better experiences for the people we are researching and designing with.

This book also has many great examples and guides for how to bring trauma-informed principles into the design and research artefacts we create, from the content we produce to the software we build. I encourage you to engage deeply with these to create meaningful impact through your creations.

Towards "trauma-informed infrastructure"

Within public sector service design, I have seen innovative applications of trauma-informed principles at the individual level, and sometimes at the level of teams. In some brilliant and progressive organisations, trauma-informed principles are being embedded and practised at organisational level. But this is often not the case.

Many industry colleagues I have spoken to feel as though they are individuals, swimming upstream against the wider organisational or system culture, and are not given the resources needed to truly be trauma-informed in their work. In the co-design workshops where we shared many of the ideas above, the discussions moved to some of the deeper issues that needed to be tackled at a systemic level. This included comprehensive training and ongoing development around trauma and its impacts, not just for UCD professionals but for anyone coming into contact with or producing products for users. As this is a field where we are always learning and refining approaches, this needs to be an ongoing endeavour.

Zooming out from the specific product or service we're designing, we also need to think about the wider policy landscape. Is the actual policy that service is there to deliver trauma-informed? Very often it is not. This creates challenges before the first bit of research work is even begun. We, as designers and researchers, can do our best to be trauma-informed in our own interactions and through our own outputs, but often the political decisions which drive our work are failing users before we even begin.

Organisational culture is another area which can leave practitioners feeling as though they are swimming upstream. Where colleagues and leadership aren't aware of the necessity of trauma-informed practice, it can be a challenge to get resources or support to enable this way of working. Being trauma-informed often means taking things at a slower pace, and this can be a challenge within some organisations.

Shifting the infrastructure of our services is both a challenge and an opportunity. It may seem insurmountable, but as we can see in the examples of accessible design and workplace recognition of mental health, better approaches are breaking through and becoming embedded.

As user-centred researchers and designers, we can do what we've always done:
- be human-centred in our approaches, showing compassion to those we are interacting with, and also to ourselves as we seek to improve our practice,
- be evidence-based, using our research insights to help shift perceptions of those around us and advocate for better ways of working,
- iterate and evolve as we learn, adopting the practices we're learning through resources like this book.

Ultimately, we can use our skills to bring people together and continue to push for wider change as we go.

References and further reading

- Kate Every, "Applying trauma-informed principles to user-centred design" (2023)
- Kate Every, "User research, design and trauma: understanding practitioner experiences" (2023)
- Matthew Bernius and Rachael Dietkus, "Cultivating Resiliencies for All: The Necessity of Trauma Responsive Research Practices," *Ethnographic Praxis in Industry Conference Proceedings* (2022)
- Harry Cerasale and Caitlin Connors, "Common standards series: post-session participant care" (2021)
- Bright Harbour https://www.brightharbour.co.uk

Chapter 8
Working with and for young people

by Steph Mann

Throughout most of my career, I hadn't thought about content in a trauma-informed way. It had never come up. But then I moved into a role as a senior content designer in a national charity. The charity's audience included children and young people, and my work focussed on website content.

Coming from roles that were very much centred on an adult audience (government and academia), this transition brought with it a steep learning curve. I have learnt that trauma-informed practice is now something we could all be aware of and build into the work that we do.

It was my role to help write content for children and young people. The projects I worked on covered topics like:
- sexting,
- eating disorders,
- self-harm,
- child sexual abuse,
- financial abuse,

- gambling,
- mental health.

Working on these topics was challenging in many ways, and I heard of things I never knew existed. It also gave me experience creating content on difficult topics for children and young people.

Trauma in children and young people

Trauma is a complex issue that can have profound effects on young people. Understanding different types of trauma and how they impact children and young people is crucial for anyone working with or creating content for them.

Trauma in childhood can last into adulthood and have lifelong effects. It impacts how we grow, physically and mentally. It can affect our feelings, thoughts, and how we behave. Children and young people don't have the same coping mechanisms as adults, nor do they have the experience to help them deal with trauma. They don't have access to the support networks that adults can find, and so they rely on what is available to them.

They tend to use the internet (particularly social media) to look for information, and that was the world I work in and where I was creating content.

Adverse childhood experiences (ACEs)

If you work in a government or policy area, you may have heard of ACEs. Young Minds, a mental health charity, describes ACEs as:

"highly stressful, and potentially traumatic, events or situations that occur during childhood and/or adolescence. They can be a single event, or prolonged threats to, and breaches of, the young person's safety, security, trust or bodily integrity."

ACEs include events or situations like:
- emotional abuse,
- sexual abuse,
- physical abuse,
- living with someone who abused substances,
- living with someone who has gone to prison,
- losing a parent through divorce, death, or abandonment.

As our awareness of childhood trauma grows, ACEs are becoming more talked about. As content designers, we can't fix a young person's trauma, but we can do our best to support them and not add to it.

It's important that we design content in a way that supports children and young people. We won't always get it right, but using the best words that we can and offering support can really help.

Responses to trauma

A child or young person can have memories that upset them, affecting their daily life. Research shows that trauma at a young age can cause harmful levels of stress, which impacts their:

- learning,
- behaviour,
- health.

These factors can affect a young person's:

- language development,
- ability to pay attention,
- ability to regulate their emotions.

Children and young people develop coping mechanisms to help them survive. If they perceive trauma in any way, their natural response is:

- fight (face the threat with aggression),
- flight (try to leave or run away),
- freeze (be unable to move or leave),
- fawn (try to please to avoid conflict).

These are automatic responses that they have no control over.

These responses make the body release hormones (adrenaline and cortisol). And these make:

- their heart beat faster,
- them feel more alert.

And you need to think about how this is relevant to your content. A young person who has experienced trauma might have these reactions when they come to your content. Even if they are in a safe place, a child who has been through trauma is always aware of danger, making daily life overwhelming.

For example, if a young person responds by fawning and has poor boundaries due to their experience, does that change how you might design a form or get their consent (if applicable)?

Knowing that they are likely to agree to something, even if that isn't necessarily in their best interest, might mean changing the way you ask questions or making it clear if something is optional.

Or if they are in flight mode, think about the impact that has on their ability to focus on information. Can you remove extra words, or create more space so they can absorb information more easily?

All of these responses can change how you design content. The way a traumatised young person reads or retains information means their user needs are different. We need to think about what this means for findability, the language we use, and how we structure content.

Understanding different types of trauma

A child or young person often experiences trauma in a relationship where they should be cared for. This means that they learn not to trust people, making it hard to build and have safe and supportive relationships.

To design trauma-informed content for young people, you need to understand different types of trauma and how it can affect them. Trauma can be:
- a single event, such as an assault or an accident,
- repetitive (occurring over years).

The impact of trauma on trust and relationships

We know that users need to trust our content, and trauma-informed approaches need to work harder to gain that trust.

You may know the saying "work smarter, not harder." Trauma-informed content needs to work both smarter and harder.

Compared to standard content design, there are additional questions that need to be answered and more research that needs to be done.

Depending on the content, context, and format, you need to think about if children and young people will:
- trust your content,

- naturally look for information on their own,
- read it in the way you expect.

Everyone who works with children, including those who design content for them, needs to understand and recognise the impact of trauma. Healthy relationships really matter to young people. They respond well to supportive and responsible adults. Your content cannot replace an adult, but it can:

- be trustworthy and supportive,
- help a young person to have some of their needs met, rather than ignored,
- be written correctly,
- help a child cope and recover from the effects of trauma by being in the right place at the right time.

The impact of trauma at different ages

It's important to change your style based on the age of your users. However, children and young people can't be put into one age bracket. Their developmental changes and needs vary greatly over just a few years, compared to an adult audience. In general, we understand that behaviour changes with age, but there are additional differences that you need to be aware of for a child who has been through trauma.

This means they have different user needs which will change how you write or display content, or whether you leave something out altogether.

Age 0 to 4

Whilst it's unlikely that a child this age will be reading content, they might still hear or see it, depending on the type of content. Children this age can respond to trauma by displaying:

- exaggerated responses, such as tantrums, crying a lot, or being easily alarmed,
- demanding behaviour, like clinging to adults for protection, even if the adult was the source of danger.

Age 5 to 12

Children this age can:

- struggle to express feelings,

- be sad or worried about safety,
- think about past events,
- be overwhelmed by noise, touch, or smell.

Age 13 and up

Teenagers may find it hard to manage their emotions and can:
- worry about being vulnerable and hide how they feel,
- feel shame and guilt and engage in harmful or risky behaviours.

Design safer content

You can use trauma-informed principles as a guide to create content for children and young people.

This means your content offers:
- safety for a young person rather than a threat,
- trust in your content and organisation as a reliable source of information and support,
- choices, so a young person feels they have their own power,
- collaboration, like co-design and pair writing, which gives young people a say in the content,
- empowerment, in that your content supports a young person to understand it and act on it independently, where appropriate.

Cultural consideration in trauma-informed practice is often about recognising things like language, tradition, culture, and values. Young people may have different sets of cultural values from their families and peers, for example.

Content design can:
- offer predictability and routine though structure and design elements like button text,
- give consistent and predictable content to help manage distress through language, voice, and tone.

Supportive content can:
- be designed to help young people regulate their emotions and understand their feelings,
- be interactive and engaging.

Research with children and young people

Do your research

One of the biggest parts of any project is research. If you have user researchers, go to their user sessions and take notes. You can get valuable insights from this. If they talk to young people, be part of the process so that you can observe and learn. Make notes on:
- the language and words young people use,
- concerns that they have,
- what they like (or don't).

When I joined these sessions, I wrote everything down because it could (and mostly did) come in handy in the future. It gives you a repository of information that you can refer back to as the product grows.

Stay close to the research and know your users

Being close to the research really allows you to understand the perspective of children and young people.

I chatted directly with young people and service workers in our research sessions. Young people were candid and shared their feedback without hesitation.. Workers gave me an in-depth look at what they expected and needed. This level of information allows you to identify gaps that you might be able to fill early on in the process, things that would have been missed if a content designer wasn't in the room.

We know that getting content designers in the room from the beginning really helps a project. And in a lot of circumstances, it is considered nice to have (mainly because it's difficult for us to get engagement that early on). But for trauma-informed content, it's something I would have as a hard rule. This is a space where your knowledge needs to grow and develop in order to do the best for your users. It isn't a nice-to-have, it's a must-have.

Knowing your user groups gives you the opportunity to really advocate for them.

Our user researchers did some scenario testing, and I volunteered to take notes. Watching young people navigate content helped me to see exactly where the problems were. In this instance, it was watching users hover over some microcopy for a second, but not trusting it enough to click through.

When I asked them about it, they just said they weren't sure why they hesitated. Digging a little deeper, it turned out that they weren't confused; it was a matter of trust, and we hadn't gained that.

I listened to what they said and the words they used. I know our user researchers would have reported this back, but there are nuances that content designers see because it's our job. Rather than having to change the whole flow, it was only a matter of adding in some hint text to the button so that users would trust the text. And in the next round of testing, users moved through as we hoped they would.

Being in the room can save unpicking or redoing huge pieces of work. Usually you can fix things quickly and easily.

Doing your own research

If you don't have a user researcher, you can still do lots of research. Desk research gives you insights into:
- what other websites are doing,
- social media platforms young people are using,
- words they are searching for,
- trends that are happening,
- gaps in the market.

You can test user journeys on other websites (if they are similar), which can help you to understand any frustrations a child or young person could have. Having an understanding of trauma-informed content changes your perspective, and you can start to identify gaps that you wouldn't have seen before.

Test everything

Testing your content is crucial. Work with services and real users to gather feedback and iterate your content. This ensures that it meets the needs of your audience and remains effective.

You can do this using methods such as:
- card sorting with young people:to group content in a way that makes sense to them,

- A/B testing: to give the choice to young people about which content they feel is more understandable,
- highlighter marking: as a quick indicator about things young people like, don't like, or find confusing,
- task-based usability testing: (to really understand how young people navigate your content,
- comprehension testing: so young people can tell us if something doesn't make sense or is complicated.

Working with young people to design content

Once you have done your research and understand your audience, you can map their needs and start to design your content.

When you're ready to write, if you can, write with young people. I found this to be one of the most rewarding things I've ever done as a content designer. Having met some wonderful young people in user research sessions, I asked some of them if they wanted to help write and fact-check content.

Talk to young people

As content designers, we know that we need to reflect our users' language back at them. Children and young people use lots of words we might not understand. You will learn a lot through desk research and social media platforms. However, I still think part of co-creating with young people should involve speaking to them at every opportunity.

Language evolves at a fast pace for young people, and trends come and go. You might not be able to reflect all of these changes in your content.

When I was speaking directly with young people, there were some words and phrases that were not appropriate to use in content online. But knowing some slang for this particular project was a key part of searchability. If we wanted adults to be able to search for a word or a phrase a young person had said, we had to know what those were.

The language in this particular project really taught me a lot. One area was learning words and phrases around online risks. It really opened my eyes to how much I didn't know about the online world and how young people interact with it. I had no idea that "pile-on" harassment was a way of lots of people targeting one person online. Other words for this were "dog-piling" and "flaming." Another example was "doxxing," which is when someone's personal information is shared online. And I had no clue money laundering is also known as "smurfing." Other terms that stood out were "loot boxing" and "skin-gambling."

But learning this by researching allowed me to use multiple slang phrases (that all basically meant the same thing) in the metadata on the page. This gave our users search results that were as relevant as possible.

You can reflect keywords and the language of young people in your metadata to help with search engine optimisation (SEO). Using direct quotations from young people in your content will also help with searchability as well as give your users context on the page. Young people also said they found this really valuable, and it helped them to trust the content more.

Talking to young people will also give you a broader and deeper understanding of how they should be spoken to. This will help you to develop the tone of voice your content and audience want and need. Principles of trauma-informed content design can be consistent across projects, but things like tone, language, and structure can differ a lot. It all depends on the topics and the context.

Pair writing with children and young people

I pair-wrote a lot of the content with young people to make sure I captured what was important to them. I also had sessions of pair writing where young people got to tell us about their own experiences with mental health and the impact that has had on their life.

Young people have told me that they loved the peer-to-peer content. They said they could really relate to it, whether it was a whole story or a call-out quotation. This all comes back to that principle of building trust, listening to feedback, and being aware that it can be a slower process than usual, but it's worthwhile.

Pair writing with young people is different to the standard approach because you have more to consider. Sharing their story with you can make a young person feel vulnerable, but if you set it up right, it can be empowering.

You need to:
- create a safe space, whether online or in person,
- give them clear boundaries,
- let them lead if they want,
- make sure you follow safeguarding procedures.

To do this, I worked with service workers who asked young people if they wanted to take part. This meant the young person was invited by someone they already knew, and this person also attended all the pair writing sessions with us. I met all the young people online and let them know what to expect, including that they could:
- keep their camera off,
- leave anytime,
- only answer if they wanted to.

I also let them know what would happen with the information they gave me.

I found that sending guidelines and content (if possible) ahead of time really helped the young person to know what we would be working on. Having a rough draft ready with some parts you know you need help with is a good starting point. The young people are the experts here, and they will tell you when something is wrong or hard to read.

For example, on the projects I worked on, we sent out an agreement to the young people we would be working with. This set out what they wanted and expected from us — and vice versa. We used these to set the tone of all our sessions and interactions.

Keep your questions to the point, but do allow yourself to wander off topic. It's more of a conversation, and you never know what you might learn.

Once you're finished, let the young person know what you will do next. For me, it was a simple process of:
1. finish the draft,
2. email it to the young person (via their worker),
3. get their feedback,
4. make changes,

5. run a final check with the relevant subject matter expert from my organisation,
6. publish.

Working directly with young people gives you an important perspective on your content.

If you can't pair write directly, you might still be able to ask a young person to:
- check the language of your content,
- give feedback.

Tone of voice

We know that young people who have experienced trauma might read content differently because of their response to trauma. One of the things you can do to mitigate this is to get the right tone when creating content. The voice you use depends on where you work, and it will likely be part of your brand.

Where you can really make an impact is through tone. You can adapt tone depending on the audience and the content. To make sure you are on the right track, you can do quick and easy tone of voice testing with users. See how it makes them feel, and iterate using the evidence. You can also do some comprehension testing to see if users understand the point of the content.

Some examples of tone of voice you might use when writing for children and young people include:
- calm and reassuring: use a gentle tone,
- empathetic and understanding: show empathy and understanding of their experiences,
- positive and encouraging: highlight their strengths and encourage them.

Thinking about the tone you use can offer stability, safety, and consistency to young people.

During some of our research, we realised that young people often found filling in forms to be hard work and they didn't trust them. To remove the burden from them, we made any interaction where we gathered data as simple as possible. And adjusted the tone to let users know this was a quick and safe process. We told them what they needed in advance, how long it would take, outlined the benefits, and gave them clear options to opt in or out.

It doesn't need to be an app

When we think of children and young people, we tend to assume that content needs to be an app or social media platform.

The young people I worked with said they access media in lots of different ways. They said that video content was helpful, and contrary to my assumptions, they did like to browse websites. If they were reading something, they often liked to go back and take their time to read some things. It depended mostly on the content. They said they preferred websites to read if the content was:

- long-form,
- helpful,
- relevant.

I worked on a website that was designed solely for children and young people. It offered advice and guidance around their mental health. I wrote content in an article format, and the site was designed with young people at every stage.

We asked for feedback on:
- design, including colours and content placement,
- language that was used, so it reflected theirs,
- topics to cover, to make sure it was relevant to them.

Getting the right subject matter expert (SME)

It's important to write trauma-informed content with an SME who is an expert in an area relevant to your content. These might be people inside your organisation, a specialist organisation, or someone you need to pay.

Here are some types of SMEs:
- Child psychologists or psychiatrists are experts who understand the mental health needs of young people. They can help make sure your content is sensitive.
- Trauma specialists are professionals who specialise in trauma. They offer insights into the needs and responses of young people, helping your content to be appropriate and supportive.
- Social workers often have direct experience working with young people in different settings and can offer practical advice on how to engage and support them.
- Educational psychologists can help design content that needs to be educational and therapeutic. They can help to make it accessible and beneficial for young people in school.
- Youth workers have experience working directly with young people. They can give feedback that can help clarify language.
- Non-profit organisations can be good partners when creating content or listing resources.

Follow safeguarding procedures

Always use the appropriate channels to get content tested. Whether that is through an agency or previous rounds of research, it is important to follow safeguarding procedures. These procedures and requirements will vary from country to country.

If the content you want to test is triggering, check with the person who is responsible for the young person's safeguarding that it is okay to test. A young person could agree to test content without considering the implications. Always keep the safety of the young person at the heart of everything you do.

Different perspectives and reading between the lines

I found that it's important to get as much feedback as possible. You learn different things from different users about the same piece of content.

One of the best ways I found to test final content in this particular project was A/B testing. At this point we had already written and fact-checked our content. One thing we had to test at the last minute was how to lay out the content.

We tested a long version and one that used accordions and headings. We asked 2 user groups: service workers and young people.

Both groups preferred accordions, but the reason why was not the same.

The young people pointed out that the long content was hard to read, and the accordions made it much easier to break it down.

Workers said that if they were reading it on a laptop or mobile, a young person might see it, and it could trigger them. The accordions were a much safer way to display the content.

We got the same result, but for 2 very different — and valid — reasons.

This is the sort of knowledge you can take with you from project to project. You learn something new, and likely something you hadn't thought about. And it can help you in the future.

Things to remember

Routines and predictability

Routines and predictability are important to children and young people. They can help young people contain distress. Supportive content can help young people manage their emotions and behaviour. It can help regulate their feelings, relate to them, and help them understand why they might feel the way they do.

Good content can help them feel comfortable, offer advice, and be safe.

Be safe and predictable

- Use a consistent layout and design across your website to create a sense of predictability and safety. Avoid sudden changes in design that might be unsettling.
- Ensure that navigation is intuitive and straightforward. Young users should be able to find what they need without confusion or frustration.

Empathy and understanding

- Use a calm, reassuring, and empathetic tone. Acknowledge their feelings and experiences without being patronising. Don't have a tone that tells them how they should feel or what they should do. Try to be supportive.

- Use tested content warnings for any material that might be triggering. This allows young people to make informed choices about what they engage with. Always test content warnings, and remember that your users might not want them at all.

Empowerment and choice
- You can include interactive elements like quizzes, polls, and comment sections where young people can express their opinions and feel heard.
- Allow users to customise their experience, such as choosing themes or adjusting text size. This gives them a sense of control and empowerment.

Collaboration and trust
- Involve young people in the content creation process. This could be through focus groups, surveys, or direct collaboration. Ensure they have a say in what gets published.
- Implement feedback mechanisms where users can share their thoughts and suggestions. Show that you value their input by making visible changes based on their feedback.

Supportive content
- Provide resources and links to mental health support services. Include articles and videos that offer coping strategies and emotional support.
- Highlight positive stories and achievements of young people. This can
- help build self-esteem and resilience.

Age-appropriate content
- Ensure that content is age-appropriate and relevant to the different developmental stages. For example, content for younger children should be simple and visually engaging, while content for teenagers can be more detailed and interactive.
- Use insights into age-specific behaviours to tailor content. For instance, younger children might benefit from stories and games, whilst teenagers might prefer articles and forums.

Get it wrong to get it right

Working with young people brings extra challenges. The cohort of young people changes every few years, and their words, preferences, and platforms change even faster. It can often feel like you get it wrong more than you get it right.

And this, for me, is one of the joys of content design. It's a job where you can keep growing and learning. Nothing is the same year after year, and I'm thankful for that. Having our assumptions challenged through our work helps us become better designers and people.

Working with young people also brings rewards, like the opportunity to create content that can truly support and help someone at a formative time. My advice is to embrace mistakes, feel awkward, and lean into learning.

References and further reading

- "Trauma," Young Minds
- "Understanding child trauma," Substance Abuse and Mental Health Services Administration (SAMHSA)
- "What is attachment theory and why is it important," NSPCC Learning
- Sharon Gray, "Healthy relationships make the biggest difference" GOV.UK (2023)
- Ingrid Clayton, "What is the fawning trauma response?" *Psychology Today* (2023)
- "Anxiety and panic attacks," Mind
- Charles A Nelson, Richard David Scott, Zulfiqar A Bhutta, Nadine Burke Harris, Andrea Danese, and Muthanna Samara, "Adversity in childhood is linked to mental and physical health throughout life," *The BMJ* (2020)
- "Psychological trauma and adversity including ACEs (adverse childhood experiences)," Scottish Government (2024)

- Elena Bozzola, Giulia Spina, Rino Agostiniani, Sarah Barni, Rocco Russo, Elena Scarpato, Antonio Di Mauro, Antonella Vita Di Stefano, Cinthia Caruso, Giovanni Corsello, and Annamaria Staiano. "The Use of Social Media in Children and Adolescents: Scoping Review on the Potential Risks" *International Journal of Environmental Research and Public Health* (2022)
- "Trauma-informed practice toolkit," Scottish Government (2021)
- "Cultural diversity and culturally competent practice" (section 3, chapter 6) New South Wales Government
- "Cultural identity and mental health," Young Minds
- "Consider culture when communicating with young people," Mental Health First Aid

Chapter 9
How trauma-informed principles can work in government

by Jane McFadyen

Dealing with government can be stressful. Many people use government services when they are in vulnerable situations or experiencing important life events. This might be for services related to a birth and death, or when applying for benefits. We often come to government content when we are dealing with a stressful thing, perhaps for the first time. If we asked people to describe government, they probably wouldn't choose words like:
- friendly,
- comforting,
- reassuring,
- encouraging.

So how do we reconcile trauma-informed design with delivering vital government services?

Designing for government

Content design for government digital services is hard.

It's a complicated mix of using research and evidence to understand users, their needs, and the journeys they make. We have to understand the processes and systems behind the scenes and identify opportunities for improvement.

It's about understanding legal guidance and translating policy so services are as simple as possible to understand and use. And then we need to produce information, often using tricky legacy systems or restrictive technology.

Then there's engaging with stakeholders and acting as the voice of the user so government services meet the needs of potentially millions of people.

I work as a content designer for the Department for Work and Pensions (DWP), which is the largest government department in the UK. DWP operates on a scale that is almost unmatched anywhere else in Europe. I work in Bereavement and Care, helping teams to deliver vital services for people.

Most people in the UK come into contact with us at some point in their lives: if they need to claim a benefit, get help finding a job, or understand their pension. And in DWP Digital, we help build, develop, and maintain the digital services that enable millions of people to access the help, advice, and financial support they need.

And because DWP is a part of the UK government, it means that in our work we also follow the:
- Government Design Principles,
- GOV.UK Design System,
- GOV.UK Style guide.

We also, of course, meet the UK government service standards. That's all before even designing the content, then testing, iterating, and responding to feedback.

But as content designers, I believe there's more we can — and should — do.

Trauma-informed principles should be baked into your content design

Should we really add more elements to an already complex role?

100% yes, we should. Following trauma-informed principles will improve your content design and the user experience for everyone.

For example, using the GOV.UK design consistently for government content helps people trust the services they are using. They recognise them and know they are official and secure, and perhaps already understand how the components behave. The standards are compliant with WCAG 2.2 accessibility criteria, which helps improve general accessibility. And content should follow GOV.UK style guide around clear, concise content.

By using these design standards as a foundation, and then applying trauma-informed principles, content designers can create services that are efficient, accessible, and meet users needs. So if you use these designs and style guides, you are already starting from a positive starting point.

And I'm not forgetting the diligent content designers working elsewhere! GOV.UK's success has empowered other public and private sector organisations around the world. Many are now working towards a similar unified and consistent approach to design standards. And the GOV.UK design system and guidance is available online for anyone to access and reference.

Applying design systems

A valid concern with using any design system is that it might be too restrictive. Some might assume that working in a well-defined system would be too limiting and not flexible enough to allow designers to incorporate trauma-informed principles.

But actually, I believe it's more about *how* you apply design standards.

We research regularly with people who have been recently bereaved, so we can design and iterate a service based on our users' needs. Our research means we can understand the impact that dealing with a death has on a person, and how this can affect the way they interact with a service.

Dealing with a death is always a unique experience for an individual, and it can cause a lot of emotions. Our users experience a complicated mixture of:

- anxiety,
- anger,
- depression,

- despair,
- fear,
- frustration,
- guilt,
- helplessness,
- numbness,
- overwhelm,
- panic,
- regret,
- relief,
- resentment,
- sadness,
- shock.

All of those emotions can affect a person's capacity to think or do things. And this can show up in people as:

- absent-mindedness,
- confusion,
- detachment,
- disbelief,
- disorganised thinking,
- insecurity,
- lack of concentration,
- lowered self-esteem,
- preoccupation.

Just one of the things listed here could affect how well someone can do a task or make a choice. This can affect that person's ability to do something that ordinarily they would do without thinking. And from our research, we know that bereaved people often experience several of these emotions at the same time.

When someone dies, there's a lot of (new) things to do and sort out. There are organisations to speak to, paperwork to complete, friends and family to deal with — often all at once. All of that is in addition to coping with the bereavement, grieving, and supporting others.

With so much going on, there's an endless combination of emotions and tasks. And since grief is personal and different for everyone, it requires a careful approach to avoid causing harm or making things more difficult for someone.

But we are working within the restrictions and guidelines of government design. Is there room to incorporate trauma-informed principles?

Well, yes, there is. Our research findings show that what people need aligns with a trauma-informed approach. And that has given us opportunities to include this thinking in our work.

So let's take each trauma-informed principle, and I'll show how we can apply GOV.UK design standards to align with the trauma-informed practice framework provided on GOV.UK.

Safety and trust

Clear and simple language, active voice

During a bereavement, our research showed that people really needed and appreciated this type of language. They were already busy, had yet more things to do, and were stressed — so being told clearly what to do (and more importantly, what they didn't need to do) was helpful.

This is incredibly similar for people in crisis or experiencing trauma — clear and simple communication is best.

Your content can help create a feeling of safety and trust for a person. The GOV.UK style guide uses the active voice, combined with Plain English. Following these principles helps make your content clear, consistent, and simple — and that's great, because if somebody can't understand something, they can't trust it.

Using clear and simple language enables inclusive design. It also allows content to be more accurately translated into other languages. Remove any ambiguity in content:

- write out an acronym in full the first time you use it on a new page or screen, unless it is well known the majority of your users, like "NHS,"
- do not use euphemisms (for example, "late" if you mean "died") or idioms (for example, expressions like "by the book" or "red tape"),

- consider not using any contractions, because these add complexity to understanding your content for people with limited English and are harder to translate.

By doing the hard work to remove or reduce complexity in content, we can improve understanding, and that improves trust. We try to make sure:
- our content becomes specific, rather than general,
- we avoid jargon and use everyday words,
- we use short sentences and paragraphs,
- we are clear.

And we need to regularly review and maintain content to make sure it is up-to-date and accurate. Trust is immediately lost if your information is wrong.

Hyperlinks and onward paths

If you have an onward path from your digital service, include a link. Make it easy for the user of your service to continue their journey, know where to go next. Make it clear where the link will take them and always use a descriptive link text, so it is accessible. For example, use:

> Your payments will be paid into your <u>bank, building society, or credit union account.</u>

Do not use:

> Your payments will be paid into your bank, building society, or credit union account. <u>Read more.</u>

If there's no onward digital path, then make sure any information, telephone numbers, or addresses provided are correct and kept up-to-date.

Make it less overwhelming

Learn about the barriers to using your service. People are more likely to use a service if you can reduce the level of concern, worry, or unknowns. So tell them what the service is for, what they have to do, and what will happen next.

Really, *really* think about what you are asking your users to do. Are there any steps, questions, or information you collect right now that you don't need? Focus on getting the minimum you require.

Once you do that, you can consider user journeys and how to filter people towards the most efficient path for them. This is important because it means people are not using their time or effort to answer questions that are not relevant for them. And this reduces any unnecessary cognitive and emotional load for people.

For example, one of our bereavement services is called "Bereavement Support Payment." It's for people whose partner or spouse has died. It makes sense, then, to ask early on when they died. This means if they are not eligible for this particular support, we can direct them towards something else they might be eligible for. It also saves them the time and energy spent answering unnecessary questions when they would not be eligible anyway.

Break it down

GOV.UK design patterns recommend 1 question per screen. This works. It can mean there are a lot of screens in a service, but I've seen the user testing. People fly through the questions because the design is so simple and clear. For our bereavement service, we went even further.

We had short sections, but we also used an "In this section" screen. This is a simple screen that briefly explained what the next section was about, the questions we would ask, and why we were asking them. You can also use the screen to tell someone how many sections are left, so they know how much of the service they have completed, and how much is left to do.

By using an "In this section" screen, you can warn people about the questions you're asking next. This is important because it takes away that worry and anticipation about what is coming next. For example, in research we had a participant who was terrified they would be asked a certain question. They didn't know if they would be asked it, but they were anxious and stressed during the research because they were thinking about it.

Having the "In this section" screen means someone can choose to pause and prepare if they need to before continuing. Importantly, we also explained why we were asking a question. This helped with increasing understanding and establishing trust and feelings of safety.

Normally on a GOV.UK service, the user gets a "check your answers" screen at the end of completing a form or application. This is a chance for them to go over their answers and make sure they are happy with them before they submit. Because these screens are at the end of a service, they are often quite long lists of information to go through and check.

We decided to add a "check your answers" screen to the end of each section, instead of the whole service. This meant they were smaller and more concise, which was less overwhelming for people.

Give a time expectation

Set expectations about how long it might take to use the service. This means someone can judge for themselves how long it might take them and decide if they have the time or opportunity to do it then, or instead choose to come back later.

This is about respecting someone's time and giving them the ability to decide when is best for them. But there are inclusive ways to do this with content.

Never use "This is a simple service that will take you 15 minutes to complete."

You can't know for sure how long it would take someone. Accessibility needs, time available, technology used, a person's concentration, or their distractions can all affect how quickly someone can do something. And you have no idea if something that is simple for you will be simple for them. Calling a task "simple" that someone else goes on to find difficult can reinforce negative feelings, or even lead to someone abandoning the task. Instead, use something like "it takes about 15 minutes to apply."

I have severe Dyscalculia (a specific and persistent difficulty in understanding numbers). Giving me an estimate of how long something might take is actually quite helpful. I know it will take me much longer, so an estimate helps me to plan accordingly. If you do not set any expectations for how long something might take, this could be a barrier.

In our research we found that people dealing with a bereavement were often busy. There is always lots to do when someone dies. Understanding how long a task might take helped people plan when to do something.

They would say things like, "I'll come back when I have more time," or "I'll do it now while the house is quiet."

Help people get the information they need before they start

Provide a list of information, documents, and anything someone needs to have prepared before they start your service. You want to help them succeed, so provide this upfront.

For our bereavement service we added an additional screen after the start page, called an "interstitial" start page. This was a direct result of testing with users. We discovered people were reading the start page quickly and selecting the start button, but not remembering the information. So we added the interstitial page that estimated how long it would take to apply. It also asked "Do you have everything you need to apply?" and listed what they needed. We then added an action for people to confirm they had everything ready before they progressed.

Our additional screen provided time to pause, and users slowed down. Because this content wasn't buried in the rest of the detail a start page has to convey, it was more prominent.

But importantly, the screen also warned people that on this service, they couldn't save and return. And this was why it was so important to set a time expectation: people had to be able to complete the service in one go.

Choice

Save and return functionality

You can support people by giving them the ability to take a break. Providing a save and return function on a digital service gives people the reassurance that they can come back when they are ready without having to repeat some of the time, effort, or information they have already completed.

This functionality can help create a feeling of safety. It shows someone that they have the time they need, and that their information is saved securely for them when they do come back.

If a save and return function isn't possible (due to security or legacy technology), then put it in the design backlog. Design debt is a vital element that needs documenting and revisiting. Technology changes, opportunities arise, and then you can iterate your service to improve.

Different channels or ways to do things

People might choose to do some things at different times: at night, when they are lying awake, unable to sleep. They might choose to do something during the day when they are alone, or with someone who can help, or when they feel safe, or just when they have the opportunity.

Sometimes people choose to use a service to give them something to do, or even remove them from a stressful situation. We had people using our service on New Year's Eve and in the middle of the night at Christmas. For them, this was the right time.

By giving people different channels to use a service, you can support their choice.

What's important here is that, depending on a person's situation or circumstance, their choices can — and often need to — change. For example, let's imagine someone is dealing with something away from home. Suddenly, broadband internet isn't possible, or perhaps their phone signal is weak because they are in a remote location. Factors like these can change a person's usual ways of access.

Offering only one channel for a service will exclude people, probably at a time of need.

It could even affect if they can use your service at all.

Back buttons

Adding a back button on every screen is a simple way to support choice. It can act as a visual prompt that someone is able to go back a step or screen if they need to. Without it, people might assume they can't go back. You are enabling people to safely change their mind and change their answers.

This is critical when people might be experiencing stress. When people are stressed, they are more likely to make mistakes. By enabling somebody to go back and change their answers if they spot their mistake, you are helping them succeed.

And if people can't go back on screen, they will go back on their device or browser anyway — you are just making things harder.

Exit this page

The "exit this page" component is worth noting as it is new to the GOV.UK Design System. It was created to help people quickly leave a web page or site.

We have not used this design in our bereavement service, but having it available is a positive move to support people in vulnerable situations. It aims to reduce the risks someone might have while looking for information or trying to access a service.

Empowerment

Confirmation

A confirmation screen, email, or text is empowering because it helps give people confidence that a thing has been done, or something has been received. This reduces the burden of having to remember something, and that is a powerful thing. By giving a simple confirmation, you could help someone tick one thing off their long mental list, or give them the reassurance they can continue on to the next step in a process.

As someone who is neurodiverse, I find confirmations invaluable. My working memory is really bad, and I often forget if I have done something, or when something is due. Having a confirmation that I can screenshot, share with my partner, add to my calendar, or refer back to in my messages is a great help. And this can help everyone.

Accessible and inclusive services

Designing services to be accessible and inclusive not only follows government standards, it enables as many people as possible to use them. That is empowering.

But it is just the start. Using the GOV.UK design system is like starting with a baseline accessibility level. You will still need to research, design, iterate, and test if your service is accessible. And make sure to signpost to other ways to use your service. This enables a person to be able to switch channels if they need to, or use another channel that is more accessible for them.

Make sure your service uses inclusive language to build trust, communicate effectively, and empower people to use it successfully. For example, if possible provide an age range to select rather than an exact age to input (for a number of reasons, people might not know their true age). Design a full name input field instead of splitting into first and last name. Use neutral terms like "partner" or "spouse" instead of "husband" or "wife."

Collaboration

User research

All the best content designers I know have a great quality in common: empathy.

For me, it's *the* content design superpower: really understanding what your users' needs are. Thinking hard about what you are asking them to do (or will not ask them to do), the order of questions, and the user journey.

But as important as empathy is, it will only get you so far.

It is vital as user-centred designers to collaborate with your users to discover their needs so you can understand and empathise. Use that research to respectfully share lived experience to improve designs and to continue acting as the voice of the user.

Practise inclusive research, and reflect the real world experiences of the people who will use your service. You might start designs with assumptions, but make sure there is user research to test them.

If there is really, absolutely, no user research option, then look for evidence from desk research or from other user-centred designers. Use communities on Slack, LinkedIn, Bluesky — whatever, just reach out.

In Bereavement and Care for DWP Digital, we regularly chat with other people across government who are designing for a bereavement, often for the first time. They might not have access to research with bereaved people themselves, but they absolutely want to know how to do the right thing for them.

So, get in touch with those who have done it before, who are already in the space you need to be. They are often happy to help share insight that will help you.

A note on vicarious trauma

Our work as designers means we often spend time listening to people's stories in research. Sometimes these stories can be stressful or upsetting, and there is a risk that we could experience secondary trauma, or "vicarious trauma" as a result. Whatever your response, it is completely personal and legitimate.

Take time to consider how you and your team could be supported and protected. It might be suitable for the wider design team to explore creating an agreed-on psychological safety plan to enable ongoing support.

Cultural considerations

Euphemisms

Words matter. There are some words that are not directly translatable and, therefore, are exclusionary. During our research for bereavement services, we found that people struggled with some words often used to describe a death, like "loss" and "passed away."

Some didn't understand that "loss" and "passed away" actually meant "died." They were frustrated as these words were indirect, not clear.

Euphemisms like these are inherently an indirect way of communicating, so they are not clear. But people dealing with a death are often cognitively overwhelmed, so using euphemisms makes content difficult to understand and instructions harder to follow. And because euphemisms cannot be interpreted literally, it also makes them difficult to understand for:

- children,
- people using English as an additional language,
- some neurodiverse people,
- people with dementia or PTSD,
- people experiencing stress, anxiety, or trauma.

Euphemisms are not inclusive and can exclude people as they:
- often rely on a cultural understanding,
- are often unable to be translated into other languages.

Do not use euphemisms.

Direct simple and clear language is empowering for people when it's needed most. It lowers the cognitive load needed to process, it's quicker to understand, and it's easier to translate.

Designing for government is challenging — and rewarding

Designing for government is challenging. It might even seem thankless at times. But most people will need government services at some point in their lives. And it's often at a point where they are in a vulnerable situation, or need extra care and support.

Designing for government is also a privilege. So many people need our services, and we are in a position to interact with and help literally millions of people. If we can provide a bit of care and a bit less harm in their journey, we have done well.

References and further reading

- Taking Bereavement Support Payment to public beta," DWP Digital
- Anna Khoury, "Psychological safety – creating a safer environment for trauma informed researchers"
- "Achieving design justice through inclusive design," People Street (2023)
- "Designing content for people going through grief," Fourth Wall Podcast with Helen Lawson (2023)
- GOV.UK Design System
- "Exit this page fast with the Design System's new component," GOV.UK (2023)
- "Designing for people with limited English," UK Home Office Design System
- "Inclusive language," UK Home Office Design System

Gratitude and recognition

User-centred design is a team sport. It takes a massive collective effort over years to create services that use trauma-informed principles. For me, that's the next-level kind of design, and I feel privileged to be able to share our work in Bereavement for DWP Digital with you. It is their diligent work that has enabled services to be designed with such empathy and care to support people when they need it most. They rock.

Chapter 10

Content design in high-risk digital spaces

by Owen Leigh

What does trauma-informed design actually look like in practice? In typical content design fashion, the answer is "it depends." It depends on a lot of factors, including:
- who you're designing for,
- the trauma in question,
- what you're trying to achieve with the design.

During my career, 2 projects in particular have taught me how to apply the principles of trauma-informed design. They involved very different situations, but both were intended to provide support to people experiencing current or developing trauma. The first project, with a domestic abuse charity, was the first time I applied trauma-informed design principles to content, and it involved a lot of learning. The second is a more recent project, informed by deeper learning and experience.

In this chapter, I'll take you through some of their shared problems and, more importantly, the different trauma-informed approaches needed to solve them. These projects had 2 problems in common:

1. Protecting the user from harm.
2. Building a positive relationship with an isolated and anxious group.

As well as these shared problems, both groups of users were:
- unlikely to have strong support networks,
- often isolated,
- financially unstable.

But each project needed a different solution.

Applying a framework

Before we take a look at the projects, I want to explain how I approach trauma-informed design in general. There are several frameworks for trauma-informed practice, and they share many common principles. I tend to use the UK government's set of principles.

Within those principles, I like to think of 2 categories. There are things that:
- influence you as the designer,
- you influence.

Much of this may seem familiar to you, but stepping back and reflecting on the basics can be useful. Indulge me for a moment.

Collaboration and cultural consideration

The best work happens when you prioritise collaboration and cultural consideration. These are the things that influence you. You should maintain communication with co-workers, stakeholders, and users, building on others' knowledge and expertise. Every team is different, and how you do this will be personal. You might want to have daily meetings or weekly email summaries. Have a conversation with everyone who will be involved and see what works. Above all, just talk to each other: ask questions, give feedback, bring ideas.

You'll also need to be mindful of how culture has shaped your ideas and perspectives, and strong team communication will help here. Your collective goal is to create experiences that work for your users. This is easier when you maintain strong relationships, and constructive criticism is given and received with care.

A collaborative approach allows you to draw on each other's knowledge and identify your own biases. So build strong relationships that allow for feedback, and then ask for that feedback. Create a space that allows others in your team to challenge you when they see bias creep in. A simple chat, in a safe setting, and taking breaks if needed, will help if you have to cover a difficult topic. Again, your team shares the same goal and acknowledging you lack a skill or piece of knowledge can only help you in the long term.

You can also learn a lot about your own biases simply by asking yourself why. Why does that word or concept make you feel that way? Why did you choose not to include that quotation? Why does one image feel safer to you than another? They can be difficult questions, so give yourself some space and don't expect to have all the answers right away. Just reflect on what influences you as you work.

Safety, trust, empowerment and choice

Safety, trust, empowerment, and choice are things you create with the knowledge you gain from that collaboration and cultural consideration. These are areas you can influence with your content design practice. And they are interconnected. Trying to separate them is not useful in practice.

However you use the principles, though, remember that they are a guide, not a set of tasks to tick off. They're not linear, and as you incorporate one, you'll build on another.

The charity

I first worked with these principles as a content designer when working with a local charity. The charity supported people who experienced domestic abuse, and as such, they were very familiar with trauma-informed care and design. Founded by people with lived experience, this charity focused on peer support, moving at the user's pace.

They had recently built a support centre using trauma-informed architectural principles, full of large, open spaces that felt warm and inviting, with lots of natural light and clear exits so everyone felt safe and comfortable. They now wanted a digital rebrand that incorporated these same ideas. The aim was for users to have the same feelings of safety and care online as they did in person at the centre.

My team was small, and as the only content designer on the project, my job was to:
- find content solutions to safety concerns,
- build trust between users and the charity,
- help users to take the next steps in their own support plan.

Many people using the charity were actively experiencing abuse. They had to be careful not to leave evidence of their engagement with the service for their abusers to find. The users were also slow to trust strangers and anyone in authority. For some, there was a wariness to engage with support at all, fearing repercussions or dismissal.

By talking to the recovery and helpline support teams, we learnt that people interacting with the charity website were:
- often diagnosed with PTSD,
- hypervigilant,
- sometimes still in situations that put them at physical and emotional risk.

User research

The charity had done considerable research with the people who used their services to learn what they wanted and needed from the website. This was before my work with the project, so I started out with many questions already answered and enough information to begin developing ideas. But that didn't feel quite right. Collaboration on a project is so much more than being handed the research someone else has done. You need to share with and learn from your team, the rest of the organisation you're working with, and most importantly, your users. You'll learn the most when you collaborate with people whose experiences are different to your own, and that's when you'll create the best solutions.

So I spoke to the researchers who had interviewed the users and asked for clarifications on some of the data and quotations.

I showed them my team's interpretations of what they had said, and I listened to their ideas. Looking at the quotations from research, we had statements like "How do I know you won't..." and "How am I supposed to ..." come up a lot. We thought this suggested fear and uncertainty, but was that right? Could they explain why the users felt this way?

We were told there was fear, and some of this was because users were afraid of leaving any evidence of engaging with the charity. One said they were afraid that if an abuser did find evidence, they would contact the charity, which might give out information. They explained that after they had escaped an abusive relationship, a hotel had put them in danger by giving their abuser information.

Details like this meant we could understand how important it was for our content to be trustworthy.

I should explain that these conversations always went through the charity's user support team. The support team had an established and trusted relationship with the users, and were trained to deal with crises. When we were asking for additional details about traumatic experiences, it was sensible and safer for everyone involved to go through them.

Going through this process gave us richer data and stopped some weaker ideas before they got too far. It also meant users could directly influence the content over time. They provided feedback on our drafts and got to see how that feedback changed the content. This gave them a sense of ownership of the content. It became a living, evolving solution designed not just for them, but by them. And this helped establish trust and empowerment.

Users told us this involvement helped them to feel "respected" and "understood." They appreciated that we checked our understanding, and that we corrected ourselves when we hadn't. This stopped us from making mistakes that could be hurtful.

The users also shared how important meaningful collaboration was for them. They had experienced a lack of control in their own lives, but collaboration helped them feel heard and respected. An open conversation and collaborative design process meant users could reclaim some control and a sense of ownership over their experience and the content it was helping to shape.

Building trust and relationships

One challenge the charity faced was that some of the people it was supporting were still in dangerous situations. Accessing the website had the potential to cause them harm. They needed to be able to quickly hide their activity if they were caught using the site. We decided to create an "exit this page" interaction as a solution.

After some exploration, we settled on a design for a "sticky" banner at the bottom of screens. A sticky element stays in a fixed position when the user scrolls. Ours contained:

- emergency contact details,
- an exit button,
- a link to a page about safe browsing.

The design meant this banner was always available, but didn't intrude on the user's experience. Reminding users about danger and emergencies all the time could heighten any fear or anxiety they were feeling. Some feedback suggested seeing the emergency information all the time only served to remind users of the danger they were often in and felt they could do nothing about.

So we leaned into the choice to build trust. We kept the sticky function, so the banner would always be at the bottom of the screen and the exit button itself would always be visible. But we made the rest collapsible. When someone had read it once, they could decide whether they wanted that extra information visible or not. On collapse, only a heading to "reveal emergency information" with a chevron and the exit button would be on screen.

But while an exit button lets you leave a site quickly, it doesn't always erase all evidence that you were ever there. Without additional clear context, the button could imply a promise that couldn't be kept — that the website could not be tracked in the user's browsing history. Failing to give users this information could leave them vulnerable.

The wording we settled on to explain what the button was for was "You can hide this site quickly by using the 'leave site button.'" Then we linked a page with information on the limits of the button and specific instructions for deleting their browsing history on different browsers.

Now users had:

- a real, tangible choice that gave them control over their digital environment,

- reassurance that safety information was available if needed,
- a quick way to leave the website.

The first solution is not the best solution

Being open to change and parting with a design you thought was "final" is part of the process. Being transparent with users about the limitations of the exit button came later than it should have, after some feedback and reflection. That's the nature of design.

We had initially felt that admitting the button couldn't protect everyone in every instance would cause stress and be harmful. But in reality our users needed our transparency. It was better to be honest than to promise something we couldn't deliver. Our users were facing the potential of abuse. If we weren't honest with them, we could destroy any trust they had in us.

Building trust through language

The charity wanted to use language that placed power with the user, because one of their goals is to help users support themselves and each other. We did this in a few ways.

We spoke directly to users, addressing them as "you," and we gave clear, easily understood actions. Information about support plans emphasised that users were in control, and they could stop and start at any point. This helped them make small choices and build their confidence.

"Victims," "survivors," and "suffering"

A common question that comes up with this kind of content is whether to use the word "victim." Many organisations choose to use the word "survivor" instead.

We tested it and found that a few people thought "victim" was helpful. They found something defiant or powerful in being able to say, "Of course I'm a victim but I'm still going to survive and thrive." But others found it disempowering.

Another term we tested was saying someone had "suffered abuse." Again, there was a small group that liked it, but the majority didn't react well to either expression. They found them insulting or defeatist.

Instead of saying someone was a "victim" or had "suffered abuse," the charity preferred to say someone "had experience of domestic abuse."

But after user research and a few iterations, we agreed to keep references to abuse minimal. We used the term only to let people know they were on the right site. Our focus was centring the user as being in control of their future, rather than focusing on the past.

We wanted the people engaging with the content to feel like they were having a conversation, so we used friendly, relatable language. We tested phrases like "come in for a chat and a cup of tea," which resonated with users. If you're using language like this, remember it's contextual and you must know your audience and how they might react. In this case, though, they weren't just words — the charity welcomed everyone with the offer of a cup of tea to help alleviate nerves and start with a friendly interaction.

We also made it clear that contacting the charity didn't have to mean signing up to a weekly appointment or programme. Things like that were available, but only if wanted. Finding the right place for this took a while, but eventually alongside contact details, we tested this messaging: "If you're ready, get in touch. Nothing happens without your consent. No commitments, just a conversation." We received feedback that this made the decision to get help less overwhelming. Paired with the visual designs and other intentional language choices, the overall tone became one of a friendly neighbour, offering support at the user's own pace and in the form they wanted.

I learned a lot from this project, and when I came to the next, I had more experience and thought I knew what to expect. But working with a specialist health clinic would come with its own unique challenges.

The clinic

At the clinic, staff were working with marginalised and vulnerable adults. The clinic is a referral point for mental and physical health. It aims to help patients create a personalised support plan to address their health needs.

The clinic often had long waitlists due to:
- the specialist nature of its services,
- a small pool of practitioners,
- a relatively large patient population.

To help address these long waitlists, the clinic reallocates cancelled appointments wherever possible. They can only do this when they have advance notice that someone can't attend an appointment.

But they were experiencing a significant number of missed appointments with no warning. Many users were just not turning up, and the clinic wasn't sure why.

They initially consulted a group of other service providers, clinicians, and community members to try to understand what was happening. They learned many users struggled to use the clinic's website to find contact information. This made it impossible to get in touch to cancel or change an appointment.

But the clinic didn't know how to make effective changes to their webpage. I was asked to:
- help them understand why the contact details were hard to find,
- identify what needed to change,
- give clear guidance on how to make those changes.

The website:
- was text-heavy and inaccessible,
- used tables unnecessarily to format information,
- didn't provide clear calls to action.

It became clear that, as well as struggling to find contact information, users were experiencing a sense of disempowerment that led to them giving up.

Staff at the clinic had told me their users were known to:
- self-harm,
- have suicidal thoughts,
- experience anxiety.

The clinic knew how to handle those things therapeutically. But they didn't see the connection between these issues and the difficulty users had getting in touch. The clinic was struggling to understand how trauma was impacting their users' ability to contact them.

User research

The clinic lacked the resources to do extensive user research, but I needed to know more about the users I was working for. So I:
- asked the clinic's leadership team to explain what they could about their users,
- learned about their historical feedback from surveys,
- learned from practitioners about their collective experience and research.

I found that many users experienced hardship, directly and indirectly linked to their reasons for referral. Many were estranged from their families or had little or no support network. They often struggled to find work and faced racism and discrimination due to their gender and sexual orientation. This took a toll on their physical health, resulting in high rates of chronic illnesses that further prevented them from working and left them financially unstable. Many reported medical trauma and feeling dismissed by other health providers.

As a result, the clinic's users often had low self-esteem and poor mental health. Some didn't believe they deserved their appointment, feeling others needed it more. They felt they were a burden on the very system designed to help them. Many were distrustful of healthcare workers. They feared that if they went to the clinic, they would be ignored or told they had come to the wrong place.

Low literacy

A large proportion of people using the service spoke English as an additional language. Many also had low digital literacy. The website's language wasn't accessible to people with lower English proficiency. It was too "academic," "sterile," and "cold." It reminded them of the cold, clinical corridors of medical centres that caused some of the users significant stress in the past. In short, the language had become a barrier to access. This created a feeling of distrust amongst users.

Putting research into action

Now that I had information, I knew we needed to:
- make it easier to find the contact information,
- explain why users needed to get in touch to change an appointment,

- build trust and empowerment to help them feel comfortable contacting and attending the clinic.

There were a few things that could be improved.

Language

We knew from speaking to the clinic's staff and some community groups they had contact with that users were highly distrustful of authority, medical professionals in particular. They didn't respond well to the impassive language used to outline what:
- was expected of them,
- they needed to do,
- to bring or to fill out ahead of time.

Language needed to be gentler and clearer across the site. It needed to reinforce the importance of attending appointments, but also encourage people to get in touch if they couldn't attend. Changing the language for a gentler tone helped create a sense of trust, choice, empowerment, and safety.

This last point — safety — was particularly important. As with the charity, we needed to protect the users from harm. There were a number of factors behind this but one that caused the clinic significant concern was the potential harm in missing appointments and delaying treatment. Missing an appointment, or excluding themselves because they didn't feel worthy, ultimately harmed users because they wouldn't receive the help they needed.

And if they missed 3 appointments, they would be removed from the clinic's systems, something that they were told loudly in a banner across each page. The banner's purpose was to try to encourage attendance by increasing understanding. But its effect had been the opposite: it was increasing reluctance to engage with the clinic. In previous feedback, users explained that it showed the clinic was "annoyed" with them. One commented that they felt "told off" as soon as they arrived on the website. Another said they felt the clinic had already decided they wouldn't attend without ever having met them, making them feel "small" and like they were a "problem."

Instead of focusing on consequences, we decided to emphasise ways to contact the clinic. Centring what needs to happen, not the consequences, made the messaging less confrontational to reduce anxiety. The aim was to make the user feel in control of what would happen: they will contact the clinic in a way that suits them, and the appointment will be rearranged. Being able to offer cancelled appointments to other patients meant the clinic could see more people quickly, easing the impact that long wait times can have on physical and mental health.

Information architecture

We didn't just need to change the language. We also had to structure the website so that users could find the contact details needed to rearrange appointments. Many people struggled to locate the contact details, which were at the bottom of a page in a poorly formatted table. There were several different phone numbers and email addresses, with little to tell users which one was for what.

Behaviour analytics showed that users would often come back to the warning banner that told them about the consequences of missing their appointment. People were drawn to the banner because it was visually distinct and where they expected the information to be. So because people were already looking at the banner for information, we decided to add the contact details to it.

Helping users take this seemingly small action would help with empowerment and safety. Just a small change removed some of the friction preventing them from accessing help and meant it didn't seem as though the information was being hidden.

Improvement is the point

No 2 trauma-informed design projects are ever the same. While both the charity and the clinic involved work with people in vulnerable situations, they worked with very different communities. These communities had different experiences and needs, traumas, and risks. The solutions for each needed to be different, too. Trauma-informed design has no single or perfect solution.

At its core, trauma-informed design is about listening to the people you're designing for and responding to what they need with empathy and flexibility. As long as you're listening, adapting, and making improvements, you're doing the work.

References and further reading

- "Working definition of trauma-informed practice" GOV.UK (2022)
- "Stress in America 2023: A nation recovering from collective trauma" American Psychological Association (2023)
- Elizabeth Hopper, Ellen Bassuk and Jeffrey Olivet, Jeffrey, "Shelter from the Storm: Trauma-Informed Care in Homelessness Services," *The Open Health Services and Policy Journal* (2010)
- Katrin Starcke and Matthias Brand, "Decision making under stress: A selective review." *Neuroscience and Biobehavioral Reviews*, Vol. 36, Issue 4 (2012)
- Georgia Punton, Alyson L. Dodd and Andrew McNeill, "'You're on the waiting list': An interpretive phenomenological analysis of young adults' experiences of waiting lists within mental health services in the UK." *PLoS One* (2022)
- Matthew Limb, "Long NHS waits and rising living costs are harming people's health, show ONS data" *The BMJ* (2023)
- Alex J. Mitchell and Thomas Selmes, "Why don't patients attend their appointments? Maintaining engagement with psychiatric services." *Advances in Psychiatric Treatment* (2007)
- Naomi L. Lacy, Audrey Paulman, Matthew D. Reuter and Bruce Lovejoy, "Why We Don't Come: Patient Perceptions on No-Shows," *The Annals of Family Medicine* (November 2004)
- David R. Williams, Jourdyn A. Lawrence, Brigette A. Davis and Cecilia Vu, "Understanding how discrimination can affect health," *Health Services Research* (2019)

Chapter 11
Does this feel dignifying? Considering, telling, and sharing more ethical stories

by Morgan Cataldo

I want to talk
about what happened
without mentioning
how much it hurt.

There has to be a way.

To care for the wounds
without re-opening them.
To name the pain
without inviting it back into me.

— Lora Mathis

Stories shape our imaginations and, therefore, the realities we live in. Some are narratives that are dominant and that dominate. These often serve to perpetuate, reinforce, and entrench stereotypical and stigmatising narratives and norms: that is, the ways we understand social issues and the people experiencing them. There are power dynamics inherent in how stories are told: whose worldviews are being shared, and the frames through which we receive them. If people are the sum of the stories told *about* them and the stories they then internalise about themselves, whose imaginations are we living in, and what does it take to challenge this?

The content designer as story narrator

Content designers often re-tell stories about the people and communities they are working with. These come in the form of case studies, or efforts to make content more "real."

How then do designers share and re-tell stories respectfully, in ways that honour the dignity and uphold the rights of participants?

How might we share and re-tell stories in ways that not only benefit a service, product, or brand, but that equally benefit the people whose stories are being told?

And how do we create opportunities for people to tell and shape their own narratives about themselves and their communities?

As someone who had to use social services for many years, my story was often told on my behalf. This happened in ways that didn't capture or do justice to my life or circumstances, didn't uphold ethical principles and practice, and that therefore did harm. This harm ran deep, distorting how I understood my identity and felt about myself. At its worst, it further reinforced damaging narratives that I was trying to work myself *out* of. It had detrimental impacts on my recovery and healing, on the person I was fighting to become.

I also experienced times when telling my story was a deeply transformative and powerfully healing experience: when the ways in which my stories were held and shaped were done *with* me, in ways that upheld informed consent and honoured the narratives I was working to unearth about myself. In some special instances, where truths were told about me, it transformed how I understood and saw myself. Those truths included strengths and characteristics I had not yet perceived in myself.

This chapter seeks to unpack how we can tell more ethical stories as part of our design practices. It explains how the act of co-creating narratives, in partnership with the people and communities we work alongside, enables us to tell more nuanced and multifaceted stories in support of social and systems change, and innovation. Ethical storytelling means that we are not further entrenching cultural myths that strip people of their humanity, their multitudes, and their agency.

As part of our design work, we often invite people to tell and share profoundly personal and sacred stories with us. But we aren't always equipped with the:
- essential training, support, or understanding of trauma-informed interviewing techniques,
- space-holding capability required to facilitate these processes,
- understanding or discernment required to effectively engage with and consider cultural and other distinct sensitivities.

Are we considering what questions are appropriate to ask? What aspects of people's lives can even be considered or uttered out loud? For example, we might need to consider:
- how to approach the topic of challenging power,
- whether it's appropriate to ask someone to think critically about family or kin,
- what is allowed to be shared with people of other cultures and identities due to the sacredness of the information, story, or meaning.

For those of us working at the intersection of those with lived experience who are sharing stories, and the organisations and the media who want to use and benefit from these stories, there are 3 distinct questions I find useful to ask before we set out in this work.

1. How do we hold stories with sensitivity and care?

Set out with a stance of deep humility, having done the pre-work required to determine whether we are the right person to be asking questions of this person or community. If so, are we then capable of the quality and level of listening and holding required?

2. How do we tell stories well and in ways that lead to action and change?

The act of telling stories alone does not immediately lead to systems change. What people do with the stories that are told does. If we are asking people to share difficult and highly personal things about themselves and their lives to influence change, we must create the conditions wherever we can for these stories to lead to action and the possibility for meaningful impact.

3. How do we share stories in ways that educate, not just pull on heartstrings?

When telling stories about impact, particularly in the context of sharing about the efficacy and value of social services, pulling on people's heartstrings is a well-known tactic to move audiences to action. But value is not simply about dollars raised or reputation; it is also about our responsibility to the people and communities we seek to serve. There are real-life consequences of playing into damaging tropes for short-term gain.

With these points in mind, what should we consider when re-telling or using someone else's story in our content? How might we protect and preserve their dignity and the integrity of their stories, and how do we balance these aspects with what organisations or clients might be wanting or needing from the work?

Foundations of ethical storytelling

Let's start with the basic building blocks of how to work with a person who may be sharing their story.

Informed consent

First, does the person understand exactly what they are saying yes or no to, and can this choice or decision change over time? These are some key aspects you may wish to consider:

Who
- Which person or community is being asked to tell this story?
- Who is the person or people holding space for the story to be told, and what is their intention?

- Would the storyteller prefer the use of a pseudonym to protect their identity?

What
- What is the context in which this story sits?
- Is there a particular angle or broader messaging that is important for the storyteller to be aware of?

When
- How long is the timeline or lead-up to publishing? Is there time for the storyteller to review and approve what is being shared, and how it is being shared?
- Does the storyteller have enough notice to prepare themselves before the story goes live?

Where
- Where will this story be shared? In print or online? On billboards or the side of buses?
- Can we predict or advise how far the story might travel?

Why
- What is the purpose of this story being shared?
- Whose idea was it, and who stands to benefit from it?

Mitigating harm and mapping risk

Do we know what supports the person already has in place, or what supports they might need, as part of the process? People need a trusted network in their lives to walk alongside them when entering processes that may make them more vulnerable. This might include people to talk to, or make sense and debrief with. This is particularly important if and when painful memories arise, new information gets unearthed, or when speaking out loud about something old brings up new perspectives, emotions, and understanding.

Right of withdrawal

Does the person know that they can exit a storytelling process at any time, and that there will be no repercussions for doing so?

As designers who may be working with or representing social service organisations, a power dynamic exists. Within this dynamic, those we ask to tell stories may not feel safe enough or able to express themselves honestly, for fear of being treated differently by their support workers or the organisations they are accessing support from.

Intellectual property

Be clear about limitations of the use of storytelling content. This might include:
- how many times it can be used,
- if and where it can be repurposed,
- for how long it can be used.

It's important to be clear about the intellectual property that will be created from the person's experience. Who owns it? Even if the person was offered financial compensation for their time, who owns the content that the person's story informs and shapes?

The *how* is deeply contextual

From here, we can get further into the detail of the how.

As with most things involving people, the answer to these questions is always contextual. Over the years, I have been part of storytelling processes with people where the act of writing stories together is an incredibly powerful experience. This might look like sitting down with someone and having a guided conversation where I take notes based on what the storyteller is sharing, and then we edit together.

This is similar to the content design practice of pair writing: the storyteller is the subject matter expert. My role is like the content designer's: to help tell their story. Through a process like this, I might ask and consider questions like:
- Did you use words that you would normally use, or did I put words in your mouth?
- Did I interpret or misinterpret anything said based on my own worldview or biases?

- Is there anything you would like to add, change, or delete altogether?
- Are there any details that feel too identifying (if working to protect a person's identity)?

And perhaps one of the most critical questions I ask myself internally:
- Is there a clear enough purpose to this question, statement, or response or is it simply to satisfy my own curiosity or need to feel a certain way?

When it comes to authorisation, it is critical for designers to understand that we have power and a responsibility to ethical standards. Although we may see ourselves working to bridge between organisations and institutions and people with lived experience and communities, we must question who we see ourselves predominantly accountable to and why. We must ask ourselves: does this feel dignifying? And we must educate the people we work with if we believe a story and/or the dignity of a person is being unjustly compromised or jeopardised.

Potential difficulties to be aware of when commissioning or sharing a story

Over the past decade of supporting people as they tell their stories and helping organisations build the conditions for stories to be told, I have learnt that the act of sharing stories is a highly contextual experience. Each experience is different, and you can't just repeat the same thing you've done before. The process depends on many factors, but some main considerations are:
- where people are at in their lives,
- the levels of internal and external support and stability they have at the time,
- situational and environmental factors, like where a person is telling a story and who is around them in that place.

At the heart of this learning has come these understandings:

No telling of a story is ever the same

The way we tell stories and how we feel about the process is different for each person and community. What has worked for me or for someone else may not work for others. For example, I've moved away from sharing intimate parts of my story in public for reasons that are specific to my own circumstances. But other peers and advocates I know get a tremendous amount of strength and validation from sharing their stories. For each of us, the experience offers something distinct, and the reasons and motivations for why we share may change over time.

Sharing from open wounds versus scars

There is a fine line between sharing vulnerably and sharing in ways that are detrimental. Although it's important to understand this distinction, it's equally important to know that we learn about it through the practice of doing and experimenting. There are times when sharing from rawer wounds is entirely appropriate and necessary.

Years ago, I remember having a conversation with a peer about this topic, and I'll never forget what she said to me: "Sometimes, I see people bleeding [as they're sharing] and you can tell that they're hurting. It hurts to see that."

From my own experience, there has been at least one occasion when I was very well-supported and prepared to tell my story to a group. But when I got up to share that day, I spotted someone I didn't expect to see in the audience. This triggered an emotional reaction. I did go on to tell my story, and although this was a cathartic experience for me at the time, that outcome was very much due to the conditions:
- the place where I was in my own recovery meant I had the internal strength and external support to move through the experience in a positive enough way,
- there were many trusted people I knew in the audience, all of who were supportive and able to act as a kind of buffer to help absorb the shock of my reaction,
- it was a closed event in an intimate setting, and I had enough speaking experience to feel prepared for what happened in the moment and any fallout afterwards,
- it was also a positive experience for the audience, with many people sharing how powerful it was to witness.

In a different context, with different people, or on a day when I might have been another version of myself, this very same experience might have been re-traumatising. This is what I mean by the contextual and sometimes unpredictable nature of sharing personal experiences. And this is why it is important for us to set up supportive conditions so that storytellers are more likely to have a beneficial experience.

Parallel and corresponsive impacts

Telling stories affects not only the teller, but also listeners. We've all been moved by stories in our lives. I'm sure that if I asked you to think of one right now, you could vividly remember a story or message that has changed you somehow.

I've reflected on the safety and ethics of storytelling for those sharing, but there is equally something to be said about the experience of and impact to those receiving and absorbing what is being shared. When sharing personal experiences, I am a strong supporter of being able to speak truths — being blunt, honest, fierce, and expressing righteous anger. I have also experienced first-hand the reality that details matter, especially when it comes to sharing about traumatic experiences.

Although we are not in control of how people receive our stories, a simple forewarning doesn't hurt. This doesn't need to be content or trigger warnings, but some sort of notification or foreshadowing can help, so that audiences know to prepare themselves. It also feels critical to add here that there are certain topics that ought to make us feel uncomfortable and that we must practise sitting with; for example, when people share stories about abuses of power. To help with this distinction, I often ask myself:

- Am I feeling unsafe or am I feeling uncomfortable?
- What helps me to identify, feel, and know the difference?
- What capacity do I have to be attentive or react in a way that's consistent with my values in this moment?

I learnt something fundamental on this topic from Australian comedian Hannah Gadsby's show Nanette:

> "This tension is yours. I am not helping you anymore. You need to learn what this feels like, because this tension is what not-normals carry inside of them all of the time. It is dangerous to be different."

As people making decisions about how stories are told, we have the power to "raise the temperature" with the ways we craft narratives and messages about social issues. Those who have been "othered" by mainstream society (many of whom are survivors of abuse and systemic trauma) often hold profound tension that cannot be reconciled. They are then asked and demanded, in both explicit and implicit ways, to protect others from feeling this same tension by telling sanitised versions of their truths. There are considerations in weighing up the agency and empowerment of those who choose to share their stories, how far we push audiences to confront difficult truths, and the ways in which we approach both.

The deeply cultural, personal, and phenomenological nature of stories

Ultimately, people must be supported to tell their own stories. People and communities should be able to tell stories about their lives in their own words and ways. As designers, when we are asked to tell stories on behalf of other people, how can we use our positions to challenge the way things are done? How can we help the organisations, institutions, and clients we work with to move towards more participatory and creative approaches?

A working set of principles

I offer up this evolving list of principles as a guide for moving from the extraction of people's stories towards storytelling processes that are more dignifying and mutually beneficial.

Get underneath the story to the learning

People are often asked to share unnecessary details of what they have lived through and experienced. This is commonly done in ways that stoke inappropriate curiosity and sensationalism.

What we really want to get to is what people have *learnt* from what they've lived through: what they've learned about themselves, other people, and the world around them. Ask questions that help people to engage in a process of mutual reflection and that move to deeper levels of inquiry.

From empowering to power building

We do not "empower people," but we can contribute to the conditions and circumstances that support people to see, understand, and exercise their own personal power and agency. So instead of assuming our processes are necessarily empowering, let's work with the people who are telling the stories to understand and sense-check what powerful narratives and messages look and feel like to them.

Learn how people best express themselves

We often place dominance on the written word, but not everyone best expresses themselves this way. There are many ways of telling stories, including the use of:
- photos,
- voice,
- animation,
- poetry,
- other creative methods.

So often, people's experiences are beyond the realm of words. Help people find what feels and works best for conveying their message and the impact they want their story to have.

Illustrate people's multitudes

Impactful and memorable stories bring people to life. They don't trap them in overly simplistic boxes. It is common to represent people as one aspect of their identity or experience and to keep reinforcing it. But people are more than simply victims at one end of the spectrum, and victors at the other. People do not simply "get over" the things that happen to them, they move through them over time. We must help audiences grasp the multidimensional nature of the people in our stories, not merely draw the boundary at their circumstances.

Move beyond exceptionalism

When it comes to narratives about "overcoming disadvantage," a common trope is to make exceptions of and glorify those who achieve greatness "despite" their circumstances. This can work to further reinforce narratives of individualism and hyper-individualism. Let's not unintentionally celebrate hyper-independence. Let's instead question systems that demand an excess of resilience.

Final reflections

Over many years and iterations and evolutions of myself, I have at times experienced a strong external pressure to (as Sarah Wilson puts it in her 2017 book) "make the beast beautiful." As part of my own storytelling, I've felt pressure to:

- turn negatives into positives,
- turn the volume down on the harms and the pain,
- end on notes of hope in the hope that people will listen and be moved to action.

But sometimes power comes from saying something plainly, from calling something what it is. In not dressing anything up, or toning it down, but by simply stating a truth and letting it hang there; suspended, outstretched. To turn the insides out. Two passages come to mind:

"We do not have to romanticise our past in order to be aware of how it seeds our present" — Audre Lorde

"In order to retain our visions, to protect our imaginations, and keep our surface tension, we have to hold tightly to that space of refusal." — Ruby Oluoch

To end this chapter, I share a powerful message from advocate and 2021 Australian of the Year Grace Tame. This comes from her National Press Club address in March 2021:

> "listening to survivors is one thing – repeatedly expecting people to relive their trauma on your terms, without our consent, without prior warning, is another. It's sensation. It's commodification of our pain. It's exploitation. It's the same abuse.
>
> ... Healing from trauma does not mean it's forgotten, nor the symptoms never felt again. Trauma lives in ourselves. Our unconscious bodies are steps ahead of our conscious minds. When we are triggered, we are inevitably at the mercy of our emotional brain. In this state, it's impossible to discern between past and present. Such is re-traumatisation"

My hope is that these words echo in our minds the next time we are tasked with asking someone to share about their experiences or telling stories on behalf of others. When people are asked to delve into and return to the most painful parts of their lives, they are exposed to the risk of re-traumatisation *every single time*. This does not mean we shouldn't engage in storytelling, but it does mean that we are required to bring a level of intentionality and consideration to the lasting impacts of how people's stories are told and shared.

References and further reading

- Lora Mathis, "If There's A Way Out I'll Take It," *Instinct to Ruin* (2016)
- Hannah Gadsby, *Nanette* (2018)
- Sarah Wilson, First, *We Make the Beast Beautiful: A New Story About Anxiety* (2017)
- Audre Lorde, *Sister Outsider: Essays and Speeches* (1984)
- Ruby Oluoch, "The Last Word," Pollen
- Grace Tame, "'Share your truth, it is your power': Grace Tame's address to the National Press Club." The Guardian (2021)
- Chicago Beyond, "Why am I always being researched?"
- Karen Workman, "Whose story is it? Consider story sovereignty" (2022)
- Kate Marple, "Partnering with People to Tell Their Own Stories"
- Melissa Lucashenko, "Writing as a Sovereign Act" (2018)
- Michelle Drumm, "The role of personal storytelling in practice" (2013)
- Morgan Cataldo, "We contain multitudes: an introduction to ethical storytelling in policy and advocacy"
- Otto Scharmer, "Four listening levels" (2019)
- Our Race, "Story support resources"
- PhotoVoice, "Ethical Photography for Social Change"

- Stella Young, "I'm not your inspiration, thank you very much," TED Talk (2014)
- Tyson Yunkaporta, *Right Story, Wrong Story: Adventures in Indigenous Thinking* (2024)

Thanks

A huge thank you to Lora Mathis for the use of her exquisite poem, "If There's A Way Out I'll Take It" — the first strike of inspiration for this chapter.

Chapter 12

So you want to decolonise trauma?

by sahibzada mayed (صاحبزاده مائد)

Arriving to this space

Hello! I'm really glad that you found your way to my chapter. I am grateful for your presence, curiosity, and engagement. In this chapter, I will share reflections, musings, and wonderings on what decolonising trauma-informed and trauma-responsive practices could look like. That being said, I want to be as transparent as possible on what engaging with this chapter might feel like. Some of the topics include:
- colonial violence,
- intergenerational trauma,
- carceral systems,
- intersectional oppression,
- interpersonal and relational harm,
- exploitation.

As we move through this chapter together, you may experience a range of emotions, feelings, and responses. I encourage you to lean into practices of embodiment, moving at a pace that feels right for you. You may find it helpful to reflect on ways to self-soothe and regulate your bodymind, especially in moments of activation and heightened awareness. I trust that you will honour your own agency in choosing how (not) to engage with this chapter.

If you haven't been introduced to it yet, the concept of "bodymind" integrates the perceived split between the mind and body by understanding them as interconnected and interdependent. Dr. Sami Schalk, in her book *Bodyminds Reimagined: (Dis)Ability, Race, and Gender in Black Women's Speculative Fiction*, stretches our conceptualisation of bodyminds by imagining possibilities that break free from the social constructions of identity and oppression. I offer this as an invitation for you to tap into the rich and abundant knowledge your bodymind carries and explore it as a site of resistance, joy, and liberation.

Grounding ourselves in the present moment

At the time of writing this, I am situated on the unceded, ancestral lands of the Anishinaabe people from the Ojibwe, Potawatomi, and Odawa nations. These lands carry the memory of enslavement, occupation, and the ongoing genocide against Native and Black communities. They also embody ancestral wisdom passed down through generations of healers, land defenders, water protectors, and freedom fighters. In the present moment, we are actively witnessing multiple genocides across borders and the continued expansion of colonial empires. The wounds inflicted through colonial and imperial violence extend beyond linear timescapes and are felt across generations. As we seek to decolonise trauma, it is our individual and collective responsibility to actively confront the systems that create and perpetuate those traumas in the first place.

My histories, herstories, and relationships with (de)colonisation

I come from a lineage of ancestors, known and yet to be known, who tended to their native lands and waters as a primary form of sustenance and survival. Due to colonial violence and forced displacement, these relationships have been severed over multiple generations and cycles of loss. Unravelling the work of colonisation has led me through a process of reconciliation and remembrance — (re)learning ancestral ways of being and preserving new practices for future kin. As a first-generation immigrant-settler on Turtle Island, I commit to centering Indigenous sovereignty and the right to self-determination and resistance against occupation, settler violence, and colonisation.

Decolonisation is an everyday practice that requires us to actively confront the ways in which colonial legacies seep into our lives, relationships, social structures, and institutions. Decolonisation work cannot exist without a steadfast commitment to defend and protect Indigenous presence and futures. We must resist the metaphorisation of decolonisation, as Eve Tuck and K. Wayne Yang highlight in their seminal paper, "Decolonization is not a metaphor." Decolonial struggles must be rooted in a politic of Indigenous resurgence and revitalization.

My journey with decolonisation continues to emerge and remains imperfect. Every single day, I continue unravelling the ways in which colonial norms and legacies are ingrained in my daily practices of living. This process requires me to reckon with my own histories of colonisation and how I, too, participate in maintaining the dominance of colonial structures that exist and linger today. Before we move further, I invite you to take a moment and reflect on what practising decolonisation means to you.

What brings me to this work

Care work has always been an integral part of my life: to stay alive, to transform harm, to build peer support networks, and to keep each other safe(r) from institutional forms of violence. Navigating a world that is inherently violent to racialised, queer, femme, and disabled bodies has taught me the importance of reclaiming our bodily autonomy and creating pockets of joy and resistance. Often, we face harm and violence at the hands of the very institutions meant to provide care. In the face of such injustices, care work is a necessary and life-preserving strategy for survival.

Leah Lakshmi Piepzna-Samarasinha, in their book *Care Work: Dreaming Disability Justice*, highlights how:

> "people's fear of accessing care didn't come out of nowhere. It came out of generations and centuries where needed care meant being locked up, losing your human and civil rights, and being subject to abuse."

As someone who has firsthand experience surviving the medical and psychiatric industrial complexes, I believe that access to dignifying care should be a fundamental human right. When institutionalised care strips people of their autonomy and criminalises them, the struggle to cultivate care beyond carceral institutions is shared and ongoing.

Contextualising trauma

Trauma is often understood and defined from the perspective of an individual responding to distress, harm, injury, or violence. The dominant socio-cultural construction of trauma is based on what is considered a "normal" response to a situation or context that is activating, distressing, or violent. Often, there is a hyper-emphasis on defining and controlling the ways in which people respond, without addressing the root causes of what creates and exacerbates trauma. Dr. Samah Jabr, Head of the Mental Health Unit at the Palestinian Ministry of Health, prompts us to reflect on:

> "what is sick, the context or the person? In Palestine, we see many people whose symptoms — unusual emotional reaction or a behaviour — are a normal reaction to a pathogenic context."

Trauma as a collective experience

In order to contextualise trauma, we need to create space for multiple ways of viewing and understanding trauma itself. Trauma is often thought of in the context of one person with their individual symptoms, not a group of people with a collective experience. For example, colonial violence is rooted in the logic of separation. This attempts to sever our relationships with each other and our more-than-human relatives. I use the term "more-than-human relatives" to honour the sacred and infinite life forms that exist within the ecosystems we are part of. For many Indigenous communities, their livelihoods are deeply intertwined with the lands and waters they tend to and steward. The trauma of separation and displacement is profound and passed down from generation to generation.

As a response to colonial violence, in order to comply with and survive the colonial order, we are often forced into ways of assimilation and erasure. Over time, this becomes encoded into our bodyminds as a lasting impression that permeates our ancestral ways of being and knowing.

This is how intergenerational trauma manifests itself, continuing to change and evolve, and in some contexts becomes embedded into cultural norms. Dr. Resmaa Menakem highlights how:

> "trauma decontextualized in a person looks like personality.
> Trauma decontextualized in a family looks like family traits.
> Trauma decontextualized in people looks like culture."

This is extremely important to understand how cycles of trauma are reinforced and continue to persist over time, especially when the underlying conditions remain unaddressed.

Trauma beyond the confines of human supremacy

Many discussions around trauma are rooted in human supremacy and neglect to account for the ways in which harm and violence are inflicted upon lands, waters, and ecosystems. These narratives reinforce colonial norms, which privilege human domination and exacerbate hierarchies of control. The impact of colonial violence and plunder on the land is often ignored. In many cultures and communities, the land holds great significance as it sustains and nourishes us. The interconnectedness between all sentient beings is profound and necessary for our collective survival. Land-Based Ecologies is an interdisciplinary network seeking to understand the lived experiences of land trauma among marginalised communities. They articulate how "the land and the body are sites of simultaneous land-based violence and we feel the land-body trauma in our bodies, because we are the land, land is us." Understanding the impact of land-body trauma is necessary to contextualise the experiences of many individuals and communities whose livelihoods are deeply intertwined with the lands and waters they belong to.

It is important to highlight the trauma carried by the land and our more-than-human kin. As a result of land-based and colonial violence, they hold the memory of all they have witnessed and been subjected to. Similarly, we need to understand that the way this trauma manifests may shift and evolve over time. Our understanding of linear timescales is often rooted in a human-centric perspective shaped by coloniality. Inspired by Anna Tsing's work in her book *The Mushroom at the End of the World*, I invite you to reflect on the different kinds of world-making projects happening around us, by different species on multiple timescales. By viewing trauma as an evolutionary phenomenon, we can map out how trauma influences and shapes sociocultural change.

Exploring the root causes of trauma

It is important that our understanding of collective trauma addresses the root causes of harm and violence. Systems of oppression are built on the foundations of dehumanisation, erasure, and othering. These principles are based on separation from our shared humanity and interdependence.

An aspect often diminished is the need for co-regulation and mapping out how disruption and dysregulation can have a ripple effect beyond individual experiences. Co-regulation allows us to embrace a holistic approach to collectively tend to our nervous systems and care for our bodyminds. Dr. Jennifer Mullan, author of *Decolonizing Therapy*, traces the roots of pain and trauma to "separation from our land, our ancestry, our community, and our innate joy." This separation is intentional and by design, allowing systems of oppression to stay alive and thrive. In order to effectively respond to trauma, we need to shift toward relational practices that integrate the need for individual and collective care.

Resisting pathologisation

One of the unfortunate realities I have witnessed is how sometimes seemingly "trauma-informed" practices reduce people's lived experiences to the traumas they carry without directly acknowledging systemic and institutional contexts. When we fail to address the root causes of harm and violence, trauma can be pathologised in detrimental ways that strip individuals of their agency and dignity. This form of isolation is often weaponised as a means of control: to label and categorise whether someone's trauma responses seem irrational or disordered. In many situations, pathologisation directly feeds into criminalisation, as is the case with the medical industrial complex. Stella Akua Mensah explains how:

> "the mental 'health' system is fundamentally carceral, meaning that it is one of the many kindred systems that function to contain and surveil people, take away their locus of control, isolate them from their communities, and limit their freedom."

It is also important to acknowledge that de-pathologisation does not necessarily mean getting rid of a clinical approach to addressing symptoms arising as a result of trauma responses. In some contexts, people can find a sense of belonging or community through having a fully-realised psychiatric identity, and it may open up pathways to access institutional care. We need to hold space for multiple truths to co-exist. Wrongful de-pathologisation of the ways in which trauma manifests can lead to trivialisation or create barriers for accessing needed care and support. At the same time, we can reckon with the ways in which medical and psychiatric institutions uphold carceral practices and further cause harm, disproportionately to minoritised communities. To be clear, we are not attempting to question the validity or legitimacy of what an individual is experiencing or how that shows up in their bodymind; rather, we are seeking to deconstruct the notion of what is considered "normal."

Decolonising trauma requires us to shatter the social construction of normality and with it our dependence on carceral systems and institutions that continue to control and oppress us. The medicalisation of trauma often focuses on "fixing" the individual and getting them back to "normal." The underlying notion here is again that of control and domination. In their article "Visions for a Liberated Anti-Carceral Crisis Response," Stefanie Lyn Kaufman-Mthimkhulu shares how "medicalisation has limited our capacity to show up as curious humans, to find value or meaning in someone's state or in their words — regardless of if they 'make sense' to you or not." This is often a result of the ways in which internalised carcerality is projected onto others, contributing to systems of policing and oppression. Internalised carcerality can be understood as the "cop that exists in our heads and our hearts," reinforcing ideas of surveillance, punishment, and dehumanisation.

Before we move further, I invite you to pause and reflect on the ways in which internalised carcerality shows up for you, as well as experiments and practices to dismantle these carceral logics. As a reminder, engaging in this process may feel unsettling or dysregulating. I encourage you to move slowly and gently while tending to your own needs and honouring your capacity.

Reclaiming trauma work

As we seek to decolonise trauma, it is imperative to highlight how much of trauma work continues to be a mode of survival and resistance against institutional forms of oppression. While there is an emerging discipline around trauma-informed and trauma-responsive practices, many of these approaches have existed for time immemorial across borders, communities, and cultures.

Let's take a closer look at the Liberatory Harm Reduction movement in the United States, driven by the community advocacy of sex workers, substance users, transgender activists, and disability justice organisers attempting to survive realities where they are outcast and criminalised. In the absence of institutional support, peer and community support becomes essential to survive. Liberatory Harm Reduction, as defined by Shira Hassan, focuses on transforming the root causes of oppression. It is rooted in true self-determination and total body autonomy. A central aspect of this approach is to promote community-based empowerment and survival strategies that prioritise safety from institutional violence and reject any coercion, judgement, or stigma.

Shira Hassan highlights how:

> "we have become targets of a system that cannot make sense of us and seeks only to control us. Sometimes I think these systems have little help to offer, and other times I think these systems hoard resources from our communities intentionally and force us to fight each other for what little access we have."

This perspective is significant because it highlights the need to cultivate ecologies of care that prioritise the material and safety needs of the communities who are impacted by institutional harm and violence. Learning from the many examples of peer support and alternatives to carceral care, we must realise the need to invest in grassroots initiatives that are directly led by community members and reduce the overall dependence on carceral systems. A popular perspective that has gained momentum in abolitionist spaces is that "we keep us safe," which highlights how safety needs to be reimagined as something that grows from cultivating reciprocal relationships rooted in accountability, care, and transformative justice.

Reframing resilience

I often come across narratives of resilience that romanticise struggle in the face of adversity and trauma, rather than recognising how resilience is a necessary mode of resistance and survival against oppressive systems. This phenomenon is exacerbated for folks who experience intersectional forms of harm and violence. The glorification of resilience is incredibly harmful and can lead to further dehumanisation of individuals and communities, as violence inflicted upon them becomes more normalised. Dr. Sahar D. Sattarzadeh expresses how:

> "resilience is often understood from a lens that centres the oppressive forces that many peoples and communities face. It rarely, if ever, centres the human beings that experience and endure suffering."

The fetishisation of resilience can also mask the deep-rooted realities of institutional and systemic violence, making it seem like enduring trauma is a routine, and even admirable, outcome. This narrative shifts focus away from those perpetuating violence and oppression, absolving them of their complicity and responsibility to take action. The burden inevitably falls on those who are disproportionately harmed, along with the demand for resilience becoming an expectation.

We must ensure that the endurance of immeasurable violence and brutality is not lost on us. In some ways, resistance and resilience, too, are intertwined. Ancestral wisdom is a form of resilience that has been cultivated through generations as a means of cultural preservation and continued presence. Reframing resilience means shifting away from narratives that overemphasise struggle and instead focusing on celebrating rest, joy, and collective care.

(Re)Centering joy and pleasure

Trauma-informed practices often exclusively focus on the absence or prevention of harm, but rarely the presence of joy and pleasure. Systems of oppression are inherently violent and designed to suck the life and soul out of us. We are often denied the right to experience joy and pleasure, especially those who are forced to live in a state of continuous and perpetual trauma. Thus, joy and pleasure become necessary antidotes to keep us alive and sustain our bodyminds and spirits. A brilliant example is how Sins Invalid, a disability justice-based performance project led by Disabled people of colour, challenges conventional paradigms of "normal" and "sexy" by centering body liberation. Through various forms of artistry and storytelling, their collective efforts resist the medicalisation of bodies and celebrate the diversity of beauty that exists.

Creating space for joy and pleasure allows us to embrace the richness and abundance of our experiences. This is important because it deconstructs the narrative that portrays minoritised communities as perpetual victims that need to be saved. Our experiences should not solely be defined in relation to the harm and violence we experience at the hands of oppressive systems. Reconnecting with and remembering our cultural practices, connections with lands and waters, ancestral wisdoms, and innate capacity to practise joy is revolutionary and necessary resistance. Decolonising trauma requires us to lean into our imagination and break free from the shackles placed on us. How can we imagine, practice, and build outside the confines of the colonial imaginary?

Shifting the scales: what does this mean for designers?

Decolonising trauma requires us to critically examine the ways in which hierarchies of control and domination are (re)produced in design and research. Power is a dynamic, multifaceted concept that shows up in a myriad of ways.

One of the ways I like to think about power is when it is coupled with possibility. Where there is room for power dynamics to be exacerbated and reinforce systems of oppression, there is also space to imagine what possibilities may open up when power is leveraged to share access, privilege, and resources. As designers seeking to decolonise trauma-centred practices, it is our responsibility to shift power imbalances and actively work toward dismantling systems of oppression.

Rejecting the commodification of trauma

The commodification of trauma is something that shows up significantly in design, especially when working with communities who face intersectional forms of oppression and violence. When trauma is commodified, it loses its depth and complexity, turning people's pain and suffering into a spectacle for the sake of engagement or profit. This is made possible through objectification and stripping individuals and communities of their agency.

There is an underlying phenomenon of how the practice and institution of design has persistently extracted from minoritised communities, while community members involved rarely reap the benefits of the work. As designers, we must treat people's stories as living and breathing. It is truly a sacred gift to have someone entrust their lived and experiential knowledge to you. As such, we must act with a duty of care and relational responsibility, reminding ourselves who we are accountable to and how we can ensure reciprocal exchange to respect and value their contributions. I invite you to further explore ethical storytelling in Chapter 11.

Deconstructing colonial hegemony

As designers, we hold a fair amount of power afforded to us by our positionality within social ecosystems and institutions. This means that we often have control over what and whose stories are highlighted, how they are portrayed, what issues get prioritised or not, and so on. This form of control dictates the ways in which we may engage with the communities we partner with.

In order to understand someone's experiences, we must ensure that we are not enforcing a dominant lens or perspective. We are conditioned to view certain forms of knowledge as more credible, dismissing alternative ways of knowing and being. We need to remind ourselves that often what is considered "new knowledge" already exists within communities, and accessing that insight and wisdom should be done with utmost care, dignity, and respect.

Centering agency, dignity, and the right to self-determination

In our work, we must ensure that the identities and experiences of the people we are designing with are captured in dignifying ways that align with how they want to be represented.

An example comes to mind from a project where I was collaborating with a group of predominantly Black and Brown women who had recently been released from prison. One moment that came up during our work together was to create a shared language on how to represent their experiences with the carceral system. Through feedback and mutual consensus, we agreed upon the term "system-impacted." I remember reflecting on this moment and the impact it had on the women I was working with, particularly as they were used to being labelled as "inmate" or "prisoner." While this shift in language may feel small or insignificant, I do feel it had a profound impact by allowing someone to exercise their own agency in defining their experiences. From this interaction, I learned the importance of the right to self-determination and how changing the narrative is a crucial step for designing new possibilities.

Another example is related to a research project where an online survey was shared with a group of college students to better understand their experiences navigating mental health support. In this context, we asked each of the students to define what mental health means to them through the use of a creative metaphor. Coupled with open-ended questions to self-describe their backgrounds and identities, this approach created space for students to share their experiences on their own terms.

We must recognise and affirm that every individual is the expert of their own lived experiences. As designers, our role is to hold space for them to share if and whatever they feel comfortable with, as well as take charge of their own realities.

Embracing plurality and emergence

When working with individuals or communities that have experienced considerable harm and violence, it is important to ensure that we can honour and reflect the fullness of their experiences. Particularly in relation to narratives of trauma, we should intentionally create space for multiple perspectives and truths to co-exist. We must resist any attempts that default to monolithic ways of thinking and portray an entire group, community, or culture in a specific way that reduces complexity and nuance.

Similarly, the way we choose to portray individual or communal experiences should not reinforce tactics of control and dehumanisation. For example, if we solely choose to represent someone's experiences in relation to the harm or violence they have endured, we are unable to reflect the ways in which they may experience joy, resistance, and pleasure.

It is also important to recognise that people's consciousness and understanding of who they are and who they become is constantly changing. Thus, it is our responsibility to create space for folks to exercise their agency in shifting how they want to be represented.

Practising accountability and consensual repair

I have come to realise how harm is inevitable in our work as designers, or even as a result of it. This is not meant to excuse or justify causing harm, rather to recognise that we should be equipped to respond to harm if and when it does show up. This doesn't mean we need to have all the answers figured out, but it is essential to build capacity for engaging in reparative practice and create the conditions for accountability and care.

Responding to harm can be unsettling as it requires us to lean into discomfort and also acknowledge the impact of our engagement. What I have found helpful, based on my own experiences, is to practise transparency and vulnerability throughout any relational engagement where possible. By actively prioritising the need to cultivate trust, we are able to build deeper connections that allow for the possibility of repair. Any attempts at repair need to centre the experiences of those who have been harmed and prioritise their autonomy and safety.

In some contexts, I have witnessed how our desire to make amends can come from a place of fragility, guilt, or saviourism. We need to understand that repair may not always be possible — or even if it is, it may not lead to the outcomes we were hoping for or expecting. Repair needs to be a consensual practice and rooted in principles of liberatory harm reduction. I find it humbling to periodically remind myself of whom I am accountable to and what our shared understanding of accountability is.

Closing thoughts

There is so much left to be said, and there will always be more to say. For now, wherever this finds you in your journey toward unravelling the coloniality of trauma and decolonising your practices, I hope you feel compelled to continue moving forward. As you have probably realised by now, this chapter is meant to be a springboard to help you think and feel differently about trauma in relation to colonial systems of oppression. I hope you will build upon the ideas and provocations shared within and feed back into cultivating networks of radical care and support. I want to thank you for joining me on this journey. I sincerely welcome the gift of your feedback and would love to hear from you. If you feel compelled to do so, please feel free to reach out via email: mayed@sahibzadamayed.com

Honouring the lineages of whom we learn from

Learning is a collaborative and relational process; much of the labour, insight, and expertise that has been shared in this chapter has been realised through nurturing relationships and being present with community. I want to honour the many teachers, human and more-than-human, who have helped shape my understanding of and praxis around trauma, coloniality, and oppression. Some of these folks include Dr. Shirin Vossoughi, Dr. Megan Bang, Dr. Moya Bailey, Incia Rashid-Dawdy, Lauren Lin, Ritika Ramesh, and many more.

I also want to extend heartfelt gratitude to my partner-in-alchemy, Sabrina Meherally, who has been an amazing collaborator over the past year and a pivotal force in pushing the boundaries of what research and design rooted in care and relationality could look like. Sabrina and I have had the pleasure of working together at Pause and Effect, a decolonial design and research think-tank and consultancy based on the ancestral lands of the Musqueam, Squamish, and Tsleil-Waututh Nations. A substantial portion of the work shared here has been co-created through our collaborative visions for decolonising trauma-informed practices.

At several moments throughout this chapter, I have included quotations and references from a multitude of authors, cultural workers, community organisers, healers, and trauma practitioners. I encourage you to support and amplify their work in whatever ways you feel called to. In a similar spirit, I ask that you respect the labour that has gone into compiling this work, and hold it gently and lovingly with integrity and tenderness. I hope this is an opportunity to recognise how our work is always in flux, building upon the rich and abundant lineages of knowledge present within and around us.

References and further reading

- Sami Schalk, *Bodyminds Reimagined: (Dis)Ability, Race, and Gender in Black Women's Speculative Fiction* (2018)
- Eve Tuck and K. Wayne Yang, "Decolonization is not a metaphor," *Decolonization: Indigeneity* (2012)
- Leah Lakshmi Piepzna-Samarasinha, *Care Work: Dreaming Disability Justice* (2018)
- Lara Sheehi and Stephen Sheehi, *Psychoanalysis Under Occupation: Practicing Resistance in Palestine* (2022)
- Resmaa Menakem, "How do we heal?" (Talk Easy podcast with Sam Frogoso) (2020)
- "Collective grieving to heal land-body trauma," *Land Body Ecologies* (2023)
- Anna Tsing, *The Mushroom at the End of the World* (2015)
- Samara Almonte and Sayeeda Bacchus, "Working with our ancestors' rage: How Decolonizing Therapy can help heal intergenerational trauma" (2023)
- Jennifer Mullan *Decolonizing Therapy: Oppression, Historical Trauma and Politicizing Your Practice* (2023)
- Cara Page and Erica Woodland, *Healing Justice Lineages* (2023)
- Stella Akua Mensah, "Abolition must include psychiatry" (2020)
- Stefanie Lyn Kaufman-Mthimkhulu, "Visions for a Liberated Anti-Carceral Crisis Response" (2022)
- Shira Hassan, "Our Right to Heal: Liberatory Harm Reduction," *Yes!* (2023)
- Sahar D. Sattarzadeh, "Resoulience: Reimagining Resilience (and Ourselves)," *Journal of Critical Thought and Praxis*, Volume 11, Issue 3 (2022)
- Sins Invalid https://www.sinsinvalid.org
- Zarinah Agnew, "The prisons inside of us - on internalised carcerality, transformative justice," *Beyond_** (2024)

Chapter 13
Vicarious trauma: Protecting your spirit when doing trauma work

by Jenny Winfield

Recently I've been listening to an audiobook of *Bullshit Jobs* by anthropologist David Graeber. Despite the flippant title, the book's message is gravely serious. It "postulates the existence of meaningless jobs and analyses their societal harm." Graeber says that:

> "A bullshit job is a form of paid employment that is so completely pointless, unnecessary, or pernicious that even the employee cannot justify its existence.
>
> A lot of bullshit jobs are just manufactured middle-management positions with no real utility in the world, but they exist anyway in order to justify the careers of the people performing them. If they went away tomorrow, it would make no difference at all."

His findings were deeply provocative. According to Graeber, up to 40% of people — particularly those working in the administration, legal, and financial professions — admit feeling that they contribute nothing of value to the world. And that because of this, they're experiencing a kind of "spiritual violence." His message is that we need our lives and our work to have meaning. So much so that engaging in a charade of purpose can be "corrosive" to the soul.

"Oof," I thought, listening along, and feeling a rising wave of gratitude for the work that I do. "Imagine a job so exceedingly unnecessary that, were it to disappear tomorrow, it would not matter in the slightest. Imagine doing a job that is so pointless, that just by logging on every day, it actually becomes damaging to your spirit."

Alongside many of the other authors of this book, I practise trauma-informed design, and I believe that our work is fully necessary. But my wave of gratitude was quickly tempered by another reflection: our work can cause us spiritual harm, too.

Not because it's meaningless, but the opposite: because we value its meaning so highly. Our dedication to our design work, and the practice of sitting with the pain of others as a part of that work, makes us at risk for vicarious trauma.

In this chapter, I'll share some thinking on how and why we, as trauma-informed designers, need to protect our spirits. I'll draw on my own experience as a researcher and designer, having explored trauma almost exclusively for the last 7 or 8 years of my practice. In that time, I've researched with people in recovery from addiction, folks in prison, and those deep in grief from a suicide. I regularly do research with people who have experienced traumas like domestic violence, sexual assault, and tech abuse. I don't mind sharing that some of the stories I've heard have percolated into my soul, and not always positively. I've had my share of secondary traumatic stress (STS) and teetered on the edge of vicarious trauma (VT), too.

I'll also share some guidance from experts on how to spot the signs of secondary traumatic stress and vicarious trauma. I'll leave you with some questions to reflect on, and a sincere invitation to explore your capacity to rest. My goal is to help you stay committed to this important work — and to stay hopeful as you do it.

What are secondary trauma and vicarious trauma?

Secondary traumatic stress (STS) was a term coined by trauma specialist

Charles Figley and colleagues in the 1990s. It refers to our own experience when we witness an event that is highly stressful.

Take, for example, seeing a car accident on your way home from work. The crash happened to someone else (hence the "secondary"), yet it causes a stress response in you. Anxiety, distress, and even anger are all common reactions. You might have symptoms similar to post traumatic stress disorder (PTSD). The things that you saw, heard, felt, or smelled that day might return as flashbacks or intrusive thoughts. Over time, though, your nervous system will recover with the right kind of care and rest. The event causes you stress, but it doesn't have a long term effect on your body or your views about the world.

Around the same time that Figley and colleagues introduced the term "secondary traumatic stress," researchers Laurie Ann Pearlman and Lisa McCann popularised the term "vicarious trauma" (VT). They explored how, over time, therapists and other first responders to crises would internalise the trauma of their clients. They helped us to understand that VT can be an occupational hazard for professionals who are exposed to other people's trauma over long periods. They said:

> "Vicarious trauma is the transformation that occurs within the therapist (or other trauma worker) as a result of empathic engagement with clients' trauma experiences."

So vicarious trauma is also about indirectly bearing witness to hardships, but the difference is that some rest and relaxation alone won't set you right. That's because, as Pearlman and McCann said, you are transformed by what you've experienced, even at one step removed. In bearing witness, you actually experience a kind of trauma. (Note the difference between the word "stress" in "secondary traumatic stress" and the word "trauma" in "vicarious trauma.")

"A tiredness deep in your soul"

Laura Van Dernoot Lipsky, who wrote the brilliant *Trauma Stewardship; An everyday guide to caring for self while caring for others*, says that one of the signs of VT is "a tiredness deep in your soul." I think many of us working to support traumatised people (often while dealing with our own traumas) can relate to that. Laura works with caregivers, activists, and professionals in the trauma and social justice space. She shares some other signs of VT; for example, we might feel unable to support the people who are actually experiencing that "primary" trauma, even if we try our very best. No matter how many hours we put in, or extra miles we go, we may feel as though we have never done enough. Feeling overwhelmed is also common. The immediate systems that we're operating within can create infuriating blockers to good service outcomes — and that's before we factor in the relentless grind culture and trauma of capitalism and white supremacy.

What I love about Laura's work is that when she shares the signs of VT, she normalises how contradictory they may seem. Since VT is a type of trauma, responses look different for everyone. I might totally withdraw because that's *my* trauma response — whereas someone else might become combative at work (not to mention at home). I might feel helpless; you may feel persecuted. I might minimise the experiences I'm having ("Oh, it's nothing"), while my colleague might start to have an inflated sense of importance. This makes it vital to be conscious about the risks and signs of VT not just in ourselves, but in our colleagues, too.

A change in your worldview

With VT, instead of your nervous system flaring up and then resettling (as it does with secondary traumatic stress), it actually becomes altered. This means that you remain in a state of "dysregulation," and you might feel anxious or depressed for long periods. Not only that — your worldview changes negatively, too. You may begin to see the potential for trauma and harm everywhere. You might move from having a healthy awareness of risk (particularly in relation to the field that you work in) towards having a heightened belief in that risk.

For example, as someone who identifies as a woman and supports survivors of sexual violence, I have a strong awareness of the gendered risks posed to our bodies. I'll see a young woman taking a train late at night and, knowing that predators may be around, feel concerned for her safety. But if I were vicariously traumatised by my work, I might feel sure that there were potential predators everywhere and feel angry that no woman can ever enjoy her freedom to travel alone.

In their episode of The Cancer Professionals Podcast by MacMillan on VT, Dr Karen Campbell and Lisa Nell note that "one of the defining features of VT is that it can really, over time, not just affect our psychological well-being and our physical well-being but also our spiritual wellbeing." To me, this spirit means the way we approach the world, the values that guide us, and the way we direct our energies to what we believe matters. To others, it might mean something more religious.

Campbell and Nell go on to reassure us that the positive thing about our nervous systems (and our worldviews) is that they can adapt. So even if you have experienced VT, it's possible to feel healthy and happy in yourself (and your work) again. You can adjust the lens of your worldview back to a healthy awareness of risk.

So what has all this got to do with designers?

Historically, discussions about secondary trauma stress (STS) and vicarious trauma (VT) have been focused on workers who offer direct support to traumatised individuals. For example, people working in:
- death care,
- palliative care,
- social work,
- mental health care,
- sexual assault response,
- emergency response roles such as firefighters, police, or aid workers in war zones.

These roles are often called "frontline" services, and we'd do well to recognise the reference to warfare within that term.

These folks are at high risk for vicarious trauma because they are continually exposed to the trauma of others. It's literally their job to support people through some of the most challenging human experiences there are. Because of this, there are training programs on STS and VT that you're likely to go through if you decide that this is your career path. You'll be warned that the work can start to feel weighty, especially if you're an empath.

What's been happening in the last decade or so is that designers have also been given a seat at the table for trauma work. Designers, however, are only just starting to seek and receive education about how to conduct this work with the due care (for self and others) that it deserves. Social worker and designer Rachael Dietkus discusses this in her paper "Transforming Trauma-Informed Design: Ethical Practices, Lifelong Learning, and Collective Responsibility." She writes that it can feel as concerning as it is encouraging for those with clinical backgrounds in trauma to see designers being granted access to this kind of work. Often it's taking place without a code of ethics, a scope of practice, or even basic training in place.

The rise of trauma-informed design

A growing number of decision-makers in organisations and governments recognise that, in order to be effective, our services need to be well-designed. This doesn't just refer to how usable a service is. It means that the service should be designed with a deeper thoughtfulness and sensitivity for its users, many of whom are survivors of trauma. The need for trauma-informed service design and delivery has therefore been recognised not just in emergency services and mental health care, but across many contexts where everyday service provision happens; for example, in housing, education, and food systems. Frankly, I can't think of people more deserving of good design (that is, access to services and support that actually works) than people who have endured trauma.

It must be said, though, that culturally we're talking about trauma a lot at the moment. And with that growing awareness comes an addressable market for products. There are many private sector (often tech) companies attempting to cash in by designing for trauma experiences. Many superficial digital products are springing up which do exactly that (another mental health app, anyone?). This trend goes to show that some design work in the trauma space is going to be "bullshit work" (if we go back to Graeber's definition — offering nothing of value to the world). We'd be wise to assess the values and motivations of such companies, and these design roles, critically.

However, most of the great work I've seen in trauma-informed design is coming from the public and non-profit sector, and it's heartening. These organisations are more likely to protect their staff from STS and VT because they understand trauma, not just tech.

They know that people who have endured chronic traumatic stress have needs that must be heard and understood by designers. They see trauma as a community sickness rather than an individual issue. They want their designers to commit to understanding the root causes of trauma on a social and political level, and explore their own positionality within that.

Equity-centred user researcher Alba Villamil recently wrote about this, referring to Jamie Willer-Kherbaoui's 2019 paper "Working through the smog." She invites us to notice and challenge the ways in which white saviorism in particular is damaging to communities who are encouraged to engage in design processes or are considered the beneficiaries of them. One of Alba's reflections is that, in the design industry, we often see issues being de-contextualised or depoliticized. This is evident in:

> "The refusal to acknowledge how slavery, colonisation, public policy, and other harmful interventions have impacted and continue to impact communities, which has implications for the research questions we ask and the problems we wrongly try to solve for."

Engaging in this kind of critique is vital for designers working in the trauma space. Being willing to unlearn what you may have been taught about what good design is can bring deep discomfort. It can result in designers (especially those who haven't been formally or informally educated about the social, political, and historical context of trauma) feeling in over their heads. It is a lot to go from working on purely commercial design projects to working with trauma survivors (believe me, I've done it). This only adds to the feeling of overwhelm that can creep in as part of VT when doing the trauma work itself. To engage properly in the wider narrative of your work, and also to know when to process and rest, is a lifelong skill to learn.

Overexposed and underprepared

Kate Every, Rachael Dietkus, and I ran a study in 2024 that explores the idea of being overexposed and underprepared for trauma as design practitioners. Our survey of designers and researchers found that out of 95 respondents, 51% had experienced secondary traumatic stress in their work, with a further 24% "not sure" whether they had. Considering that many of these people don't actually work on trauma in an official capacity, these are noteworthy numbers.

Designers described being appointed as stand-in user researchers for organisations who don't employ a dedicated researcher. Some shared that they'd been underprepared for situations they found themselves in; for example, wanting to have done more to support a participant during or after a distressing research interview. Practitioners said they were well-meaning and caring, but that these attributes only go so far towards helping them to avoid being harmed or causing harm to others. 70% wanted more training, and 66% wanted more opportunities to work directly with and learn from trauma specialists from other disciplines (for example, social workers and other clinical practitioners).

Many survey respondents were frustrated at their senior leadership or organisations for failing to proactively put more structural support and policies in place to support them. 65% wanted their leaders to have more education about trauma-informed practice.

Are designers at risk for STS and VT?

In user research (my professional discipline), it's pretty well known that if you work on a trauma-related project, you'll be at risk of STS, and possibly VT, too. But what about if you're a content designer working on that same project? Does that mean you're not at risk of STS or vicarious trauma? Of course not. In fact, I think that content designers have different risk factors of their own.

One reason lies in who does the user research. If we're going to do justice to trauma-informed design work, we need to conduct excellent research as part of our design work. But who gets involved in this, and who receives the benefit of training and safeguarding? Often, it's not designers.

When we're working on design projects that touch on trauma, there are usually a limited number of places to join research interviews. Rightly so, because we don't want to outnumber the participant. We also don't rely on being able to make recordings of interviews that team members can listen back to, as participants may not want to consent to this.

So, as a content designer, you might be far less exposed to live research interviews than your team members are. The thing is, you're still responsible for putting yourself in the shoes of the user. Being a dedicated and curious person, you know there is insight out there, waiting to be uncovered. You might well turn to doing your own secondary user research without any safeguards in place.

A content designer's insight-gathering might look like getting lost in a Reddit thread about extreme poverty. They might dive into some survey data or social media content about the human experiences of war, displacement, and torture. They might spend a day forensically examining helpline call logs that have been passed over from a client partner working on child abuse. They may be exposed to a lot of harmful content, quite possibly more than a user researcher who is leading qualitative interviewing would be.

This type of secondary research isn't always formally recognised as part of the research process, and it isn't always guided or managed safely. Content designers might spend hours or days on these tasks without having any training in how to spot the signs of STS and VT. User researchers are more likely to be getting this (or at least aware that they need to be doing self-directed studying about it).

To make it worse, content designers are often doing this work alone. In qualitative research, we tend to work together with colleagues. We get to check in with participants, and sometimes we stay in touch. There's a strongly relational aspect to it. But a content designer might engage with accounts of trauma after the fact. Reading data, call logs, and Reddit threads means you can't reach out and connect with those who have shared their suffering to offer validation and support — it's often way too late. You may also feel shame at asking colleagues for support after doing such desk-related activities. We shouldn't forget secondary sources of research and how activating and risky these can be, too.

Content designers may be underserved when it comes to the safety practices of trauma-informed design, which very often centre on the needs of the user researcher and participant doing "live" research.

The cadence of design work

Trauma work should not be conducted at the same pace as "regular" design work. As a designer, it's the norm to work intensely on projects that last a fairly short time (say 2–6 months) or to work across multiple projects at the same time. This means that you may be exposed to many stories of egregious trauma for a concentrated period, and then none at all. A mix of exposure can be a good thing, when we think about how vicarious trauma is something that builds in us cumulatively over time. But when we think about the potential for STS and VT, I think we're starting to see that it's risky to dip in and out of projects without having gotten training or access to safeguarding.

Yes, the chance to take a break is good, but these kinds of on/off project set-ups often miss the deep and soulful group work that is an essential component of navigating trauma work confidently. Moving on to work on another project that is not about trauma is not the same as resting. It is not the same as healing or doing reflective practices that enable you to process, and be fully present for, trauma work.

So what do we need to do?

We start by confronting the idea that, as designers, we don't need any special measures — that we don't need to be taken care of within our profession. We challenge the idea that STS and VT only happen to people working in those traditionally high-risk frontline jobs — because we can experience these things in our work, too.

Beware of hierarchical scales of suffering, which serve to minimise our experiences and elevate others' as more "worthy" of proper care. If we find ourselves doing this, we'd do well to note that being cynical and minimising pain are, in fact, symptoms of VT.

Working in close collaboration with others is essential when your work touches on trauma. Judith Herman, renowned psychiatrist and trauma expert, talks about the isolation that trauma creates, both for survivors and for the workers supporting them. Note that the Substance Abuse and Mental Health Services Administration's (SAMHSA) trauma-informed care principles include peer support and collaboration, directly speaking to the necessity of collective care in trauma work.

We also have much to learn from the Black liberation movement, and its Black women leaders in particular, about resisting grind culture and learning how to rest. While reading Tricia Hersey's book *Rest is Resistance*, I was struck by this line: "Rest is radical because it disrupts the lie that we are not doing enough."

She discusses in detail how harmful it is to allow our bodies to be treated as machines, purely there to be economically productive under capitalism, and traces this back to chattel slavery. The idea of "never doing enough" is perpetuated by grind culture. It's the modern day expression of those same white supremacist and capitalist ideals, and it's pertinent to this chapter's topic. The mindset that we are only "worthy" when we have worked and produced, that we are not enough in and of ourselves, is a massive risk factor for VT. Anyone who has grown up being taught that they are not enough will be more likely to experience VT because their natural instincts will be to pour in more energy, more of their spirit and soul, to gain approval in a system that is not designed to grant it.

Often it's those supporting us, whether through formal supervision or more informal connecting, who help us to see that we are doing all we can. They share the load of helping us assess if and how we could do more.

Growing our consciousness

I work at Chayn, an organisation that works with survivors of gender-based violence (including domestic violence, sexual assault, and tech abuse). Although we apply the principles of trauma-informed design in our external services, we're also constantly experimenting with applying them to our internal working practices.

If we want to exude collective care, we know that we need to cultivate it in ourselves as individuals. We need to cultivate it in our culture, too. There is a strong awareness in the organisation that we do challenging work. We know that this can wear us down over time, and may well activate our own traumas. So why shouldn't our day-to-day policies and practices be trauma-informed, too?

Our founder, Hera Hussain, adapted SAMHSA's trauma-informed principles and created our own, tailored to the context that we work in: gendered violence. Both sets of principles are listed at the start of this book. Chayn's are (currently):

- safety,
- power sharing,
- agency,
- privacy,
- equity,
- plurality,
- accountability,
- hope.

I use these as a framework below to share some questions that we tend to think about and ask ourselves in our work. Exploring some of these questions with your team could allow you to understand your needs and advocate for yourselves. Perhaps you might ask for the time and support that you need.

I'd always start with curiosity and seek to explore your experiences and feelings. The earlier on in your work that this happens, the better.

Safety
- Do I feel safe enough to do this work?
- If I begin to feel unsafe in my work, do I have options? What are they?
- Do I know what will bring me back to a felt sense of safety?
- If I feel unsafe during or after an experience at work, do I have a way of sharing this with colleagues and learning from it?
- Is regular supervision (speaking with a therapist to discuss what comes up in my work) available to me, and if not, can I request this?
- How can I share with my team what it looks, feels, and sounds like if I am not doing OK?

Power-sharing
- How can we plan this work so that no one feels they're "going it alone"?
- Are we sharing the responsibility for a good research experience and good design outcomes with each other?
- How are we planning to support each other and the participants that we meet?

Agency
- Am I conscious of the choices that my team or I have to make changes in our work if we are feeling overwhelmed?
- What are we practising to help ourselves?
- What are the tools that we would like to try? How could we build them into our work?

Privacy
- How might I enquire and explore topics with survivors while respecting their privacy and not overstepping?
- How might we communicate our personal feelings with our colleagues, knowing that this can also bring discomfort?

Equity
- Am I conscious of the elements of my history and identity that might make me feel particularly vulnerable to being harmed or harming others on this piece of work?
- What are they and how might I manage and navigate them?
- How might I share my experiences and support others?

Plurality
- Are we remembering that coping and not coping looks different for everyone?
- Am I aware of the different types of trauma responses that there are?
- Have I thought about how my responses might change day-to-day or over time, depending on what else is going on?

Accountability
- Am I in a position today to safely engage with survivors and show them the compassion and validation that they deserve?
- Am I clear about what my responsibilities to survivors are and where the limit is?
- Do I have clear professional boundaries, and have I communicated these with participants?
- Do I know what is "mine" and what is "not mine" to respond to and solve?

Hope
- Do I still feel hopeful?
- If we feel a sense of hope slipping, do we know how to restore that faith in the work we're doing? Who can we turn to to share our feelings?

How's your spirit doing?

I hope this chapter will serve as an invitation to tune into your souls and spirits and curiously ask them how they're doing. Committing to taking care of them is a hopeful and lifelong process.

If you and colleagues are already applying principles of trauma-informed design in your work, you've already done important work to create the support that survivors of trauma need. I'd encourage you to think about how you can also apply the same principles to your working practices. If your organisation doesn't have a group that is already talking about STS and VT, try starting the conversation with a fellow researcher or designer. Ask for the space and resources that you need before you *really* need it. If connecting outside of your workplace feels right, there are lots of online groups that provide peer support. Whether it's advice, solidarity, or learning opportunities you're after, the many trauma-informed design spaces online are free to join and very welcoming.

I think the goal for many of us (doing jobs which we don't believe are bullshit) is to continue to do this trauma work that we care about for a long time. We need those of us who are already doing this meaningful work to stick around; because if we're working in trauma, we're probably not addressing problems that will be solved by next week. We should remember, though, that it's precisely because our work is full of knotty problems and has so much meaning for us that we are going to be at risk of VT.

If we are going to manage STS and VT when it comes knocking, we need to deeply nurture our capacity and confidence to define what the limits of our work are and hold boundaries around it. To keep going, we must decide to actively — and collectively — protect our spirits and our souls.

We must get to the work, while not letting the work get to us.

References and further reading

- David Graeber, *Bullshit Jobs: A Theory* (2018)
- Charles R. Figley, "Compassion fatigue as secondary traumatic stress disorder: an overview," *Compassion fatigue: coping with secondary traumatic stress disorder in those who treat the traumatized* (1995)
- Laurie Anne Pearlman and Lisa McCann, *Psychological Trauma And Adult Survivor Theory. Therapy And Transformation* (1990)
- Laura Van Dernoot Lipsky with Connie Burke, *Trauma Stewardship, An everyday guide to caring for self while caring for others* (2009)
- "Secondary Trauma: Recovering from Compassion Fatigue with Laura van Dernoot Lipsky," Being Well Podcast (2022)
- "The weight of empathy: Understanding vicarious trauma in cancer care (Part 1)" *MacMillan Cancer Care Podcast*, Episode 5 with Dr Karen Campbell and Lisa Nell (2024)
- "2024 Post Traumatic Stress Disorder fact sheet," World Health Organisation
- Jamie Willer-Kherbaoui, "Working through the Smog: How White Individuals Develop Critical Consciousness of White Saviorism" *Community Engagement Student Work* (2019)
- Judith Herman, *Trauma and Recovery: The Aftermath of Violence — From Domestic Abuse to Political Terror* (2015)
- Tricia Hersey, *Rest Is Resistance: Free yourself from grind culture and reclaim your life* (2024)
- "6 Guiding Principles to a Trauma Informed Approach Infographic," Centers for Disease Control and Prevention (2022)
- Hera Hussain, "Trauma-informed design: understanding trauma and healing" (2021)
- Alba Vilamil, "What are the ways (white) saviorism manifests in our research and design practice, particularly in the equity design space?" (published on LinkedIn) (19 September 2024)
- Rachael Dietkus, "Transforming Trauma-Informed Design: Ethical Practices, Lifelong Learning, and Collective Responsibility" (published on LinkedIn) (14 February 2024)

Chapter 14

Crisis communication: A crisis is more than a moment in time

by Miriam Vaswani

A person in crisis needs information that is:
- directive and unambiguous,
- from a trusted source,
- at the right time,
- through a reliable, accessible medium.

Those needs apply equally to a person in a conflict zone and a person hearing the notification of an SMS from their stalker. They might also apply to a person who is about to open their bank statement. Or to someone whose child has a rising fever.

Imagine this.

You're a university student in Uganda in the 1970s. The president has ordered your entire community to leave the country within 90 days, including families like yours who have lived and built businesses in the country over several generations. There are severe limits on what money and belongings you can take with you.

You look for refuge. It's a hostile process. You have to fill out lengthy paper forms asking for the same information several times, in different ways. It's like a test to see whether you can sign your name in a small box and choose the correct kind of pen.

The forms would be difficult on an ordinary day. But the situation is one of the most stressful you've experienced. You are struggling to sleep, and often feel overwhelmed by panic. You have no idea when or how this crisis will end.

Even after reading the questions and instructions several times, they don't make sense. And many of the people who manage immigration systems seem to take pleasure in watching the process fail.

If you fail, you will have to start again. Or lose your chance of safety entirely.

Eventually, you get through the process and arrive in a safe country. Over the next few decades you build a career, raise children, and become a prominent member of your new society. In public life, you're known as a capable, intelligent person. And you are.

But for decades after gaining refuge, you struggle to open letters. Sometimes you leave them for a long time before you're able to read what's inside. Forms are especially difficult. You feel nauseous when you have to fill one out, and it makes ordinary things near-impossible, like renewing your driver's licence or organising your child's swimming lessons.

Trauma and crisis are different, but they often live together

A crisis is an event.

During a personal crisis years ago, a friend described it as a thing that "pulls the ground away." Another way to look at it: it's an event that needs unusual resources if we are to get through it.

If, for example, your home is destroyed in a fire, you'll need resources you wouldn't use otherwise. You'll have to find shelter, clothing, rearrange your usual routine, and deal with your insurance company (if you're privileged enough to have insurance). You might have to cope with the loss of things, and possibly people or animals you love. And you might have to recover from or learn to live with injuries.

Trauma is one possible result of a crisis.

Trauma is the experience of the crisis and its effect. Individual experiences of a crisis can be extremely different, as can the experience and effects on communities, animals, or our environment.

As the pioneering psychiatrist and author Judith Herman describes it, "Psychological trauma is an affiliation of the powerless. At the moment of trauma, the victim is rendered helpless by overwhelming force."

That helplessness can happen during a crisis with clear parameters, like a road accident. And it can happen during a long period of helplessness, like years of intimate partner violence or childhood abuse.

And an ordinary, routine event could force you to relive a crisis.

Marylou Fonda survived the '60s Scoop, when the Canadian government took Indigenous children from their parents as part of a wider genocide. Children including Marylou were forcibly adopted by white families, or abused and murdered in "residential schools" run by the Roman Catholic, Anglican, Presbyterian, and United churches.

Talking to Global News, Marylou described being asked about her medical history at medical appointments. "Sometimes it's downright traumatising when you're in a doctor's office . . . You have to say 'no' because you don't know."

In her essay "Eye to Eye: Black Women, Hatred and Anger," Black feminist writer Audre Lorde described surviving the many-layered violence of her childhood. "My light-skinned mother kept me alive within an environment where my life was not a high priority. She used as many methods as she had at hand, few as they were."

To survive both crisis and trauma, we need resources. Money, for example. Or a strong reputation. Self-respect, physical strength, and a loving community are also resources. And we may have imperfect resources that harm us as much as they help.

"My mother taught me to survive from a very early age by her own example," wrote Audre Lorde. "Her silences also taught me isolation, fury, mistrust, self-rejection, and sadness. My survival lay in learning how to use the weapons she gave me also to fight against those things within myself, unnamed."

A crisis is not always obvious

Some things are always a crisis; war, intimate partner violence, natural disaster, poverty. Other crises are less visible. 20 years after a traumatic cervical screening test, a person might spend the hours leading up to the same procedure in a state of crisis. They might be unable to concentrate, navigate their own home or city safely, or connect with other people in the most basic ways.

As a communicator, I have worked with people experiencing conflict, mass evacuation, abuse, and major political or diplomatic change. As a designer, I've solved problems for people who have complex, fulfilling lives and responsibilities, but are immobilised by a routine notification from their doctor. Or people who can't bear to open utility bills, despite having the money to pay them.

Crises may look distinct to the communicator. A medical appointment is fundamentally different from a terrorist attack. Opening an electricity bill is not the same as navigating a flooded city. But to the person in crisis, they have a similar effect on the mind and body.

A person in crisis has an enormous cognitive load. They're able to make fast, life-saving decisions, but struggle to plan a sequence of actions or deduce information from broad or vague statements. They will remember facts and events differently.

Most crucially, they will make decisions differently from a person who is not in crisis.

Be directive and unambiguous

Now imagine this. Or maybe you don't have to imagine.

You're a driver for a foreign embassy. Over the last couple of decades, international military forces have been in your country. It's a complicated relationship: they have been responsible for major human rights violations and have collected biometric data from almost every person in your country, including you.

They are also keeping another, far more abusive regime from taking over your country.

Now the international coalition is leaving. Members of the other regime are massing outside cities. Today you heard rumours of police giving up their stations without a fight. It seems likely that your country's rule of law will be overcome.

The embassy you work for represents a country whom the regime considers an enemy. Some of your colleagues have made their way to staging points for evacuation. But you are sceptical about whether, as a contractor rather than an employee, you'll qualify for refuge in your employer's country.

You have the keys to a relative's house near a land border, far from the staging points. You believe your best chance of survival is to ask for refuge at that border.

You get to the house safely. Along the way your phone's screen was cracked, but there is electricity in the house to keep it charged. After trying for a few hours, you find a signal to use WhatsApp.

Immediately, messages appear from your embassy's communication team. You contacted them during your journey and gave them basic information about your plans. They say they are trying to find out whether you can safely ask for refuge in the neighbouring country.

An hour later, a new message appears. It says:

> It is not safe to cross the border tonight.

You read the message several times. Then you gather your belongings, walk to the border, and ask for refuge.

The brain in crisis works differently

Why would a person ignore, or misunderstand, such a clear message?

In crisis, our brains prioritise the skills that will keep us alive. We can make fast decisions with limited information, but we have less access to skills like critical thought, long-term planning, and taking meaning from complex information.

Although the message is technically simple, it's asking too much of a person in crisis. It's asking the person to do 2 things:

- understand that the country and its border are unsafe for you right now,
- make a plan based on that knowledge.

And it uses words that could be misleading, unless a person can process the entire sentence. When we design for people in crisis, we have to allow for the more rapid, fragmented way a person gathers and acts on information.

A person could easily look at the sentence:

> It is not safe to cross the border tonight.

And understand:

> Safe, border, tonight.

A person in crisis needs more than simplicity

Now imagine you're the communicator who sent that message to the embassy's driver.

You woke up to a phone call early this morning, then logged into the first of many crisis calls.

Part of your role in the crisis team is to communicate directly with your colleagues and partners in the country. You're also responsible for keeping track of everyone you're communicating with and the way their rapidly changing environment is affecting their options for communication. And you're tracking which mediums of communication people are relying on, hour to hour.

Until the embassy's driver contacted you to say he was making his way to the border, he was unaccounted for. When you got his message, you decided with the crisis team to find out which border he intended to cross. Then, to tell him whether or not it was safe. A security expert in the team had been giving updates on routes out of the country and their relative safety.

You made that decision because you and the crisis team knew the information could change quickly. You also knew it might be a while before your message got to the driver because of poor connectivity and the uncertainty of his journey.

And you knew you could put him in danger if someone else saw his screen. For example, on a bus, or if he were arrested.

When the driver contacted you from the house near the border, you gave him the most current information quickly, in the simplest language:

> It is not safe to cross the border tonight.

And you were right. It's simple language. But the driver didn't just need simplicity. He needed direction, and absolutely no room for uncertainty.

People in crisis need directive, unambiguous communication

These messages are equally simple, and more helpful in a crisis:

> "Stay where you are."

> "Wait there. I will send more information soon."

A person would not have to make a plan if they received either of those messages. They could simply follow the instruction and wait for the next piece of information.

And there are no misleading words. It would be very difficult to misunderstand either message, regardless of a person's cognitive load.

Sometimes, the most important message is not an instruction. In that case, a simple but unmistakable key word is helpful. Like in this version of the same message:

> Danger across the border. Stay where you are.

Even with a basic understanding of the language, the word "danger" is hard to miss and easy to translate.

Trust (or mistrust) changes everything

People in crisis need more than information. They need trustworthy information.

That's especially true for people experiencing trauma — whether that trauma is immediate, or a culmination of damage, or a more complex generational trauma.

Trust has to be built over time, long before a crisis happens, so it must be part of every interaction. If trust is damaged, a person, institution, or company might never recover. That is one characteristic of a crisis; it threatens viability. Honest, timely communication is often what reduces harm.

When trust has been damaged, a sincere, fast apology and answers to people's questions show that the person or organisation responsible is not only dealing with it, but also that the people affected are entitled to dignity and care.

This is the process I go through when responding to something that could become a crisis:
- learn the facts,
- find out who is affected and what they need to know,
- acknowledge what happened,
- apologise, if an apology is due,
- say what the people responsible are doing about it,
- answer people's questions clearly and honestly as soon as possible,
- if important information isn't available yet, say you're trying to get it,
- say when more information will be available.

There is a point at which you can't regain trust. Policing, worldwide, is an extreme example of an institution whose reputation will never recover from the trust it has broken with people and communities over centuries. That reputation is built on a culture of violence combined with a consistent failure to tell the truth and fix what's wrong with the institution, including:
- the RCMP's (Royal Canadian Mounted Police) systemic violence against Indigenous people,
- decades of sexual torture in Tunisian police cells,
- Ohio police shooting a 12-year-old Black child dead while he played in a park,
- a London police officer kidnapping, raping, and murdering a woman.

In 2021, retired Anglican priest Mina Smallman told London police that her 2 adult daughters were missing. The police refused to search for them. Mina said, "I knew instantly why they didn't care. They didn't care because they looked at my daughter's address and they thought they knew who she was. A Black woman who lives on a council estate."

Her 2 daughters, Bibaa Henry and Nicole Smallman, had been murdered in a London park. Nicole's partner Adam was the first to find them.

Mina later said, "Two officers were told to guard the scene where a young man, a stranger, had stabbed my daughters 28 and 8 times respectively. Instead, they took photos of my daughters' corpses, one of them superimposing his face on to create a selfie-style image, before sharing them in WhatsApp groups full of misogynistic and racist chat."

It wasn't just the police's immediate response that Mina Smallman recognised as untrustworthy. It was the history of broken trust behind it, based on a system of abuse.

You can ruin trust with a few words

The violence I've just described isn't the only way people and companies break trust.

In the summer of 2024, American software company Intuit destroyed their reputation with one long-winded sentence that no one needed or believed:

> "We've significantly raised the bar on our expectations of employee performance, resulting in approximately 1,050 employees leaving the company who are not meeting expectations and who we believe will be more successful outside of Intuit."

Immediately, former Intuit employees and prominent people in the tech and design industry defended the employees and condemned the company, telling stories about their leadership team's incompetence.

It became a significant story over several days, worsening each minute that Intuit failed to address the crisis they had created for themselves.

Or you can spend hundreds of years destroying trust

Trust becomes more complicated — and more important — when there are serious inequalities in a crisis.

The British Museum made their own crisis in 2023. They used Chinese diaspora writer and translator Yilin Wang's translations of the Chinese feminist Qiu Jin's poems, uncredited and unpaid, in the exhibition China's Hidden Century. Yilin Wang took the matter to Twitter, and people quickly spoke up in support of them.

The British Museum chose to defend the 2 white curators of the exhibition, and then to remove Qiu Jin's poems along with Yilin Wang's translations from the exhibition. Public anger grew over the next few days, as did media interest.

It wasn't the first time. Early one morning in 2017, the British Museum's Twitter account introduced "Jane Portal, Keeper of Asia," and invited people to ask questions using the hashtag #AskACurator.

Someone asked why Asian deities, who have many different names in different languages, are only called by a few of those names on placards. The British Museum's Twitter account, temporarily under Jane's name, replied:

> "We aim to be understandable by 16 year olds. Sometimes Asian names can be confusing, so we have to be careful about using too many."

The public demolished both Jane and the British Museum, as did many journalists.

The British Museum's misuse of Yilin Wang's work and their racist tweet weren't stand-alone crises. They were part of a much bigger crisis that began nearly 300 years ago, with its first acquisition. Since then, the institution has become widely known around the world as a house of stolen wealth, cultural heritage, and sacred objects, including human remains of subjugated peoples.

Even if the British Museum decided to address the harm they've done to the world, it would take generations to regain what they've lost through systemic breaches of trust.

Crisis communication is useless without trust

I spoke to Anushka Seth, Asia-Pacific head of communications, about trust, and its presence or absence in crisis.

Anushka has worked on many public health crises, and has researched best practice in crisis communication for Ebola and AIDS. Although the

World Health Organisation declared Ebola a public health emergency of international concern, it has had a far more devastating effect on West African countries in this century than on the rest of the world.

There was a "very deep mistrust of these international organisations and foreign health workers coming in," Anushka told me, referring to Ebola, "exacerbated by a history of exploitation and colonialism that led to resistance when it came to adopting health measures like quarantine and vaccination."

"This mistrust and poor communication," said Anushka, "led to a greater spread of misinformation, attacks on health workers, and reluctance to follow public health guidelines, which contributed to the prolonged spread of the virus."

"We saw the same early in the AIDS epidemic. Messages were not culturally sensitive. A lot of early public health campaigns failed to address the cultural context of affected communities, leading to ineffective prevention and treatment efforts."

The solution was to work with local leaders who had built trust in communities. "We found there was a deep level of trust in community leaders," said Anushka.

Working in India at a time when cervical cancer was on the rise, Anushka and her colleagues partnered with ASHA and Anganwadi healthcare workers, who had spent years working and building trust in rural communities. "Everybody was assigned a couple of villages and went door to door in some of the worst hit parts of Uttar Pradesh and Bihar."

They served the community's public health needs, Anushka said, far better than a foreign development organisation could have.

Trustworthy information solves a whole problem

Imagine this.

You're a 17-year-old student. You want to apply to a university in another country. To be accepted, you have to pass an exam administered by a European company in addition to your usual school exams.

Both your parents have taken extra jobs to pay for tutors and the exam itself, and you've invested hundreds of hours in studying and mock exams.

A week before the exam, you wake up to this notification. It's partially cut off when you see it on your screen, because of its length:

> Unfortunately due to issues beyond our control with this year's new electronic exam marking system, exams for overseas candidates will no . . .

The notification doesn't give you much information, though there is enough to cause you enormous stress. So you open the message.

> Unfortunately due to issues beyond our control with this year's new electronic exam marking system, exams for overseas candidates will no longer be individually marked and will instead be based on an aggregate result. For more information contact your relevant institution.

It's written in English and you speak the language very well, but you're struggling to understand. So you look at social media to see if other exam candidates have been getting similar messages. They're frightened and angry, and sharing conflicting information.

You go to the exam provider's website. There, you scan the screen for information about the exam, your grade, and whom you should contact. But there's nothing. You have no idea whether or not your education — and years of hard work — are lost.

Take a moment to consider the panic this very young person is probably feeling. Their time, money, and ambition might have been wasted, as well as their family's and community's. It is both terrifying and humiliating.

For the student, trust was broken long before the SMS arrived. It is broken again daily by the unfair systems of transnational education they are navigating. And it was broken again by self-serving communication.

A change like this at exam time would always be alarming. But we can help by giving the person only the facts they need — and a meaningful way to get more information:

> We have changed our exam marking system. Contact the school where your exam is booked to learn how the change affects you.

Know what people need

Crisis communicators, before we write a word, should understand the most probable risks for the most vulnerable people — and the factors that increase those risks. For the exam candidate, those might be:
- a generational trauma,
- their youth,
- high family and community investment with little control over the outcome,
- inequalities between students applying for the same university places,
- the perceived value of different countries' educations, based on historic inequalities.

A healthy communication team gathers that information consistently, in several ways.

Sentiment analysis is one method. There are tools for measuring sentiment broadly, but they are dependent on strong human analysis. So, communicators need to take a critical view of what we learn through sentiment analysis.

Fast, helpful interaction with journalists and the public builds trust in itself. It shows us what people need to know on a regular basis, and how trustworthy people find different voices (individual and institutional).

Knowledge of place and history is also important. We must make it our business to understand how trust varies between communities, depending on who holds power and status. We might not be able to change it, but we can know it and communicate accordingly.

If we can't give information, say why

There are times when people have a legitimate need for information in a crisis, but providing that information would put someone else in danger, or disrupt a process that outweighs the need for information. The solution is to say why you're limiting the information you share.

One example is a terrorist attack. If the attack is ongoing, and a person is trapped in the area where it's happening, others will reasonably want information about that person's wellbeing. But sharing information could put the person in danger.

In that situation, the decision doesn't belong to the communicator. That, as global head of safety, security and continuity James Hankey says, is an operational decision. A communicator's contribution is to advise on what to say instead. Often, it's sufficient to say you can't share information while the situation is ongoing.

I spoke to James about his years of experience as a crisis manager. Careful information management, which James calls "crisis discipline," is also an internal way of working. "I invite subject experts in to talk about a specific issue or to make a specific decision", said James. "And then dismiss them from the crisis team."

"Nobody has had a problem with that," he said. "And it allows me, as the crisis coordinator, to keep tight hold on information."

James also spoke about the reasons why people wanted information about their colleagues during a recent evacuation. "People were asking because they genuinely care about their colleagues' welfare. So we told people how their colleagues were being supported."

As soon as the colleagues were safe, the crisis team sent a pre-agreed message saying the same.

"Ignoring people never works. You give as much as you can."

James' approach of giving as much as you can is similar to the principles behind Estonia's healthcare system. "Trustworthiness is built into the system's design," says Amy Lewin, writing for Sifted (Financial Times).

For example, people can lock or unlock their medical records. So people not only have a full view of their records, but can choose who sees them. If a person wants an unbiased opinion from a clinician, they can lock the previous clinician's notes and diagnosis.

And, each time someone views a person's medical records, it's digitally logged and visible to the patient. A very small proportion of people in Estonia has chosen to lock their records, which may indicate greater trust in the system.

Timing and medium

While I was writing this chapter, I flew from Edinburgh to Geneva. While boarding, the queue stopped abruptly in an overheated departure area. People were at a standstill in the tunnel. The airline staff were trying their best, but they told us nothing.

It wasn't a crisis. But it could easily have become a crisis if someone in the tunnel had had a panic attack, or if an infant too young to regulate their body temperature had been in the crowd. And to a person with limited money or passport privilege, the consequences of not getting on the plane at all could have been terrifying.

In the first minute or so, we needed a message to acknowledge the delay. Then, frequent updates to say what progress they were making in solving the problem. And we needed to know whether or not we could leave the queue to go to the toilet, get water, or sit down.

A big part of a communicator's job is noticing when we're nearing a crisis, and communicating usefully before that happens. I have never seen fast, honest, clear communication fail.

By contrast, nothing fuels a crisis so well as silence.

Tell people what they need to know, when they need to know it

Writer and broadcaster Leila Latif wrote about the UK Government and British Embassy's bad communication while she and her family evacuated from Sudan in 2023.

Writing for the Guardian, Leila said, "Friends texted me sounding thrilled, as the headlines were giving the impression that we would be rescued in hours. In reality we knew nothing, and were getting automated text messages asking us to fill out the same form that we'd already filled out."

Eventually, she and her family evacuated themselves, relying on her sister in London to have visas approved as they waited by the Egyptian border. Even then, they were still getting messages from the Foreign Office telling them to stay inside.

The worst damage can't be undone

Three years earlier, a man killed 22 people in Portapique, a small town in Nova Scotia, not far from where I grew up. He had a long, unchecked history of intimate partner violence. People in his community, including 2 neighbours who had served in the military, had reported that he was stockpiling weapons.

During the 2020 massacre, he drove a replica police car and wore a police uniform. He hunted and killed people including entire families, and set buildings on fire. And then he was shot dead. There was an independent inquiry in 2022 with over 100 recommendations as an outcome. The crisis communication response was strongly criticised, as well as the police response to intimate partner violence.

During the crisis, it took 12 hours to tell the public the man was driving a convincing replica police car. It's difficult to know why it took so long to give the public this information. But it's clear that stereotypes about rural people played a part. The RCMP's head of communication told the inquiry she believed people in the community would attempt "vigilante justice" had they known, on the basis that her grandfather may have reacted similarly. Others in the RCMP shared similar assumptions.

The medium of communication was not fit for purpose. Despite having access to an emergency alert system, which community members believe would have saved lives, the crisis team chose to use Twitter as a primary medium of communication. It was an unreliable medium. Not everyone in the community had an account, and not everyone with an account was checking it for information. And in rural Nova Scotia in 2020, not everyone had reliable internet access.

We will never know if the outcome would have been different if people had had accurate, timely information.

All my experience tells me people are more likely to make safer choices if they understand and trust both the message and the medium.

Make design accessible for a person in crisis

While communicating during some public health crises, Anushka Seth told me she and her colleagues used radio. In many rural areas, it was the medium people chose, trusted, and relied on.

"We often used local radio and SMS," she said. "Nothing else; no press, no social media."

"Trust in the messenger and medium can significantly influence how well the message is received and acted upon."

Choose trusted, accessible channels of communication

Before a crisis, learn which mediums of communication people choose, trust, and have reliable access to. And plan for technical or logistical failure. If, for example, WhatsApp is people's trusted medium but the internet fails, plan to deliver messages through trusted humans, or other mediums like radio and television.

Plan for delays

Plan for delays as well. During one crisis I worked on, we communicated with people by SMS. However, some people received our messages immediately, while others had a delay of several hours.

In a situation like that, where there is no alternative medium, tell people there are delays. For example, you can manually write the local time in the message you send, so people will know exactly how old the message is. It's not perfect, but it might be the safest solution.

Research devices and plan for low battery life

Low battery on a device is a problem in many kinds of crisis. People experiencing poverty, violent conflict, unplanned power outages, or lack of housing probably won't be able to keep their device charged.

In those situations, people could use several strategies to preserve battery life. For example, they might keep a device switched off or use flight mode as much as possible.

Communicators can help by keeping messages brief and timely, and putting crucial information inside a single message. Images, attachments and links are unhelpful because they use more energy and time.

And people might rely on notifications to get important information. Using the shortest words possible and starting with the most important information is helpful. And, before a crisis begins, test messages on a variety of devices (including really old ones) to understand how many characters will appear in a notification.

People who share devices, often due to poverty or limited resources, must be able to easily log out of applications and opt out of notifications for privacy.

People who have coercive partners, live in conflict-affected places, and are under surveillance might not have control over who sees their screen. In those situations, language and medium can be as damaging as the message itself. For example, a coercive partner might quickly recognise the formal tone of a lawyer or social worker in a message. And during war or conflict, a message written in an enemy state's language could put a person in danger.

Keep messages concise

Some crises, like being unhoused or becoming a refugee, force people to spend a long time without shelter. The glare of the sun can make a screen unreadable. So can rain or snow. And extreme cold can zap a phone battery in minutes or seconds. Keeping messages minimal and using short words and sentences will give people the best chance of getting the information they need.

This approach helps everyone, not just people in crisis.

If a design is usable for someone who has a coercive partner, it will also work for someone who is on a crowded bus. If you can get information to someone who has no electricity because of unplanned power outages, your design will also work for someone who forgot to bring their charger on a long train journey. If a person without shelter can read your SMS in the glare of the sun, so can a person who works outdoors.

A content designer's role in crisis communication

Content designers are not often part of a crisis team. But designers, researchers, and developers can change the outcome of a crisis by using their expertise in specific ways, before and after a crisis.

Content governance

During one crisis, I learned that a website had information that could endanger people in hundreds of publicly-available PDFs, unsearchable in the content management system. There were also several unbranded sites built for projects and events, never archived and with no named owner.

Over time and without ownership, information on those sites had become outdated, but was still findable in theory. Information like the names of conference speakers that had once been low-risk, now put those speakers in danger. The risks increased the longer that information remained online.

Not only was the information dangerous, destroying or archiving entire sites could also put people at risk. In some cases, people relied on it as evidence for refuge and asylum claims.

Without ownership or well-designed information architecture, it was nearly impossible to find, assess and manage that information.

Strong content governance can prevent that situation with:
- manageable information architecture,
- logical naming conventions for screens and URLs,
- no duplication or outdated information,
- a no-nonsense archiving policy,
- named content owners with authority to say what is and isn't published or archived.

Scenario planning

Crisis teams plan scenarios and act them out to strengthen their crisis readiness. These are also known as tabletop exercises.

The person running the exercise gives everyone in the room the first part of the scenario, and people work through what they would do and what resources they would need. Then, they get the next part of the scenario. If there are weaknesses in the approach or disagreements about decision-making, a desktop exercise is a better place to find out than during a real crisis.

If designers, researchers, or developers are involved in scenario planning, they could spot weaknesses that others might miss. For example, I once went to a desktop exercise and learned that everyone in the room thought we could delete any web page — including parent pages — quickly and with no consequences. By demonstrating why this was not the case, we were able to make a more realistic plan.

Research

Researchers can help communicators understand people's needs, and how those needs might change in different types of crisis. For example, a researcher can find out which mediums of communication people trust the most, and why. They can also assess which mediums are most likely to work or not in different scenarios.

Researchers also have the skills to learn what did and didn't work directly from the people affected by a crisis, without causing further harm to people who have been through serious trauma.

Go to the wash-up

A crisis is both horrible and unique. You can't make it nice, and you can't plan for everything.

But you can learn something from each crisis that improves the outcome of the next one.

James Hankey told me how he prepares and runs a wash-up, which is similar to a retro.

> "I keep a live log. Anybody involved in the crisis can jot down a couple of notes about what didn't work or worked really well.
>
> Once the crisis is complete or we're at a critical time, I give everybody a link and a defined time to put their thoughts in. It needs to be within a week or 2.
>
> Then we turn those lessons identified into lessons learned. We review all crisis policy, update it, and put what we've learned into practice in the next crisis. We typically have multiple crises running at the same time, so the next crisis might be happening already."

Designers, researchers, and developers can ask to contribute to a wash-up if they have been involved in crisis planning or communication. And, as James told me, it's a way to draw a line under a potentially traumatic piece of work.

Trauma-informed design can change the outcome of a crisis

Design and crisis communication are different fields of expertise that rarely operate together.

I want to change that. Because in collaboration, design teams, technical teams, and crisis teams can better provide information:
- that is directive and unambiguous,
- from a trusted source,
- at the right time,
- through a reliable, accessible medium.

The pressures of a crisis give communicators almost no room to test and iterate. And although we can make a lot of decisions through experience and attention to what's unfolding in front of us, we're less able to do thorough research and evidence-based iteration.

Designers, researchers, and developers have the time and expertise to define problems, then design, test, and iterate solutions. And we have the methodology to ethically gather information after a crisis without causing more damage to survivors.

Crisis communication that incorporates the best of everyone's skills might look like this:

Everyone:
- talk regularly about risks and ways of mitigating them.

Designers, researchers, and developers:
- talk to communicators and crisis managers about new or iterative designs and how they might affect reputation and safety,
- include communicators at stages during design with a clear purpose, beginning with discovery,
- give communicators the evidence they need to justify trauma-informed communication to sceptical stakeholders,
- do ethical, trauma-informed research with survivors during- or post-crisis to understand their experience of the crisis and its short-term effects,
- do follow-up research to understand the mid- and long-term effects of crisis.

Communicators:
- talk to designers about crisis plans, roles, and responsibilities,
- incorporate the well-researched principles of content design into crisis communication,
- bring designers, researchers, and developers to the wider crisis team as trusted experts — for example, during desktop exercises.

I'm advocating for something unusual. A crisis team, like a design team, has rules that govern its structure, membership, timeline, and decision ownership.

But expertise is not just knowing the rules. Experts know how to break the rules to achieve something better.

So decide what you want to achieve, and what you can do with your expertise, even if it hasn't been done before. And find your place in a crisis.

Thanks

With thanks to Anushka Seth, James Hankey CSyP, Georgina Cade, and Yasmin Alibhai-Brown for contributing their insight to this chapter.

References and further reading

- Judith Hermann, *Trauma and Recovery: The Aftermath of Violence: From Domestic Abuse to Political Terror* (2015)
- Eric Hanson, Daniel P. Gamez and Alexa Manuel "The Residential School System." *Indigenous Foundations* (2020)
- National Centre for Truth and Reconciliation
- "'We're invisible': Amid residential school reckoning, '60s Scoop survivors in B.C. want action," *Global News* (2022)
- Audre Lorde, "Eye to Eye: Black Women, Hatred and Anger." *Sister Outsider* (1984)
- "The RCMP was created to control Indigenous people. Can that relationship be reset?" *Global News* (2019)
- "Tunisia: Truth Commission Outlines Decades of Abuse," Human Rights Watch (2019)

- "Tamir Rice: police release video of 12-year-old's fatal shooting," *The Guardian* (2014)
- "Sarah Everard murder: Wayne Couzens given whole-life sentence" *BBC News* (2021)
- "Bibaa and Nicole: The life after death of two sisters" *BBC News* (2021)
- "Mina Smallman: 'My Daughters' Murders Moved Me To Begin A New Mission" *British Vogue* (2024)
- Katrina Collier, "Cruel CEO Playing With People's Lives" (2024)
- "The British Museum Tweeted That Asian Names Were "Confusing" And That Pissed A Lot Of People Off" *Buzzfeed News* (2017)
- The British Museum on X (formerly Twitter) (13 September 2017)
- "The British Museum Has Reached a Settlement With a Translator Whose Work Was Used in an Exhibition Without Her Permission," Artnet (2023)
- "Minutes of meeting of the Trustees, 'Request for repatriation of human remains to New Zealand,'" The British Museum (April 2008)
- Amy Lewin, "Inside Estonia's pioneering digital health service," *Sifted* (2020)
- Leila Latif, "I am finally out of Sudan with my family, and safe — no thanks to the British government," The Guardian (25 April 2023)
- "Why RCMP managers defend using Twitter — and not an alert — during the N.S. mass shooting" CBC News (2022)

Chapter 15

Compliance is just the start: Accessibility for trauma-informed outcomes

by Josh Kim

Hi! I'm Josh. Thanks for making your way here. I'm excited to have you around.

Is it ok if I ask you 3 questions? You don't have to answer them. Just think about them.
1. How are you feeling? If you're not feeling too great, you're welcome to put this down. This chapter isn't going anywhere. Check in whenever you're ready.
2. What does disability mean to you? Do you have a disability? Does someone you know have a disability?
3. What does accessibility mean to you? How has it showed up in your work as a content designer, if at all? How do you approach it?

If we polled everyone reading this chapter, there's a good chance we'll all have different answers to these questions.

Personally, I'm not even sure how I should answer the second question: "What does disability mean to you?"

That might need some context.

I have complex post-traumatic stress disorder (CPTSD). In plain language, it's a long term trauma that continues or repeats for months or years at a time. For example, a common chronic situation that causes CPTSD is long-term child abuse. This is unlike post-traumatic stress disorder (PTSD), which is often a short-lived trauma from an event like a car accident or a natural disaster.

Here are some common symptoms of CPTSD identified by The National Center for Post-Traumatic Stress Disorder:
- alterations in emotional regulation, such as persistent sadness, suicidal thoughts, explosive anger, or inhibited anger,
- changes in self-perception, such as helplessness, shame, guilt, stigma, and a sense of being completely different from other human beings,
- changes in one's system of meanings, such as a loss of sustaining faith or a sense of hopelessness and despair.

Growing up in my household, I was conditioned into believing these symptoms were a matter of character. Of weakness. Not disability.

At the time I'm writing this, the Diagnostic and Statistical Manual of Mental Disorders (DSM-5), a key reference for the diagnosis and treatment of mental disorders, agrees. It does not recognise CPTSD as a diagnosis.

So what is it then? Are people with CPTSD disabled? And, more practically, how might that impact our interactions with the real world, where accessibility is both intentionally (and unintentionally) designed, developed, and litigated?

The answers may depend on how you, your team, or your client chooses to define, measure, and practice accessibility in their work.

A positionality statement before we start

I'd like to share a little bit about myself. I grew up in a religious, military, Korean immigrant family and spent the majority of my life in a single-parent household. I also grew up around disability. My CPTSD is a product of my family's intergenerational trauma.

As an East-Asian cis man, in a white and East-Asian cis man-dominated tech industry, I benefit from unearned privileges.

The majority of what I know is derived from my experience working as an accessibility lead with Veterans at the US Department of Veteran Affairs.

Simply put, I don't identify as an expert, nor could I ever be, as disability is complex. I encourage you to push back, argue, and engage with what I'm going to write.

What is accessibility, and does it address trauma?

Accessibility is everyone's responsibility. Every choice we make (or don't make) from a content, design, and development perspective will have real consequences for the people who use our products and services.

But what is accessibility? Who is it for? Does it address trauma?

We might start by examining some popular definitions:

- The W3C (an international organisation that develops standards for the web) defines web accessibility as when "websites, tools, and technologies are designed and developed so that people with disabilities can use them. More specifically, people can
    1. perceive, understand, navigate, and interact with the Web and
    2. contribute to the Web."
- The International Association of Accessibility Professionals (IAAP) defines accessibility as "designing products, services, and environments to ensure equal access for everybody including people with disabilities."
- Laura Kalbag, who wrote *Accessibility For Everyone*, says accessibility is "the degree to which an environment [or website] is usable by as many people as possible."

At a glance, these definitions are a tad blurry, perhaps intentionally so. In some cases accessibility is an outcome, in others a process, an experience, or a discipline. We could argue that some of the definitions address trauma. But in a capitalist world with business needs, human biases, and international law, the outcomes may be starkly different to the ideal of products and services that are trauma-informed. For example, while the IAAP argues for equal access for everyone, the material on which it tests and certifies its accessibility professionals:

- heavily references the DSM-5, which is known to have a Western bias that can fail to address the needs of underrepresented groups (like failing to recognise CPTSD as a diagnosis),
- generalises trauma into the larger bucket of cognitive disabilities without touching on its unique qualities.

So instead of focusing on how to answer this question from a theoretical lens, let's consider a practical one instead. How do organisations strategically define, measure, and practice accessibility? And how does that include (or exclude) people who experience trauma?

We can start with a common thread between all these definitions: their relationship with the Web Content Accessibility Guidelines (or WCAG for short). The W3C curates them, the IAAP tests on them, and popular authors reference them as standards.

WCAG, as a standard, has helped motivate a common strategic approach towards accessibility that is centred around compliance, which we'll evaluate in this chapter.

WCAG what?

The Web Content Accessibility Guidelines are published by W3C.

In more plain language, they provide general guidelines and develop testable standards for accessibility based on an exhaustive list of test criteria. Meet a certain amount of test criteria and you are able to "conform" to a version (for example, 2.0-2.2) and a level (for example, A, AA, and AAA).

WCAG success criteria are also a common go-to reference for the law.

As a result, many organisations approach accessibility through a compliance framework, motivating their stakeholders on the basis of legal requirements and penalties. Two reasons for this approach include:
- **liability:** in 2020 there were more than 3,000 web accessibility lawsuits filed in US state courts alone,
- **objective criteria:** WCAG provides a list of "testable criteria for objectively determining if content satisfies them."

This pairing is an easy sell: here's a measurable checklist of requirements to provide access to disabled people, and if you don't follow them, you're going to get sued.

The good: WCAG's mutual benefits

Let's start with the positives. WCAG provides cover to an incredibly wide range of disabilities. It says that they include recommendations on "accommodations for blindness and low vision, deafness and hearing loss, limited movement, speech disabilities, photosensitivity, and combinations of these, and some accommodation for learning disabilities and cognitive limitations."

It goes without saying that there are natural overlaps with a trauma-informed approach, ranging from directly applicable trauma-informed success criteria to general access for people with disabilities who also experience trauma.

Trauma-informed success criteria

Many of the more subjective principles for a trauma-informed approach cannot be reasonably covered by success criteria that must be objectively testable. However, both the principles of safety and empowerment still benefit from WCAG's breadth of coverage and legal backing.

Safety

Some examples of success criteria that ensure users feel more emotionally, psychologically, and physiologically safer when using your product may include:

2.3.1 3 Flashes or Below
- Don't have content that flashes more than 3 times per second.
- Consider eliminating all flashing content from your website to provide safety to people with photosensitive seizure disorders such as epilepsy.

3.2.6 Consistent Help
- Don't have critical help resources like crisis lines inconsistently placed throughout your website.
- Consider providing help resources in consistent, easy-to-discover areas like your header and footer to assist people who are currently activated and experiencing difficulty concentrating.

3.3.4 Error Prevention
- Don't have legal or medical submissions that can't be double checked or are irreversible when submitted.
- Consider allowing users to undo the submission of any legal or medical paperwork they may regret or feel uncomfortable with.

Empowerment, voice, and choice

Some examples of success criteria that ensure users are in control and have choice in interactions may include:

2.2.2 Pause, Stop, Hide
- Don't have content that auto-plays, moves, or updates without any user control to pause, stop, or hide said content.
- Consider avoiding having any auto-playing, moving, or updating content throughout your website to mitigate unexpected interactions that may reactivate someone's trauma.

2.4.5 Multiple Ways
- Don't have only one way of navigating between pages.
- Consider providing choice in wayfinding by building a search or site map in addition to typical navigation methods.

3.3.8 Accessible Authentication
- Don't require authentication through the use of memory, transcription, or cognitive tests alone.
- Consider allowing for email-link or call verification, as some people who are actively experiencing trauma may struggle to solve puzzles, recall a username and password, or retype one-time passcodes.

The intersections of disability and trauma

Identities like gender, race, class, sexual orientation, and disability are all interconnected. For example, someone who experiences trauma may also:
- have a broken wrist,
- be Deaf,
- have low vision,
- all of the above.

If an organisation has met all the success criteria required to be accessible from a legal perspective, they have arguably improved the experience for many people with trauma who also actively identify with another disability.

This is particularly relevant given trauma's proximity with other kinds of physical and cognitive disabilities; for example, the many physical disabilities acquired in war, genocide, and domestic abuse.

No matter how trauma-informed your design process is, it will be significantly less effective if people who experience trauma can't access it in the first place.

Access mitigates trauma

Failing to design usable products for disabled people can in and of itself be a root cause of trauma. For example, take blind author Robert Kingett's experience with his email inbox:

> "The email subjects soon became a repeating question. What access hell would I need to endure in order to read this email? Is it worth opening just to be confronted with an inaccessible email? Probably not, so why should I even bother with this one when I already experienced 3 inaccessible emails today? . . . I examined this feeling I was having all morning. I couldn't quite pinpoint it, but I could describe it. A visceral reaction to a hostile environment. Knowingly or unknowingly. Flashbacks of a previously inaccessible experience, putting me back into that feeling of ache and emotional pain."

He phrases this as "access trauma" which is activated by "the feeling of the world constantly reminding us that the world we're forced to participate in wasn't designed for us."

Kingett's "access trauma" reminds me of my own CPTSD. Despite not being caused by a significant, short-lived trauma or being classified medically as a disability, it is trauma nonetheless. Simply by meeting the bare minimum requirements laid out by WCAG's success criteria, designers can reduce the continual trauma people with disabilities experience daily on a web that's largely inaccessible.

The bad: WCAG's inherent limitations

But just because WCAG improves access to some does not mean it improves access to all. While the many improvements are appealing on paper, focusing too much on a compliance approach centred on objective test criteria has its consequences.

Compliance isn't always accessible

To offer a concrete example of what a dystopian application of the compliance framework can look like, consider the accessibility overlay, a technology that aims to improve the accessibility of a website.

Companies that develop overlays often use a compliance framework that focuses on liability (don't get sued) and objective criteria (WCAG). For example, AccessiBe, an overlay company founded in 2018 and funded by private equity, boldly claims it's the "#1 Web Accessibility Solution for WCAG and ADA Compliance."

But can an overlay designed to address WCAG criteria truly improve access for people experiencing trauma?

Before even broaching the topic of trauma, many disabled people will already disagree. As summarised by a user on Twitter, "Accessibility overlays are not the answer, and AccessiBe is no exception. As a screen reader user, numerous sites have become less usable for me with this overlay."

So much for mitigating access trauma.

Even if we assumed AccessiBe could guarantee legal compliance by meeting all relevant success criteria, reading WCAG's documentation will suggest an underwhelming reality:

"Content that conforms at the highest level (AAA) will not be accessible to individuals with all types, degrees, or combinations of disability, particularly in the cognitive, language, and learning areas."

In other words, compliance doesn't guarantee access, especially for people with cognitive disabilities.

Given that cognition may be the most relevant criteria for people who experience trauma, what gaps might that suggest in a compliance approach designed around WCAG success criteria?

Consider this hypothetical example of a disability benefits form (based on a real one I've encountered). It requires people who experience trauma to recall an event that triggered their PTSD in order to apply for disability benefits.

Human Healthcare   Apply for disability benefits

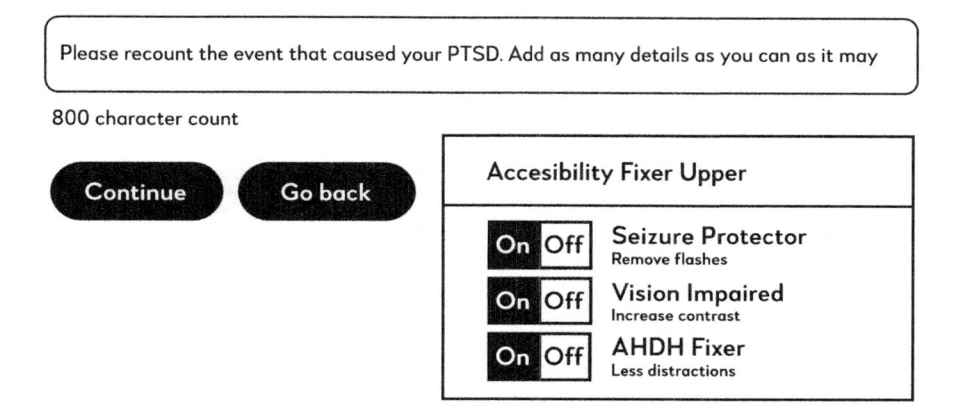

> Please recount the event that caused your PTSD. Add as many details as you can as it may

800 character count

[Continue] [Go back]

Accesibility Fixer Upper

On	Off	**Seizure Protector** Remove flashes
On	Off	**Vision Impaired** Increase contrast
On	Off	**AHDH Fixer** Less distractions

This example technically meets all 50 success criteria listed in WCAG's 2.1 AA specifications and is supported by an accessibility overlay. However, placeholder text can cause issues because:
- people in an activated state may struggle to recall the original question, as it will be lost as soon as they begin typing in the field,
- it (barely) meets the minimum levels of WCAG (4.5:1) but it may still be unreadable in certain scenarios. For people with low vision or people accessing this form with a phone in a dimmed power saving mode, the minimum contrast requirement may not be enough to read the critical instructions provided.

More critically, someone may be forced to relive and describe their traumatic experience under a slowly reducing character count. WCAG cannot address this need. But why?

Objective failures

At the root of WCAG's failure to fully address trauma is its rules for success criteria. According to WCAG:

- all success criteria must be testable,
- the training required to meet the success criteria should be able to be acquired in a week's training or less.

When it comes to anticipating what may re-traumatise someone to the point in which a product becomes unusable or inaccessible, WCAG fails on both counts as:
- trauma is experienced subjectively. What activates someone may not activate someone else. What activates someone in a moment may not activate them at a separate point in time. Furthermore, as Ted Hirsrch argues, even in a qualitative research setting, "it is virtually impossible for researchers to predict participant vulnerability or topic sensitivity [in advance]."
- trauma-informed practice should not be oversimplified. It's unlikely a week of training (or less) can prepare a team to address trauma when, as social worker and designer Rachael Dietkus wisely warns, "every design project and individual and team experience demands a contextual and nuanced approach."

Simply put, because WCAG's success criteria must be objectively testable, it cannot account for the subjective experience of re-traumatisation.

In context to the prior example, it cannot require product teams to:
- provide exit mechanisms or access to crisis lines,
- detail why this information must be collected in the first place,
- examine if there are better alternatives to collect medical information directly from a doctor instead of requiring users to input it themselves.

As a result, while some facets of trauma-informed principles can be integrated into WCAG success criteria, trauma holistically can never (nor should ever) be addressed through objective testing criteria.

Corporate misinterpretation

Finally, at a strategic level, focusing too much on a compliance framework based on WCAG success criteria can set the wrong expectations or pique the wrong interests within stakeholders and leadership.

As Lainey Feingold, a prominent disability rights lawyer argues, "the fear of being hit with a lawsuit motivates many organisations to look for quick and cheap solutions." Focusing too much on the legal repercussions can tempt your leadership to reach for shallow and quick accessibility fixes like AccessiBe.

What results is a series of levelled ceilings based on legal criteria, not disabled needs, especially for people who experience trauma.

This is cruelly unfortunate, and as web accessibility expert Eric Eggert notes, WCAG's success criteria are only one half of the whole:

> "I sometimes think WCAG should be 2 standards: The guidelines that give web designers and developers information on what to look out for, and 'testing rules' for verifying that the guidelines are followed. Unfortunately, in practice, most people learn of the guideline part of WCAG only after being confronted with the guardrails part. The tragic situation is that people would crash into guardrails less if we taught them the guidelines first."

Focusing too much on the guardrails (success criteria) gives the false impression that accessibility can be "completed," that all bugs can be resolved, and that disabilities can never have contradictory needs. At best, accessibility will be framed as quality assurance; at worst, an automatable feature.

All of these can prevent teams from being able to mature their approach towards accessibility using alternative frameworks that better consider the needs of disabled people, including people who experience trauma.

The journey ahead

I started this chapter by asking what accessibility means to you. We've talked about how it's defined theoretically and how it's applied strategically, and we've examined some of its biggest shortcomings for people who experience trauma when we frame it strictly from the objective lens of compliance.

So what can we do?

It depends. Disability is complex, and trauma is subjective.

But I can confidently say that attempting to flatten these experiences into a single framework, tool, or checklist isn't the answer, nor is it an instinct we should lean into.

Instead, how might we embrace, explore, and uplift disability's complexity? Trauma's subjectivity?

What benefits might we unveil if we centred disabled people, not success criteria, in our approach towards accessibility?

As a content designer navigating accessibility and thinking about trauma, therein lies the key.

The more you can commit to define, measure, and practice accessibility through an-ever evolving subjective lens, the better. That might mean:

- learning and applying accessibility basics (yes, the kind that WCAG covers), but resisting the urge to overfocus on or centre legal success criteria,
- continuing to ask questions, test assumptions, and broaden your understanding of disability. For example, if you conduct research with one person who has a disability or experiences trauma, don't assume their experience will be representative of everyone else,
- continuing to re-evaluate and evolve your approach towards accessibility. Explore different frameworks like inclusive design and design justice. Learn about their strengths and weaknesses. Be willing to toss them or adapt them to your project's needs.

As a lover of qualitative research, one of my favourite textbooks is *Qualitative Research and Evaluation Methods* by M.Q. Patton. He introduces a character "Halcolm" (pronounced "how come") who guides scholars through research. I'll end with Halcolm's wise words from one of his comics. I hope these act as a guiding principle for your journey with accessibility, too:

> "Two great deceptions are asserted by the world's self-congratulators, that the hardest and most important step is the first, and the most resplendent step is the last!
>
> While every journey must have a first and last step, what ultimately determines the nature and enduring value of the journey are the steps in between!

Each step has its own value and importance. Be present for the whole journey.

Be present for the whole journey."

References and further reading

A heads up. This chapter was written to serve as an introduction to the intersection of (mostly) digital accessibility and trauma for content designers. If you're already familiar with the benefits and weaknesses of a WCAG-centred approach, I recommend reading my longer piece "Broken Frames." It takes a more critical stance towards the issues that systemically unravel popular accessibility frameworks like inclusive design.

- Julia M. Whealin and Laurie Slone, "Complex PTSD," *National Center for Post-Traumatic Stress Disorder, Department of Veterans Affairs* (2013)
- Rachael Dietkus, "Transforming Trauma-Informed Design: Ethical Practices, Lifelong Learning, and Collective Responsibility" (Published on LinkedIn) (14 February 2024)
- Lainey Feingold, *Structured Negotiation* (2021)
- "Understanding Conformance," W3C (2023)
- "Overlay Fact Sheet" https://overlayfactsheet.com/en
- "PTSD and DSM-5," U.S. Department of Veterans Affairs (2022)
- Eric Eggert, "WCAG 2: Guidelines and Guardrails" (2023)
- "Design Justice Network Principles," Design Justice
- GrahamTheDev. "I was shocked that placeholder text on an <input> (instead of a <label>) might TECHNICALLY PASS WCAG!? Do you agree?" (2021)
- Robert Kingett, "Combating access trauma" (2024)
- Michael Quinn Patton, *Qualitative Research and Evaluation Methods: Integrating Theory and Practice* (Fourth Edition) (2014)
- Andrew Wales, "Halcolm's Research Parables" (21 April 2010)
- Josh Kim, "Broken Frames: Navigating imperfect accessibility frameworks for trauma-informed outcomes" (2024)

Thanks

Nothing I write about is new. Many of the points you've read here were contributed by a community of folk who edited this chapter: Silvia, kon, Annie and Andy, Soren, Jan, Sarah, Rachel, Michelle, and more. Love y'all to bits.

Chapter 16
Trauma literacy in content design

by Rachael Dietkus

As designers, we can shape experiences through the:
- words we choose,
- interactions we create,
- methods we trust,
- content we present.

The experiences we shape are not neutral. For some, they might carry the invisible weight of past trauma. For others, it may be dramatically different. Trauma can show up even in the most ordinary interactions with our content. In design practice, I believe having a trauma literacy can add depth to our work. This powerful observation by Peter Levine in *Waking the Tiger: Healing Trauma* underscores the need for trauma literacy in a field like design:

> "Trauma is perhaps the most avoided, ignored, belittled, denied, misunderstood, and untreated cause of human suffering."

Understanding how trauma shapes the human experience requires designers to adopt a literacy of trauma. This framework can equip us to anticipate and respond to the diverse needs of trauma-affected individuals.

When we deepen our practice to include a trauma literacy that builds from our sensitivity, we can actively consider how trauma can impact people's engagement with content. This chapter explores the practice of trauma literacy, how we can expand our awareness, and why our work must prioritise care, trust, and safety.

What is a trauma literacy?

In simple terms, having a trauma literacy is twofold. First, it means deeply understanding trauma, including its variances, impacts, and how it develops and manifests in individuals, teams, organisations, communities, and society at large — particularly as a result of structural and systemic harm.

Second, we take this deep understanding and thoughtfully and ethically apply it in our design contexts. But this is far easier said than done. It's important to note that having a trauma literacy goes beyond a foundation of basic information about trauma and trauma-informed care; it involves so much more.

Trauma is unique to the individual

It's essential to understand that many experiences can lead to trauma. Consider how you might recognise different forms of trauma and how it uniquely affects people. What are some common and normal reactions to stress and feeling overwhelmed?

A single traumatic event can result in vastly different responses. One person may feel overwhelmed, another experiences trauma, and a third remains unaffected. This underscores the complexity of trauma and our perceptions of it, particularly in the face of global crises. Pandemics, natural disasters, and political conflicts can magnify and diversify traumatic responses across communities.

Recognise trauma responses

Understanding that trauma is unique means understanding it doesn't always look the same. Recognising trauma responses means being aware and attuned. What are some common and normal reactions to stress and overwhelm that we could anticipate with our content? There is a wide range of normal emotional, psychological, and physical responses to trauma, including how trauma might manifest in our behaviours, decision-making, and interactions with systems or content.

Compassion and reflexivity

In addition to this awareness of trauma, a trauma-literate designer must have compassion and reflexivity. These traits allow us to approach work compassionately and understand that trauma may affect individuals and communities differently. They also involve regularly reflecting on one's role and biases in interacting with others, especially when designing content for services that may impact trauma-affected individuals.

Trauma-informed principles and practices are integrative, not additive

With these skills and understanding, we can look at our practices. Integrating trauma-informed principles ensures that environments and interactions do not intentionally and unintentionally re-traumatise or alienate those with traumatic histories. These principles do not need to be prescriptive.

A good starting point is the 6 guiding principles from the Substance Abuse and Mental Health Services Administration (SAMHSA), a U.S. government agency that promotes mental health and substance use care through resources and support.

Many designers grapple with understanding trauma while learning about trauma-informed care principles. As awareness grows, designers can begin to apply trauma-informed care principles more thoughtfully. This shift is helping to bridge the gap between understanding trauma and integrating these principles with depth and intentionality.

For example, Chayn is a global nonprofit run by survivors and allies worldwide. It creates resources to support the healing of survivors of gender-based violence and has adapted trauma-informed principles to include ones relevant to their context and scope of work.

Take a moment and consider the context you are working within. Are your projects focused on known or nuanced sensitive subject matters? The context you work within will inform the principles you may need and then choose to integrate. The safety principle may apply in every context, regardless of the topic. It is important to remember that the principles are in constant relationship with one another.

Trauma models

Numerous models exist for understanding trauma, each offering a unique perspective on its complexities. Many of these models significantly influence how trauma-informed care is approached within design practices. While most trauma-informed care stems from the medical model, it is helpful to explore other key frameworks.

The **medical model** categorises trauma primarily in terms of medical experiences, ranging from life-threatening emergencies to routine procedures. It acknowledges that trauma can emerge in various forms and that psychological effects may vary depending on the care received. However, the model focuses heavily on clinical intervention, which may limit its application to understanding trauma in non-medical contexts.

The **biopsychosocial model** integrates biological, psychological, and environmental factors to explain what is commonly seen as mental disorders. While it presents a more comprehensive view, some critics argue that it has evolved into a predominantly biomedical focus, often overshadowing the psychological and social components.

The **trauma-informed care model** prioritises creating a safe and supportive environment by considering past trauma when delivering care. It emphasises avoiding activations and offering sensitive, empathic approaches that recognise the long-lasting effects of trauma on mental health.

The **social model** shifts the focus from individual pathology to the broader societal context, recognising that social structures, cultural norms, and systemic factors significantly contribute to trauma. It highlights how external factors, rather than individual deficiencies, can exacerbate the impact of trauma.

The **anti-pathology model** reframes trauma as a natural, valid response to harm. The anti-pathology model emphasises resilience and recovery without medicalising or pathologising individuals. This holistic approach avoids stigmatisation, focusing on healing without unnecessary labelling or clinical intervention.

Creating a new model for design

As we consider these various models for understanding trauma, it becomes clear that design offers a unique space to move beyond the constraints of traditional medicalised approaches. By integrating insights from the social and anti-pathology models, design can address trauma more holistically, acknowledging its roots in systemic and structural influences. This opens the door to creating new frameworks that prioritise empathy, care, and resilience in ways many other disciplines have yet to fully embrace.

By embracing the social and anti-pathology models, we can shift our practices to prioritise care, trust, and empowerment. We can move toward building a trauma literacy that supports and empowers individuals, teams, and communities. In the following sections, we'll explore what building a trauma literacy social model in design means and how this approach can deepen our understanding and expand our practice.

Social model of trauma literacy

The social model of trauma literacy represents a paradigm shift in understanding trauma. Rather than viewing trauma as a purely individual psychological or medical issue, this model situates it within the broader societal and systemic contexts that create and often perpetuate it. Trauma is not an isolated experience; it is usually shaped by external forces such as:

- racism,
- sexism,
- poverty,
- ableism,
- colonialism,
- other forms of systemic oppression and marginalisation.

These forces intersect and compound, creating environments where trauma is more likely to occur and where its effects are more difficult to overcome. By adopting this broader perspective, designers can address trauma not only through individual care but also through systemic change and societal accountability.

For instance, in a community-centred design project aimed at creating content for the public, applying the social model could involve partnership through ongoing participatory or co-design throughout the whole process. This approach can foster co-production, ensuring the community's needs and experiences are met rather than imposing top-down decisions.

Let's look at the central components of the social model more closely.

Trauma as a collective experience

Trauma extends beyond the individual and can be a shared experience across communities. Social conditions such as economic inequality, discrimination, and marginalisation intensify trauma, making it both a personal and collective issue.

Challenging structural inequities

Trauma is deeply intertwined with systemic structures. The social model emphasises dismantling these inequities by recognising their role in perpetuating trauma. Addressing systemic issues like housing instability, healthcare access, or racial discrimination becomes central to trauma-informed work.

Community-centred approaches

Healing is not solely an individual journey. The social model advocates for collective, community-based solutions where those impacted by trauma are empowered to participate in creating systems of care. This approach recognises the value of shared responsibility and peer-to-peer support.

Designing for systemic change

Within this model, trauma-informed design aims to create systems that prevent trauma by addressing root causes. Design can play a critical role in creating digital or physical environments that foster healing by challenging harmful societal norms and offering more equitable experiences.

Anti-pathology model of trauma literacy

The anti-pathology model moves away from viewing trauma through a clinical lens that seeks to "fix" or pathologise individuals. Instead, this model frames trauma as a natural, valid response to harmful experiences and emphasises the inherent resilience of those who experience it. It advocates for a non-stigmatising, strengths-based approach that shifts away from medicalisation and toward holistic care. This model has 5 critical aspects.

Trauma as a response, not a disorder

In this model, trauma is seen as an adaptive response to adversity rather than a disorder that needs to be cured. It challenges the notion that trauma should be pathologised, emphasising instead the importance of understanding and contextualising trauma responses.

Resilience and strengths-based approaches

Rather than focusing on deficits or things that are wrong or not working, the anti-pathology model emphasises human resilience. It acknowledges people's ability to adapt, recover, and thrive, often by drawing on their inner strengths and support systems.

Avoiding over-medicalisation

This model resists the tendency to rely solely on medical interventions (like medication or clinical diagnoses) to address trauma. Instead, it advocates for alternative healing methods, including:
- social support,
- mutual aid,
- collective care,
- peer networks,
- culturally responsive practices.

Trusting and empowering survivors

Central to this model is the agency of trauma survivors. It encourages individuals to reclaim ownership over their healing journey and supports them in defining what recovery means on their terms.

Challenging stigmatisation

The anti-pathology model seeks to de-stigmatise trauma by framing it as a normal part of the human experience, particularly in communities disproportionately affected by systemic harm.

In content design, this might translate into creating resources or platforms that use inclusive and empowering language, ensuring that narratives around trauma do not pathologise but acknowledge strength and recovery. For example, your content might focus on normalising discussions about trauma, emphasising communal healing and shared experiences while providing clear, accessible pathways to support.

Each of these aspects highlights the role that social structures contribute to trauma and works to remove the shame often attached to traumatic experiences. In a recent social care and trauma-informed initiative, designers worked with trauma survivors to create a digital tool prioritising participant autonomy. Rather than focusing on clinical diagnoses or prescriptive paths, the tool allows participants to engage with content on their terms, reinforcing the anti-pathology model's focus on resilience and agency. Participants noted that the tool empowered them to navigate their healing journey at their own pace, feeling both seen and supported. This further validated the importance of autonomy and resilience in trauma recovery.

Integrating these models into trauma-informed practice

When applied to design, both the social and anti-pathology models of trauma literacy offer transformative approaches beyond conventional frameworks. By integrating these models into practice, designers and other professionals can:

- shift from seeing trauma as an individual pathology or problem to understanding it as a product of social systems and structures,
- prioritise both community and systemic healing, as well as individual care,
- empower individuals by recognising their strengths and resilience rather than focusing on dysfunction or disorder,
- challenge and work to dismantle the societal structures that perpetuate trauma, advocating for systemic change and new structures of care that foster healing.

Building a trauma-responsive practice

In addition to being a designer, I am also a licensed clinical social worker, and I approach trauma-informed practice from a discipline grounded in a strict code of ethics, practice standards, and ongoing education requirements. These essential safeguards guide care professionals like me in ensuring ethical and responsible care. However, these same professional standards do not bind most design practitioners, including content designers.

Adopting trauma-informed practices in design is not a requirement. But opting into these practices can profoundly impact the individuals and communities we design with and for. Embracing trauma literacy is a conscious choice to prioritise care and ethics in design, even without formal obligations or mandates. By doing so, we can ensure our work respects and honours the complexities of the human experience while recognising the boundaries and limitations of our professional capacities.

While designers are not bound by the same ethical standards as licensed professionals, embracing trauma literacy requires heightened ethical responsibility. Designers must recognise the limits of their expertise and collaborate with trauma experts when necessary, ensuring that the work respects and supports the well-being of trauma-affected individuals. If you want to work in this way:

- recognise the limits of your expertise around trauma,
- collaborate with trauma experts when necessary,
- make sure your work respects and supports the wellbeing of people who are affected by trauma.

The need for sensitivity in design

As designers, our responsibility extends beyond creating experiences that look nice and work well. When we commit to trauma-informed work, we must consider the emotional resonance of every element we introduce — a choice of words, an interaction, or a visual detail. What may seem insignificant to some can profoundly affect others, evoking emotional, psychological, or even physical reactions. This is where a trauma literacy becomes crucial. It allows us to approach our work with a deeper understanding of how trauma shapes human experience and how design can alleviate or exacerbate those impacts.

Designers, in particular, can play a crucial role by embedding these principles into their work. Through thoughtful design, we can create environments and experiences that promote healing, build trust, and foster a sense of safety for trauma survivors. By doing so, we move beyond functionality and aesthetics to create designs that genuinely support human well-being.

The role of trauma literacy in design

Trauma literacy, in essence, is about recognising the complexity of trauma and applying that understanding in meaningful, sensitive ways. It's not enough to simply be aware that trauma exists; trauma literacy demands that we comprehend trauma's distinct forms and how trauma uniquely shapes individual experiences. This understanding helps us to be more attuned to the varied emotional, psychological, and physiological responses trauma can activate and allows us to design with greater empathy and care.

Trauma literacy also calls for reflexivity: an ongoing evaluation of our biases, roles, and the potential impact of our work. Whether designing digital systems, creating content, or developing physical spaces, we must remain conscious of how trauma may appear in our participants' experiences and ensure that we create environments prioritising safety, trust, and empowerment.

However, trauma literacy isn't just a practice for individual designers; it should inform how organisations approach design processes. Organisations can encourage a more empathetic, ethical, and inclusive design culture by embedding trauma-informed principles into team workflows, decision-making structures, and client relationships.

Trauma literacy as a design imperative

Trauma literacy is not a static skill. It requires a commitment to lifelong learning and growth. As designers, we are uniquely positioned to contribute to a world where healing, safety, and empowerment are prioritised. By integrating trauma literacy into our practice, we can design experiences that foster environments where individuals feel supported, respected, and valued.

In this way, trauma literacy becomes imperative in design. It challenges us to think deeply about our ethical responsibility and design in inclusive and sensitive ways, creating content that is responsive to our participants' diverse experiences of trauma. Through this lens, we can create work that makes a difference and offers care and support to those who need it most.

Inclusive and accessible design

Proactively inclusive and accessible design anticipates how design, language, and interactions could activate trauma responses.

Trauma literacy empowers practitioners to design in ways that cultivate ease, not friction. Inclusive and accessible practices in design should be at the forefront and never considered afterthoughts, optional, or nice-to-haves.

Trauma literacy is always growing

Lifelong learning and trusting your "inner knowing" acknowledge that trauma literacy is not static and requires continuous commitment through:

- self-study,
- ongoing reflection and self-awareness,
- mentorship and guidance,
- communities of practice,
- formal training and workshops,
- cultural humility and learning,
- peer accountability.

We also must understand the limits of our knowledge, which is something all designers can do with a scope of practice. One framework for a scope of practice could include the following elements.

1. **Role and responsibilities:** Clearly define your role as a designer, including the boundaries of your expertise and the responsibilities you are taking on within a project or with a team.
2. **Competencies and skills:** Identify the specific skills and competencies you bring. This helps clarify what you can deliver and where you may need support or collaboration from others.
3. **Limitations:** Acknowledge areas outside your expertise or capacity. These might include topics like trauma care, clinical knowledge, or technical skills that require other experts.
4. **Ethical boundaries:** Outline the ethical standards you uphold in your content design work, especially regarding trauma-informed care and considerations for vulnerable populations. These may also be things you cannot, do not, or choose not to do.

5. **Collaboration and referral:** Establish guardrails and guidelines for when and how you will collaborate with other professionals, and identify situations that may require referring to experts in other fields, such as mental health or legal support.

This simple scope of practice framework allows designers to operate within their expertise while staying mindful of the need for ongoing learning and collaboration.

Next practices: building together

While much of trauma literacy requires individual commitment to growth and ethical practice, this work is also deeply embedded in social contexts. Trauma doesn't happen in isolation, and neither does trauma literacy. The social model of trauma literacy emphasises that our understanding of trauma is built collectively through relationships, shared experiences, and community engagement.

Collective learning and shared experiences

Trauma literacy is not something you can learn solely from books or theory; it's something you build through engagement with others. Whether through collaboration with trauma survivors, dialogue with mental health professionals, or learning from peers, the social model recognises that trauma literacy grows in the community.

Shared experiences are critical to this process. Trauma is deeply personal, yet it's shaped by social and systemic factors — factors that we can only understand through collective learning. We deepen our understanding and become more attuned to the nuanced ways that trauma manifests by:
- listening to others' stories,
- engaging with trauma survivors,
- learning from those who have worked in trauma fields.

The social model reminds us that our trauma literacy is never complete. It's constantly evolving as we engage with new perspectives, learn from each other's experiences, and participate in shared learning environments.

Community and Peer Support

The social model of trauma literacy also emphasises the importance of peer support and community engagement. Just as trauma is often experienced within a larger community, whether that's a family, workplace, or cultural group, so too must trauma literacy be developed and sustained through community.

For example, engaging in communities of practice offers a space where designers and trauma practitioners can share insights, reflect on challenges, and offer peer support. These communities are not only places for learning but also for sustaining trauma-informed practices. It can be emotionally challenging to work in trauma-informed spaces, and having peer support systems allows for reflection, growth, and accountability.

Trauma-informed work is best done in collaboration, where everyone brings unique perspectives and experiences. This collective approach to trauma literacy helps ensure we don't burn out, become isolated in our efforts, or miss critical insights from shared experiences.

Engaging with broader social systems

The social systems and structures around us profoundly shape trauma. Racism, sexism, ableism, classism, and other forms of systemic inequality all contribute to trauma. A social model of trauma literacy encourages us to engage not only with the individuals experiencing trauma but with the systems that perpetuate it. This means recognising that trauma is not just an individual experience but a social one shaped by power, oppression, and historical injustice.

In trauma-informed design, this means thinking critically about how the systems we're part of are either contributing to or alleviating trauma — whether it's a workplace, a government institution, or a social service. How are our designs interacting with these larger systems? Are we reinforcing oppressive structures or creating spaces for healing and justice?

The social model of trauma literacy pushes us to think beyond the individual and consider the broader societal impact of our work. Trauma literacy, in this context, means advocating for systemic change and designing ways to challenge the structures that cause harm.

Fostering a culture of accountability and care

Trauma literacy is not just an individual responsibility; it's a shared responsibility. Organisations, institutions, and communities must be accountable for creating trauma-informed environments. It's not enough for individuals to be trauma-literate; there must be a collective commitment to building systems of care and accountability.

This means nurturing trauma-informed cultures where everyone understands trauma literacy and integrates it into daily work. Organisations should:
- provide trauma-informed training,
- create peer support networks,
- ensure that trauma survivors are given spaces for voice, agency, and autonomy,
- establish clear reporting and feedback mechanisms for addressing trauma-related concerns,
- develop trauma-informed policies and procedures that are regularly revisited and updated,
- foster leadership commitment to trauma-informed principles by ensuring leaders model care, trustworthiness, and accountability,
- create spaces and time for rest and recovery to prevent burnout and secondary trauma.

Building trauma literacy through a social model means acknowledging that trauma recovery is not a solo journey. It's collective and requires institutional courage, community support, and a culture of care. As designers, we are part of that broader system, and our trauma literacy should reflect our commitment to creating supportive content and experiences at every level of design. As we move forward, trauma literacy will continue to evolve, shaping what's next for trauma-informed design.

Emerging models for trauma literacy: what's next?

As our understanding of trauma continues to evolve, so too do the models we use to build trauma literacy. New approaches are emerging that challenge traditional design frameworks, pushing the boundaries of what it means to design with trauma in mind. These models are about responding to trauma and anticipating and shaping future design practices that align with evolving societal needs.

The climate crisis, in particular, is already revealing new layers of trauma that designers must anticipate and respond to. From climate displacement to eco-anxiety, the psychological effects of environmental destruction will shape how people engage with the world around them. The trauma literacy of content designers will be crucial in crafting language that supports affected populations, whether through the design of communication for disaster response services, community rebuilding efforts, or social service interventions.

As global crises such as pandemics, political upheavals, economic instability, or climate-related disasters continue to emerge, the need for a trauma literacy in design will become even more pressing. Designers will continue to be called to respond to large-scale trauma on a societal level, working to create an information architecture that is resilient, adaptable, and capable of fostering collective healing. By anticipating how trauma will intersect with future challenges, content designers can ensure that their work is responsive and proactive, addressing trauma at its roots and creating pathways to recovery and resilience.

References and further reading

- "6 Guiding Principles to a Trauma Informed Approach," Centers for Disease Control and Prevention (2022)
- "Cultures of Care," Othering & Belonging Institute
- Resmaa Menakem, "Notice the Rage; Notice the Silence," *On Being with Krista Tippett* (podcast) (2021)
- "Identifying your current scope of practice" Health and Care Professions Council (2024)
- Centre for Institutional Courage: https://www.institutionalcourage.org

About the authors

Morgan Cataldo

Morgan dedicates her professional life to developing and advocating for participatory practice and peer education as essential levers for creating true, lasting, power-shifting change in services for systemically neglected communities. She is the founder and principal consultant of morgan&co. Morgan has over 15 years of personal and professional expertise collaborating with individuals, communities, and organisations to reimagine the role those who experience systematic exclusion play in social change.

Rachael Dietkus

Rachael is a social worker, trauma-responsive design strategist, and advocate for embedding ethical care into civic tech and design practices. She is the founder of Social Workers Who Design, where she specialises in trauma-responsive systems, integrating her expertise to create environments that prioritise healing and safety. Rachael's nearly 25 years of experience spans government, nonprofit, and social impact sectors worldwide, where she focuses on promoting trauma literacy, community engagement, and social justice through responsible design.

Rachel Edwards

From dabbling in food writing to working as a librarian, Rachel has spent the best part of 2 decades working with words. As a content designer she has worked extensively with parliament, and government, helping people understand their rights. Her interest is how to create better content for people experiencing stress, anxiety, and trauma. Originally from Canada, Rachel now lives in Scotland with her 2 children.

Kate Every

Kate is a user-centred design leader specialising in inclusive and ethical design and delivery within the public sector. Her academic background is in human rights practice. She holds a master's degree in fieldwork, and she has done extensive research into restorative justice and survivor-centred approaches to criminal justice. She is also a trained Rape Crisis support worker. She brings these lenses to her work as a human-centred designer in government and healthcare.

Sarah Fathallah

Sarah is an independent designer and researcher who specialises in applying design to the social sector. Their work with vulnerable communities leads them to question the harm and ethics of design. They serve as faculty at the California College of the Arts and UC Berkeley, and they engage in organising, mutual aid, and political education that challenge and inform their work. Born and raised in Morocco, Sarah now calls xučyun (aka Oakland, CA) home.

Michelle D. Keller

Michelle is a content designer who led on content for bereavement services at a nationwide hospice in the US. She specialises in designing clear and compassionate content for people who are grieving. Having experienced hospice care with her own family, she is committed to providing trauma-informed digital content at a difficult time. She currently lives near the Blue Ridge Mountains of Virginia, where she enjoys good wine, good coffee, good mountain views, and time with her family.

Josh Kim

Josh is a qualitative UX researcher turned accessibility designer, committed to re-centering civic service away from technology and towards historically underserved people. Through his personal lived experiences with CPTSD and work with disabled Veterans at VA.gov, he strives to broaden accessibility's impact through a trauma-informed lens.

Owen Leigh

Having witnessed the effects of severe trauma within his family, Owen became aware of the effects of inaccessibility and inequity in society at a young age. This, and his own experiences as a transman, led him to realise the impact inaccessible and non-inclusive digital content can have on people's lives. Now, as a content designer, Owen works to create mindful content experiences in the hopes of making people's lives easier.

Jane McFadyen

Jane is a design lead working in bereavement and care services for the UK government. A genuine user centred design fan-girl (yes, she even has a badge), Jane is passionate about using research, evidence, and empathy to create simple and clear content design for people dealing with really tough things. She also works towards improving accessibility and awareness of dyscalculia (a neurodiversity) and has helped designers worldwide by co-creating guidance.

Steph Mann

Steph is a lover of words. For over 20 years she's been a freelance writer and a content designer. She is an advocate for users, testing, and getting content wrong (to get it right). She wants to help people understand how to write for different audiences who have different experiences. She's worked in government, the private sector, higher education, and the third sector. She lives in Scotland with her family.

sahibzada mayed (صاحبزاده مائد)

mayed is a decolonial researcher and designer, committed to dismantling oppressive systems and cultivating pathways for collective liberation. Through genderful fashion, they create spaces to celebrate the beauty of diverse gender expressions and disrupt the gender binary. mayed's identity is shaped by their background as a Muslim immigrant of Afghan, Indian, Pakistani, and Persian heritage, as well as lived experiences of queerness, disability, and neurodivergence.

kon syrokostas

kon is a software developer who also designs. For the past few years he's been curious about the impact of trauma in people's lives and the pathways to healing. Now, he combines his background in software development with his interest in trauma-informed design to create safer, more healing, and more inclusive digital experiences. kon holds a master's degree in computer engineering. He lives in Patras, Greece, and when he's not working, enjoys reading, long walks, and rewatching old sitcoms.

Miriam Vaswani

Miriam Vaswani is a lead content designer, researcher, and fiction writer, with several years' experience of crisis communication with international impact. Her trauma-informed design practice is influenced by her work in crisis communication. She's from Canada, where she grew up on the traditional unceded territory of the Wolastoqiyik and Mi'kmaq Peoples. She lives in Scotland, and has also lived in Germany, Tunisia, India, and Russia.

Jax Wechsler

Jax is a trauma-informed designer, researcher, educator, and coach committed to fostering positive change for people and the planet. Her work focuses on the intersection of inner development, personal growth, and systemic transformation, with much of her practice centred in the social change sector. Jax integrates trauma, wellbeing, and inner development into her approach to change, teaching at universities and independently. She lives among the gum trees on Yuin country in Australia.

Jenny Winfield

Jenny is a researcher and strategist from the UK, focused on taboos and trauma. She's led design research on a range of issues that tend to be hushed up, from medical misconduct to sexual dysfunction, suicide, incarceration, and addiction. Jenny works as the Head of Research and Impact for a feminist organisation (Chayn) that supports survivors of gender-based violence around the world. Jenny is interested in the personal and collective journey of learning how to rest.

Thanks

To the authors, who gave their time, energy and wisdom so generously. Their passion for the subject and the people they design for means there is now a book to hold in our hands.

Special thanks to kon for the website, and Laura Copestake, Steph and Miriam for the editorial support.

Anna Kruse is the most talented, thorough and thoughtful proofreader I could ask for. I know if I let her check that sentence she would be questioning my lack of an Oxford comma and ending with a preposition. Thank you for the thousands — yes, thousands! — of comments and corrections.

Sarah Winters and Helen Lawson have been my content heroes from the very beginning. To have them involved and supporting this book means the world to me.

I met our designer, Taryl Guenter, in an 18th century lit class some 25 years ago. She will understand that I must thank her in heroic couplets:

Most artful designer, acquaintance of mine
You made this epistle both shapely and fine
An artistic nymph with talents immense
My thanks for turning a vision into sense.

To Rachel Murray, my friend and colleague who first explored trauma-informed content with me. Thanks also to Emel Harper, Brian Moss, and all the others in the design team and Scottish Government team. We learned so much together, and I'm grateful to all of you.

To my mum, for reading early drafts and commenting tirelessly. And to dad and Julia who said not to edit a book, but understood when I did.

To Chris, for listening to me go on and on about this project.

To Leo for making me cups of tea, and Rosa for problem solving and letting me tell her story.

And finally to the nurses, doctors, and everyone in the Lochranza Ward at the Royal Hospital for Children and Young People, Edinburgh. You deal with trauma every day with grace, kindness, and strength. Thank you for giving life, hope and love.

– Rachel

Printed in Great Britain
by Amazon